Horns of the Goddess

By
Dolores Cannon

For permission, serialization, condensation, adaptations, or for our catalog of other publications, write to Ozark Mountain Publishing, Inc., P.O. Box 754, Huntsville, AR 72740, ATTN: Permissions Department.

Library of Congress Cataloging-in-Publication Data

Horns of the Goddess by Dolores Cannon -1931-2014
     The past lives of three volunteers who went back to the time of the Druids.
1. Hypnosis 2. Past-Lives 3. Mother Earth 4. Metaphysical
I. Cannon, Dolores, 1931-2014 II. Metaphysical III. Past-Lives IV. Title

Library of Congress Catalog Card Number: 2022940619
ISBN: 97819569452018

Cover Art and Layout: Victoria Cooper Art
Book set in: Microsoft Himalaya & Times New Roman
Book Design: Summer Garr
Published by:

PO Box 754, Huntsville, AR 72740
800-935-0045 or 479-738-2348; fax 479-738-2448
WWW.OZARKMT.COM
Printed in the United States of America

Message from Nancy

My mother, Dolores Cannon, first started receiving this information in 1983. At that time, she was still honing her craft and there were several who wanted to assist with letting her have sessions with them. Along this journey, she uncovered several stories that contained information that was unknown to us: ways of life, beliefs, how people were treated for their beliefs and the secrecy that had to be kept for survival, not only for the self but for the beliefs and ways of life. The time period she uncovered was a time when you were not allowed to believe what you wanted but what you were told to believe. Dolores held onto this material for many, many years for the sole reason that she felt she would be crucified herself for bringing it to the surface and telling the secrets of what actually happened during that time period. Yes, today you are allowed to speak what you want and believe what you want, but deep down inside aren't we still like those people many years ago who wanted to spread the word but who were afraid that speaking up would bring an end to not just our lives but also to the knowledge that was so precious? In those days the people, not the rulers or those of importance, were so much closer to nature and God than I believe we are today. This is something that needs to be brought forward. Our Earth, nature and God are and should be held as what is most important in our ways. We should never again allow others to make us afraid of believing in what is right. For without this Earth, where will we be?!

Nancy Vernon
January 3, 2022

Every effort has been made to protect the identity and privacy of the clients involved in these sessions. The location where the sessions were held is accurate, but only first names have been used, and these have been changed.

As you read this work, you may notice that Dolores has used words that we don't use today. This is because when she is speaking with a client that is in a past life, that person is communicating as that person in that timeline. Many times there have been words spoken and Dolores could only print them phonetically. Sometimes this was due to the strong accent the person was speaking with from that lifetime.

Table of Contents

Introduction
The Time Traveler

Yes, I consider myself a time traveler, because I found a very effective way to traverse time through the method of regressive hypnosis. More accurately, I call myself a reporter, a researcher and an investigator and accumulator of lost knowledge. This has been accomplished through the use of a hypnosis technique which I have perfected over thirty years of working in this fascinating field. My roots in hypnosis go back in the 1960s when the older, time-consuming methods of induction were used. Hypnosis was used mainly to help people stop habits: e.g., stop overeating, stop smoking, etc. The idea of using it to help people through past-life regression therapy was unheard of. Even in the 1970s it was frowned upon by serious therapists. I have been a participant all during this time and have watched it evolve to where now it is an accepted and valuable form of therapy. Such is the way it is: methods that were once considered radical are now coming into wide use, because their value has been proven. In the 1960s there were no books to help any therapist understand this phenomenon. The only book at that time was *The Search for Bridey Murphy*, which was the story of one therapist stumbling across the idea of reincarnation. The book created a great deal of controversy at the time of its publication. Such a book would not even see print today, because it would be considered too common and mundane. I and many other therapists in this field encounter these simple cases constantly during our work, and the idea of reliving past lives is no longer considered extraordinary. That book was a groundbreaking concept at its time. A book for the appropriate time in our history.

I also stumbled across the idea of past lives and reincarnation in 1968 while working with a woman who was trying to lose weight. With the help of her doctor, my husband and I were attempting to help her nervous eating that was causing kidney problems. During the course of treatment, she suddenly slipped into a past life in Chicago in the 1920s, the flapper era. Since there were no books printed at that time to guide a hypnotist about what to do in such cases, we had to invent our own rules. With nothing to guide us except our curiosity, we took the woman through five lives. This story of my beginning was told in my first book *Five Lives Remembered*. That book has never been published, because I now consider it to be too mundane. It is the story of my beginning, but my path has taken me to unimaginable and incredible adventures since then. It may be printed one day, because people are always asking at my lectures about how I started, how I began on this fantastic journey. The journey that has taken me through time and space and dimensions, and around the world several times since that humble beginning. It is a path that I never would have dreamed of in the 1960s when I was busy being a Navy wife and mother of four children. It illustrates that anyone's life path can take a 180-degree turn, and the future can hold unimaginable adventures, if only you trust in the unknown plan of the universe.

** Update: This book, *Five Lives Remembered*, has now been published due to the overwhelming request from Dolores's readers. She felt it would seem mundane, but everyone wanted to know "how did it all start?" **

I had to wait until my children were grown and creating lives of their own before I could devote full time to hypnotherapy and investigation in 1979. I could never have dreamed that the people who were coming to me with problems would supply the information that resulted in nineteen books. Sometimes it may be better if we don't know what the future holds for us, or we would never start down the path. Along the path I was offered many chances to stop, turn around or detour. Any of these times my life would have been changed and I would have gone in a different direction. I called these years my "testing times." Fate was trying to see just how committed I was to the path I had started down. The path that led to an unknown future clouded in mystery. But once the commitment is made, there is no turning back. One of my readers sent me the following quotation that I considered to be very appropriate. It hangs over my desk and reminds me daily of the task I have volunteered for. The task of presenting unknown and lost knowledge to the world.

Until one is committed, there is hesitancy.
The moment one definitely commits oneself, then providence moves. All sorts of things occur to help one that would never otherwise have occurred.
A whole stream of events issues from the decision raising in one's favor; all manner of unforeseen incidents, meetings, and material assistance which no one could have dreamed would have come their way.
Whatever you do or dream you can do, begin it;
Because boldness has genius and power and magic in it.

~ Johann Wolfgang von Goethe

I now know that there have been unseen forces gently guiding my path all these years. They have been there to help, and I have had wonderful evidence of their care. They have never given me more than I could handle at the time, and I know my path would have been much rockier without them. Fantastic people have been brought into my life, and my books are now translated all over the world. Nothing that has happened could be considered accident or coincidence.

Since 1979 my work in past-life regression therapy has grown and evolved. I developed my own technique and have perfected it over the years. I found that much of the normal hypnosis techniques were time-consuming and unnecessary, so I began cutting out the procedures that I thought were not needed and was able to shorten the induction process. Then I gradually developed a technique that places the subject into the somnambulistic state of trance. This is the level from which I like to work, because I have found access to all knowledge there. Many hypnotists are afraid to work in such a deep level, because they say strange things can happen there. Those who have read my books about my adventures know that strange things *can* and *do* happen there. The somnambulistic state of trance is the deepest possible level. To go deeper causes the person to fall asleep, and it is difficult for them to respond. The somnambulistic level is attained by everyone at least twice each day. It is the state you pass through when you are going to sleep, and when you are waking up. My job is to take the subject to that level and keep them there during the session. It is said that one out of twenty or thirty people will spontaneously go into this state during hypnosis. Yet in the technique that I have developed the opposite is true: one out of twenty or thirty will *not* go. During most past-life sessions the person is placed in the lighter levels of trance. In this state they will remember what they saw and upon awakening think they made it all up or imagined a story to please the hypnotist. This is because the conscious mind is still active and acting as a censor and kibitzer. When the somnambulist state is reached the person does not remember anything. The conscious mind interference is totally blocked off and cannot influence the person with thoughts of "This is silly. You are making this up. You saw it in a movie, or you read it in a book." In the case of past-life regression, with the conscious mind out of the picture, the person *becomes* the other personality in the past *totally*. This lifetime no longer exists. They are only familiar with what is in the other lifetime. I have proven this many times in my other books. If you mention something in the present lifetime that does not exist in the past one, they will not know what you are talking about. The subject becomes the other personality so totally that, if they can write, for instance, I have had the handwriting compared to their present writing by handwriting analysts. They say they could not have been written by the same person. I have had them suddenly begin to speak in other languages, and even unknown or dead languages. When the person awakens from the regression, they have no memory of what has transpired. They will often say, "Oh, I'm sorry! I must have fallen asleep!" They have no feeling of the passage of time and the fact that I have two hours recorded on tape.

The majority of my clients go into this deep level, and we are able to find the cause of their problems in this life, because most of the time it can be traced back to other lifetimes. These cases of therapy would fill many volumes, and I use many examples when I teach my hypnosis class. But even though they reach this deep level and become the other personality, the majority of the lives were simple, mundane. This is a parallel to people's lives today. There are far more ordinary people than those who get their names in the newspaper. They will only be able to tell you what they know from their own life experience. The farmer in the field will not know what the king is discussing in his castle. They can only report what they are familiar with. This gives their stories more validity, because they do not claim to have been some important personage. The skeptics say that the person always claims to have been some famous person like Cleopatra or Napoleon. I have never found this to be true. Out of thousands and thousands of cases over more than thirty years I have never found anyone who was "the" important person. But I have found those who might have known or been associated with "the" person, or who might have lived in a historical time period. This is what I have written my books about.

Over thirty years I have accumulated an enormous amount of information. This has resulted in my nineteen books which cover all phases of the paranormal, from prophesy to history to UFOs and metaphysics. There is still a huge amount of information that has been waiting for the proper time to be inserted into a book. As I travel the world doing sessions, I find pieces of information that eventually form parts of a puzzle. I find a piece in one country, and another piece years later somewhere else. I try to arrange it according to subject matter. I now have so much and am still accumulating it that there is no danger of me running out of material to write about for many years to come.

That is where the information used in this book came from. I have encountered many people who had past lives in ancient societies or gnostic groups that had tremendous knowledge and abilities. This had to be kept secret for their own safety. There have always been groups down through history who desired mystic knowledge for their own use. These people were not allowed to have the information because they often wanted to use it negatively. In my book *Jesus and the Essenes* it was shown how the Essenes allowed themselves to be tortured and killed before they would reveal their secrets to the Romans. This has been the case through history. Many of these groups had powers and abilities we cannot even approach or understand today. But it is coming back in our time, because it will be needed in the new dimension we are evolving into. I have many clients who want to retrieve this lost knowledge that they knew in past lives. Doctors want to remember the psychic healing methods, therapists want to remember the use of energy to heal, and herbalists and similar workers want to bring back their knowledge of plants, herbs and oils. Artists want to regain their artistic abilities and techniques, as do musicians. I have found this is easy to do. All information is stored in the subconscious mind. If the person had a lifetime where they practiced these ancient arts or abilities, the knowledge is never forgotten. It is stored as in a gigantic computer and can be accessed if it is *appropriate*. That is always the key: if it is *appropriate*. The subconscious is the judge of that, whether it is advisable for the person to remember these abilities. In my technique I communicate directly with the subconscious mind, and it makes the decisions about whether the ability should be allowed to be returned to our time period. The majority of the time it will comply because it knows the person's motives better than anyone. Thus, I can see our world benefiting from this and I think it will help improve and change the world. This is what

I call "a groundswell" or "undercurrent" that the average person is not even aware of. Many of my clients are opening healing centers all over the world. These centers will use ancient healing methods based on long-destroyed societies, and even healing machines from ancient Atlantis. These are being reconstructed, as are free energy machines that were in use in Atlantis and on other planets. I have found people all over the world who are working on these things that come from other lifetimes and which will greatly benefit our present world. My part in all of this is to act as a mediator to allow the person to access their own lost talents and return them to our time. The knowledge and abilities of ancient times was incredible, and we have not even begun to develop these talents. But we are on the path to regaining it, and it will come about in our time. We will live to see this in our future. Of this I am certain.

In this book I will present some of the cases I have found over the years of lost information and knowledge. The "little people," fairies, elves and leprechauns were real. They were a part of everyday life. It is said they still exist, but we are too involved in our hectic lifestyle to be aware of them. The people in the past lived a more agriculturally based lifestyle and were much closer to nature, thus these beliefs were very real. Today in our modern technological society we laugh at these beliefs until the gremlins get into our computers and play games and create havoc.

The old religions were also very close to nature and knew how to work with the forces of the Earth that were very real to them. Magic was and is real. It is just the use and manipulation of energies. The results of this manipulation can be either positive or negative. The problem is not with the energy, but with the manipulator. They can steer the energy into any direction they want it to go once they know how to use these methods. It should always be remembered that the use of energies creates feedback and karma. The wise manipulator or practitioner knew that whatever way the energy was sent out that it would return to themselves tenfold. So, they were very careful not to use the energy for negativity, because the results on themselves could be devastating. They respected the use of this power.

The picture painted of these ancient gnostics and practitioners that has come down to our time is one of negativity, but the wise ones knew the cost of having these powers and would not use them in negative ways. But so often down through time these people were misunderstood, and when people found out about their abilities they were persecuted or killed. No wonder the souls today are hesitant to revive these powers and knowledge for use in our time. They subconsciously remember how dearly they paid for their abilities. In certain time periods the church was very diligent in trying to wipe out practitioners of anything they considered to be against the church. So much of this work had to be done in secret out of fear for their lives. As I have said in my lectures, "They hung us, burned us at the stake, killed and tortured us, but *we're back!*" They thought they destroyed the knowledge when they destroyed the body, but it is never lost. It is stored within the subconscious mind awaiting revival.

~ Dolores Cannon

** This is one of the books that Dolores was working on when she passed. She felt that now was the time for these stories to be told. **

Section 1
Life as a Druidess

Chapter 1
The Druidess (Karen)

I was fortunate in the early days of my work to work with several excellent somnambulistic subjects. This was during the time that I was still exploring and discovering what was possible to accomplish with this form of deep-trance hypnosis. Much of the material I uncovered in these early days has already been put into books. Much more is waiting for the appropriate category. During 1982 and 1983 I worked with Karen on a regular basis. I discovered the true meaning of time travel during my sessions with her. We eventually explored thirty different lifetimes, and the detailed information that poured from her was phenomenal. She was able to so totally become the other personality that she supplied historical information as well as cultural and theological. With my reporter's curiosity I asked every question I could think of about whatever era we found her in. Karen was a young twenty-two-year-old girl who had left school at seventeen without graduating because she wanted freedom. She soon found that freedom didn't come that easily. Jobs are hard to find without an education. So, she joined the army and became a computer expert in the early days before computer literacy became common. After leaving the service she settled in our area of northwest Arkansas and got a job in a company that was just beginning to use computers. Her lack of education was to be an asset to our work however, because she had not been influenced enough to fantasize stories in faraway geographical places. Skeptics always say that the subject under hypnosis will always describe events in a location and timeframe that they are familiar with, or have some knowledge of from books, movies, TV, etc. I have found that this is not true, because many of my subjects report detailed lifetimes in time periods and locations about which little is known. I have to do extensive research to verify their accounts. This is why I consider myself the reporter, the researcher of "lost" knowledge. I am regaining information about little known cultures and societies. In the case of this book, societies that had gnostic knowledge and forgotten abilities.

My work with Karen was often done at the home of my friend and fellow hypnotist, Harriet. She has been with me for over twenty years and has been a trusted confidant in my explorations into the unknown. She would sit in on the sessions and sometimes ask questions. Her energy always added an extra dimension to the adventure through time.

These sessions were a part of the series with Karen. At that time, I was still under the belief that time was linear and was working from that angle. I was trying to be organized and orderly about my approach. It would be at least fifteen years later before I made the discoveries that resulted in the "Convoluted Universe" series. By that time, I found that time does not exist at all. It is merely an illusion, and everything is existing at the same time. But in the early 1980s this concept had not yet been presented to me. I thought going backward in linear time was exciting, and I thought I had all the answers. I thought at that time I had the whole concept of reincarnation figured out. Little did I know that it was merely my baby steps into the unknown, and I was to have many shocking and mind-boggling concepts presented to me as I grew in my research. At any time, I could have stopped and declined to explore further, because my basic beliefs were being threatened. But I had the curiosity to explore further, and now in my work there are no limits to what I can discover, as long as the human mind can accept them. But in the early 1980s when I was working with Karen, I thought I was being very daring by taking her backward through time in 100-year jumps. These explorations resulted in my books, *A Soul Remembers Hiroshima* and *Jesus and the Essenes*, but the many other lives we discovered have not been put into books until now. They were waiting for their proper niche.

When I was making these jumps through time, I never knew where she would end up. I was making notes, so I knew all of the other entities that we uncovered as we progressed backward. It became so obvious that all I had to do was say the year and the same personality would emerge. These were always the same and never changed. They became quite familiar to me. I soon began to recognize the different personalities by their speech patterns and mannerisms. In some cases, even her facial expressions would change. They began to seem like old friends as each emerged. But we were still going backward, and I didn't know which new personality we would encounter next. This was our first time to encounter the Druidess. I am not even sure if the dates are correct, because I have since learned that the soul does not recognize time and the limitation of years, as we do. We had completed conversing with an entity in what we thought were the 800s. So, I had her jump back one hundred years to the 700s. After I finished counting her there, I asked what she was doing.

K: We go to the isle. 'Tis in the Sea of Mists.
D: *(This was confusing.)* *In the Sea of Mists?* *Oh, I'm not familiar with that.*
K: It is the isle of the lady.
D: *Where are you? Does this place have a name?*
K: Britain. (She frowned and was unsure of the answer.) This is what it is called. We call it the land. This is the name that someone gave it. (Her voice was very soft. Britain was pronounced: Britn.)
D: *Then you do not really call it Britain?*
K: It is just our land.
D: *How are you going to the isle?*
K: We walk across the pathway. It is a bridgeway. It is the time of the moon and the path has been cleared. The other times the water comes and rises, and it is covered.
D: *Oh, I see.* *Then during other times of the month, it is covered by water?* (Aye) *And then in the time of the moon, it is above*

water and you can walk across? What is your name? What do people call you?
K: It is Arania (Phonetic).
D: Are you a male or a female?
K: I am a woman.
D: Is this where you live?
K: No one lives on the isle but the lady. It is the chapel.
D: Where is your home?

She hesitated and had difficulty explaining. Then she said abruptly: "We must not tell."

D: Why? Is it dangerous to do that?
K: Many wish to find it so that they would *use* us for power.
D: Then you must be secretive of what you do, is that what you mean? (Aye)

This has happened at other times when I contacted people who were members of secret groups (especially the Essenes in my book *Jesus and the Essenes*). They distrust strangers and I knew I had to gain her confidence. Karen knew me and felt comfortable with me, but I was not speaking to her in the twentieth century, but to her former personality where the individual had a different set of morals. It is difficult to have the individual go against their morals, whether in the present life or a past one. This shows how closely the person identifies with their past-life personality. It becomes dominant.

D: But you know you can always tell me things because I don't tell people. I'm not someone who wants to hurt you. I try to help you.
K: We live in the hills with the Old Ones.
D: Then you don't live in a city or a town. (She frowned.) Do you know what a city is?
K: I know fort. We do not live at fort.
D: A city is where lots of people all live together in one place.
K: This sounds like fort to me.

D: *Could be. A fort, as I understand it, is a place that has a wall around it?* (Aye) *Where people live and are protected within the wall?* (Aye) *That would be very similar, yes, to what a city would be.*

K: We do not go there.

D: *Is it dangerous?*

K: It 'tis not done.

D: *Who lives in the fort?*

K: The ones from across the water.

D: *So, you live in the hills? You don't have a city of your own?* (No) *Do you live in houses in the hills?*

K: We find shelter in caves or sometimes huts.

D: *And you don't have a place where you stay all the time?*

K: No. We must always move.

D: *Why?*

K: They try to say what we do is wrong. And perhaps they slay us.

D: *Why would they think you did wrong things?*

K: Because we are not like them.

D: *In what ways are you not like them? Do you look different? Act different, or what?*

K: They are *darker* than us, but they say that it is wrong to worship the spirits and the fey and the ...

I didn't understand that word and asked her to repeat it. The dictionary spells it "fay" and it means: fairy.

** Upon further research we found "the fey" to be the world of the little people, leprechauns, fairies, sprites, brownies, etc. **

D: *The fay? And they think these are bad things?*

K: They say that we are from what they call their "demons," or something like that.

D: *Oh, is that true? Do you worship demons and things like that?*

K: (Emphatic) No!

D: *Do you think they just don't understand what you really do?*

K: They do not wish to. They know we have power, and they wish to either corrupt us or destroy us.

D: *So that's why you must hide?* (Aye) *This sounds like it's your belief, your religion? Do you know the word "religion"?*

K: It has no meaning to me.

D: *It's a belief. What you would worship and what you would believe in.*

K: Worship, yes.

D: *Do you have a name for your belief? I mean, do you call it something?*

K: The others, some of them call us Druids, but this is not what we call ourselves. We are just the ladies of the goddess.

D: *That's what I meant. A religion is what you believe in. You know, that you would consider your god, or your ... Well, it can have many meanings, do you know what I mean?*

I was only confusing her more by trying to explain the word, so I gave up.

D: *But you are one of the Druids? Is that what you call yourself? (She pronounced Druids a little differently than I did.) And you worship—I guess that's the right word—worship the Lady of the island?* (Yes) *Does the Lady have a name that you call her?*

K: She has a name, but it is never spoken, for it is not allowed on a mortal's lips. It is very holy.

D: *You cannot speak her name.*

K: To speak the name is to have power that has not been granted mortals.

D: *Even during your ceremonies you don't speak it?* (No) *These people who are trying to do these things to you, do they have a name?*

K: They are from Gaul. I have never met them.

D: *They're from across the water?*

K: Yes. They come in and they destroy the things of our friends, and they cry out to us. And when we strike at them, they try to kill us.

D: *But you're not a violent people, are you?*

K: *We* are not. I've heard of those who make sacrifice of people they captured. But we do not do that. The Old Ones, they do not like this.

D: *Well, you said you were crossing to an island on a bridge that is like a land bridge.*

K: Yes. The water rises and it covers it with the coming and the going of the moon.

D: *You mean, like with the tides?*

K: I know not this ... The water, it comes up and it is like it is not. But then there are times that it is for all to see.

D: *The water will go down at certain times, and then you can see the bridge to go across?* (Yes) *Well, when you get over there, do you have to wait before you can come back?*

K: The ceremony is done this night before the water rises again.

D: *Oh, you have to do it quickly then, in one day?* (Yes) *And then go back across the bridge before the water comes up?* (Yes) *You said there was a lady who lived there?*

K: The Lady. Not *a* lady. *The* Lady.

D: *I'm trying to understand. You must be patient with me. The Lady lives on the isle in the Sea of Mists? Is that correct?*

K: Yes. This is her place of power. And we are her children.

D: *Oh, she is not a real person. Is that what you mean?*

K: (Sigh) She is as real as you or I, but she is much more. She is greater.

D: *And then on this one night ... is it once a month?*

K: It is once a month.

D: *Once a month you go there and have a ceremony. Is that in her honor?*

K: In her honor? Yes. To show her ... to let her know that we remember and hold her in awe and ...

D: *Yes, I think I know what you mean. It's just hard for me to put it in words that you understand. You said, you are her chosen people? Would that be correct?* (Yes) *What do you have to do for her? Does she require things of you?*

K: We keep watch and we listen for things that she would perhaps need to know, and we help the folks that need it. The Lady, she is a healer, and if someone needs us, we would go and do this.

D: *Then she really is a flesh-and-blood person. I was thinking of maybe a spirit.*

K: (Sigh) She is not like me, she is much greater. She enters into the priestess and directs her. She is not a person as you would think of. She is a child of creation.

D: *A child of creation. But she is not a person like you or I that would require food and drink and a place to live.* (No) *Does she show you how to heal?* (Yes) *If you were going out to heal someone, how would you do that?*

K: If we are called, we must go, and while we are there, we would prepare a fire. And in drawing this fire into ourselves, we would draw the power and then we would ... (She had trouble finding the word.) channel this energy into the person who is ill. And sustain them while the herbs and the things that we had put together would then do their work.

D: *You use herbs too.*

K: Yes. The fire is something to gaze upon, to visualize, so that we would draw it into ourselves. This same fire, only greater and we would become part of *her*. And it would be her power and her energy that would be channeled through us.

D: *Then the fire is only used for you to look at, for you to concentrate on.* (Yes) *And when you put your hands on someone who is ill, you can direct power to that person to heal them. And you also give them the herbs. I'm just trying to understand. It's a little difficult for me.*

K: It's ... I'm not very good at explaining things.

D: *I think you're doing a very good job. Do you use any stones in healing?*

K: We use the purple stone that is found in the hills. Sometimes, if it is gazed upon, it has part of the fire, and then this is good. Sometimes if there are different things that are wrong, perhaps we would use the pink stone that is here too. It is shaped ... (She made hand motions.)

D: *Odd-shaped, you mean?*

K: Yes, and it also has part of the fire. By the feel of these things we would know where to find them. And each of us has our own personal stones, because there are several others that are used. But we find one thing on which to focus, that does not necessarily have to be the same for every person. We would find something that we would use to draw *our* energy, if perhaps there was no fire to start.

D: *Are you talking about a real fire, or are you talking about energy? Would that be a word you understand?*

K: The fire is started with power, but there is a real fire. It is made from different things. It is held in the bowl and it is lit through the energy. But it is a focal.

D: *Because you talked about there being fire in the stones.*

K: No, no. The stone is an extension of the fire. It is something that magnifies what we can put through our self.

Harriet was motioning to me.

D: *There is someone here who would like to speak with you and ask you some questions. Is it okay if she asks you some questions also?*

K: If I can answer, I shall try.

Harriet (H): Can you tell me if stones are used along with the fire? Are they placed over the fire to help you concentrate?

K: Usually they are strung, and they are hung about our neck, and over the point of light. They are on a long string and they are hung from where your essence of light comes. And they take that light and they amplify it. And this is how they are used.

Was she referring to the solar plexus chakra as the point of light?

H: *And that stone does change from person to person. Is this because different people have a different rate of energy?*

K: And some seem to work better with one stone than the other, yes.

H: *How does the individual find their correct stone? Do you go by the feel of it?*

K: Some stones, when they are taken into the hands, they repel, and you know that this is not good. And others, you feel the warmth and, almost like love radiating out of them, and this is the fire. And you know that this one is the right stone.

H: *Then does this stone stay with you constantly, or do you put it away?*

K: It stays with you, yes. Because the more that it is with you the more that it tunes itself to you and you tune yourself to it.

H: *Are different stones used for different types of illnesses? In other words, if one person has a purple stone, is that only good for certain types of healing?*

K: It depends on how much power this person can focus through the purple stone. If they have a very high level of being able to sustain the power, they can heal many things with this. But then there are those who have perhaps, maybe lower level of energy that they can focus, and they would only be able to heal certain things with their ability.

H: *Is there any way they improve their power, to increase it?*

K: By opening yourself to what is around you. To use focusing exercises every day, in which you focus on a certain point of yourself. The light center that is in all of us. When you learn to touch this and to hold the touch, then you will be able to release all your power.

H: *When you say touch, do you mean actually touching with your hands, or touching with your mind?*

K: No, it is drawing your mind into one's self, and focusing to this point until you see it and recognize it for what it is. And then you would reach out to hold it and lightly caress it, and this is the joining of yourself with the energy that is *all*.

H: *And this will help to increase your ability to share it with another person?* (Yes)

D: *These do help to make it stronger?*

K: Yes, but the original drawing must come from within. They cannot teach you to draw upon it.

D: *Are there any precautions you should take, so that when you try to use this energy, you won't hurt yourself?*

K: Place yourself in a very calm state and surround yourself with good will and protection, knowing that you are surrounded.

H: *Do shapes have any significance? For instance, triangles, pentagrams?*

K: The triangle has the points that draw *in* the energy, and so the central point, the center of this triangle is the focus point. The pentagram is in the same manner. A great deal of interest has been put upon the shape of, what is known as the … (She had difficulty finding the word.) ah, pyramid. In the very center of this, there is a *great* energy focus. I have heard that those that have similar knowledge, that they use this. It is said that the people who came before us, used these shapes to a great advantage. But there is also danger in the fact that they can amplify the power so much that great damage can also be done.

D: *The larger the pyramid, you mean, the larger the shape, this generates more power?*

K: Yes, the difference, it is stone or whatever it is made of.

D: *That's why the danger if you had a very large one, because you could generate too much energy?* (Yes) *Does it matter what material the shapes are made out of?*

K: It helps if they are made out of something that is pure. Crystal is good because it is basically pure. There are different stones that are also good.

D: *I mean, if they were made from wood or from a stone.*

K: A stone is perhaps better than the wood.

D: *You mean like a stone of the ground or a jewel?*

K: Yes. You see, if you use a jewel, perhaps, the focus links are not as in tune with what you are wanting to use it for. Like you would not use the crystal in the same way that you would use the aquamarine.

D: *But you could use a rock or a crystal, and it would work?* (Yes) *What about wood, if you carved …*

K: It is not as good.

D: *You said there was exercises that you do every day?*

K: Yes. Like the one that I described. There are also those in which you would go around and spin in circles this way (She made hand motions.) until that you could not go any longer. It opens oneself to the energy fields that are around you.

D: *Do you mean you spin your body?* (Yes) *Wouldn't you get dizzy?*

K: Each day you increase it until you could do it more and more, so that you are able to control the dizziness. And soon you will just feel the energy rather than just dizzy.

D: *I think it would make you fall down.*

H: *When you do this, do you move in what we would call a counterclockwise direction?*

K: You move wintershins.** (Phonetic. Maybe: withershins?)

** Another term might be "widdershins." This is a motion that is in a left-handed, wrong, or contrary direction (counterclockwise; compare deasil). **

There was some confusion here over the word, because it was strange to us.

D: *We don't understand that word. What do you mean?*

She moved her hand counterclockwise.

D: *The way your hand is moving now would be what we call counterclockwise. That's an odd word, isn't it?*

H: *You call it wintershins.* (Yes)

Naturally she didn't understand our word. She was obviously speaking from a time period that didn't have clocks.

D: *What do you call the other direction? Do you have a word for that?*

She was confused.

H: *Would you have any benefit by moving in the other direction?*

K: It is a blocking-off. We wouldn't use that direction.

H: Are there areas where it's better to do this circular movement?

K: If you're out in the meadow or under the canopy of the trees where you have an area that you could do it in. Anywhere that there is Earth power that you could open yourself to.

D: You wouldn't do it indoors then.

K: Where? In the cave? No. Where there is Earth power, you would use this.

D: I still think when you do it you would fall down. I probably would.

K: (Laugh) When we first started, there was many of us who fell. But it is no longer.

D: Do you do this every day? (Yes) *It's one of the exercises you have to build up then.* (Yes) *Are there many of your people?*

K: There are fewer than there used to be. It has become dangerous to become one of us. They do not wish us to survive, because our power threatens their security. They wish to take the people of this land. And when the people look to us for their help and guidance, if we are still here, then it is very dangerous for them.

D: Do you think this is why they spread these stories that you are bad, so the people will fear you? (Yes)

H: Why would they want to take your people? Where would they take them?

K: They just want to control them. They want them to do as they wish. They wish to rule.

D: So, they want you to use your powers to help them.

K: This is what they wish, but we shall not do this.

D: Even if they took you, you would not do any of these things that they want?

K: We would rather die.

D: So, it wouldn't do them any good. (No) *But you couldn't teach them anything anyway. They're probably the wrong kind of people.*

K: You cannot teach someone who is closed since birth, how to open one after it has been closed for many, many years. If they had no desire to learn it. Especially if it is for bad. The spirits know when a person is being honorable with them.

And if you are not, then they will not come.

D: *Well, there are bad spirits too, I have heard.*

K: Yes. But you must just protect yourself with the light and they cannot ... What you would consider a bad spirit is of the darkness. And where there is light, all darkness is repelled.

D: *How do you use this light? I'd like to try it. Would it work for me?*

K: If you are able to touch that which is the center of yourself. You just make this light come outward until it surrounds you.

D: *And no one can hurt you whenever you use that protective light? (No) I've heard of that. I call it the "white light." Would that be accurate?*

In my work in metaphysics, I have been taught to visualize a white light surrounding myself and my clients for protection against negative influences. I use this during my sessions, and also visualize it around my house and my car when I am traveling. I have been told in my work that the white light is a very powerful protecting force, and nothing negative can approach near it. I have encouraged many of my clients to also use this visualization as a protection.

K: Some people visualize it as being white. I see it as being every color in the rainbow. It encompasses all.

D: *There are many other stones besides the ones you talked about. I've heard of white ones. They're clear, you can see through them? (I was thinking of crystals.)*

K: I have heard of them being used to gaze in, but not as much for healing. They're not as common here, so we do not use them. Perhaps they are good. I do not know.

D: *Then the pink ones and the purple ones are better?*

K: They are the ones that are found here. This is what we use.

H: *Do you have a way of cutting the stones, or shape them into shapes?*

K: It is said that long ago, when we first came to this land, that there were those who with their essence could shape the stones. But for us, the only thing that we can do is to roughly shape them by using stones that are harder.

D: *And make a hole so you can put them around your neck?* (Yes)

H: *Is there any benefit to certain shapes?*

K: It is said that some shapes perhaps amplify the power even more by giving it a point to focal out of or in. It magnifies, yes.

D: *Are there any certain stones that you can wear for protection, or do you just use the light?*

K: Mostly we just use the light. It is much more powerful than a stone.

D: *Do you wear any particular type of garment?*

K: It is made out of white weave from the sheep. It has long sleeves and it is gathered at the waist with a cord.

H: *Do both men and women wear the same garment?*

K: There are no *men* who serve my Lady. There are men who serve others. We serve my Lady and there are no men among us.

D: *I've heard there were men who called themselves Druids.*

K: There are men who do terrible things and they are not good. It is said that originally when we came to this land, that we were always one people. And that over the years, there were people who saw that there were possibilities of ... were aimless in drawing the power of the dark side. And there was a rift and we went one side and they went the other.

D: *It's the same but they all went different directions.*

K: Yes, we would not hurt anyone.

D: *I believe that.*

H: *How are you chosen to do this?*

K: One of the ladies comes to the village where we are. They have been told that we are there, and they take us. We are exchanged for something of value. Our parents do not try to stop them.

D: *Is it an honor to be chosen for this service to the Lady?*

K: When I was chosen, it was a great honor.

H: *How old were you?*

K: Six.

D: You were a little girl. Then you have grown up with this?
(Yes)

H: Is it known when the child is born that they will be a servant of my Lady?

K: It is said, the priestess is told where to find the child. And, yes, it is known from their birth that this is the path they will take.

D: And when you are doing your studies, so to speak, is that when you are living in the caves? Or is there a certain place that you are taught how to do these things?

K: Sometimes during the later part of the training we go to the isle and spend the month.

D: The whole month?

K: And there many things are taught that are shadowed from other eyes, so that they would not know that power is being roused.

D: I thought you had to have a school, if you know what a school is, a place to learn.

K: We have teachers, but there is no ... building. (She had trouble finding that word.)

D: Can you tell us about the food that you eat?

K: We eat the fruits and the berries off of the trees, and nuts and some grasses.

D: Any meats?

K: (Shocked) No! To kill an animal is to kill something that lives and something that is part of the whole. Why would you wish to injure something that is part of nature?

D: A great many people do eat meat. But it's all right to eat things that are planted?

K: To take of the fruit of the tree or the nuts, it does not kill that which is alive. And we always leave enough so that there will be more. This does not harm anyone. They are for the good of the Earth. But to take and to kill something that is alive, to *kill* it, that is *wrong*! (She shuttered all over.)

D: If it upsets you, don't think about it. There are many people in the world, and they do many different things. Some people plant what is known as crops. Do you know what they are?

K: I have seen people that turn the ground, to put seed into the ground and this is good. As long as there is always more seed to place into the ground the Earth is willing to share her essence with all. As long as you put back as much as you take away.

I moved her ahead in time until she was on the island having the ceremony. I reassured her that she could trust us, and that we wouldn't reveal anything she shared with us.

K: All of us form a great circle around the altar in the glade. And we all, holding the candle, circle to the round while we chant. And we all are focusing our energy onto the altar. So that our love and part of our essence is focused to my Lady. And it is through this the power is then brought back to us, so that we receive greater, through the sharing and blending than we have given out. The altar is black, but in the center, there is a stone that is very clear. But it shines, it gives off a blaze of light. It is a center of the focus. It is used as a focuser. Also, an amplifier.

D: *Will the Lady come when you do this chanting?*

K: She will, if it is her wish, enter her spirit into the high priestess, so that we may know her will.

D: *Then she will speak through the high priestess?* (Yes) *And after you do the chanting and the going around in the circle, she will appear at that time?*

K: If she has chosen, yes.

D: *What type of chanting do you do? Is there a special sound or words that you use when you chant?*

K: It is not a word. How does one describe it? It sounds like the wind as it rushes by or the waves as they strike the rocks.

D: *Can you make the sound for me?*

At first, she declined, then hesitated. She was undecided, but finally she said: "It is an ahhhh sound, but it has a maaaa. But it is not allowed to tell ... I cannot!" She seemed disturbed. Apparently, she was stepping over the line of secrecy. I reassured her.

D: *Thank you for sharing the information. We don't want to get you into any trouble. We can be trusted, because we aren't going to do anything to hurt you. But this sound does help you all focus together as you all say it at the same time?* (Yes) *You said you go to the island at the time of the moon. Is it the full moon or what?*

K: Yes. It is the time of the new moon, when it is there, large in the sky.

D: *Oh, the moon is very big then. That is the time whenever the bridge appears, and you can go across.* (Yes) *Wouldn't it be dangerous if these people knew when you were out there, because they would know where to find you?*

K: The island is protected. It is not *here* to other people.

D: *I see. That's why they call it the Sea of Mists?* (Yes) *They cannot always see it.*

D: *There's a place I've heard about that's on your land. I don't know if you would call it the same name I call it or not. Have you ever heard of a place called Stonehenge? Do you know that name?*

K: (Pause) You mean the Giants' Dance. It stands in the middle of the plain, and it was built not long after we first came, and it was a place of study. Of focusing powers and learning about the universe.

D: *I've heard they have large stones and they are in a circle? Is this the same place?*

K: Yes. It is said that it was raised by music. This is true. By using certain sounds great weights can be lifted and moved. And it is said that before this was lost that this was built.

D: *There are many stones that stand upright and there are stones across the tops too.*

K: And then there are the, what has come to be known as the altar stone or the king's stone. And then there are the chalk pits that surround it.

D: *What is the purpose of those?*

K: The only thing that it is known to us now, is to chart the days.

D: *What was the purpose of building it to begin with?*

K: It is said that it is to mark the time ... to the end. That when the mystery has been remembered, that then it will come time. This is a legend.

D: *Because many people have wondered why it was built and what purpose it ever served. It is a great mystery. Why to go to all the trouble to build it and then not have a reason?*

K: When the reason has been remembered ...

D: *Then you don't really know the reason why it was built?*

K: It is said that it will be known on the last day.

H: *You said your people came here from another place. Do you know where your people came from originally?*

K: It was a place across the water, that is said to have been destroyed. It is said that they angered the gods and they were misusing the abilities that had been given to them. And the gods threw their wrath down upon them and scattered them to the four winds.

D: *Do you know how the country was destroyed?*

K: Just that it sank into the sea.

** In many stories, it is said that the people of Atlantis had very strong psychic abilities/powers which may have contributed to the destruction of that area. They were able to lift heavy stones and even mold stone with their minds. Here in Karen's life as the Druidess, her belief is that Stonehenge (Giants' Dance) was raised just after the fall of Atlantis, apparently by some of the survivors. **

D: *Then the people spread to many places? That's why you have remembered the powers your people had in those days?* (Yes) *I think we were talking of the same place. It's just that where we live, they call that place Stonehenge.*

K: I have no knowledge of this name. It is just known as the Giants' Dance.

D: *Today people think it has to do with the times of the year.*

K: Marks the time, yes. But there is also greater meaning. The altar stone is lit with the fire of the sun at the mid of summer. It is this that is the mystery.

D: *But your people don't use that today?*

K: The people of my Lady have never used this. This was back long, long ago.

D: *Then your people, the Druids, did not build it?*

K: The people we came from built this, but not those you would consider to call Druids now. We did not build it. It is old even now.

D: *That's the story now where we live, that the Druids built it many, many years ago.*

K: No men that walk the Earth now remembers the power to lift the stones.

D: *Do you think it was built at the time when the country existed that fell beneath the sea?*

K: It is said that it was built by the people who came from there.

D: *Then they still had the power.* (Yes) *It is very old and very mysterious.*

D: *About how old are you at this time?*

K: Um, perhaps ... twenty-four, twenty-five.

D: *Then you are still a young woman?*

K: I am approaching middle-age.

D: *You are no longer a child anyway. The women in your group, are they ever allowed to marry?*

K: It is very rare that any of the women have a desire to do so, but if they come and find that this is in their path, if the Lady gives her permission, then it is granted.

D: *Then you are not strictly forbidden.* (No) *But it doesn't happen very often?*

K: Who would exchange a life of that for this? And a chance to serve my Lady and *all* men rather than just one.

H: *What kind of life would a young woman lead that wouldn't be chosen for this service to my Lady?*

K: Work in a field or just raise children and help her husband and ...

D: *She would live a normal human life, in other words.*

K: What knowledge is gained from this; I do not know.

H: So, these women don't really have the opportunity to learn. They merely serve by producing more children? (Yes) *But yours is a service that can help from a healing standpoint and raising the level of the mind?*

K: I hope to.

H Really then you are protecting the power and maintaining it. If you were not here to do this, this power would be lost.

K: The Lady would never be lost. But perhaps forgotten. And it is very important that they be remembered, because it is through love that we give in the need and to go on and exist.

D: You said you come to the island once a month and you live in caves or wherever you can hide. What do you do with the rest of your time?

K: We travel and if there is someone who needs us, we go out to find them. We spend time gathering foods and always learning new things. Gathering herbs and drying them. Making different things to heal with, yes.

D: But isn't that dangerous whenever you go where other people are?

K: We would not be called if they did not wish to have us there and to protect us.

D: The people will protect you?

K: Yes. When they have need of us, we are safe from harm.

D: How do they get word to you if they don't know where you hide?

K: They just let it be known that there is someone who is ill and we will know.

D: The message is given mostly through the Lady? She tells you where to go?

K: Or the Old Ones.

D: The Old Ones? You said before that you lived with the Old Ones in the caves.

K: Yes, sometimes they share the caves with us.

D: Who are the Old Ones?

K: They are the people of the hills. They have always been here. They were here when our people came. They follow the old gods and keep them from being forgotten.

D: *Are the Old Ones people?* (Yes) *I thought maybe they might be like the Lady. And these can be both men and women?* (Yes) *That's all they're called, is the Old Ones?*

K: It is said that the Old Ones are descended from the gods. A long time ago before man set foot on this Earth, the Old Ones walked the Earth. And life was good. And then there came men and women from who knows where, and the gods found this pleasing that there should be others also and some of the women found favor with the gods. And it is said that these are their children, of these women and the gods. And each one is named after the god of their family.

D: *Then they are called the Old Ones not because they are very old, but because they come from these old ...?*

K: It is this dying race. There are fewer and fewer born each year. And they are being pushed back into the hills, because of all the other things, the strangers such as come to this land. And they are being pushed back like we. And it is through fear and superstition that many of them have died of just hunger.

Each of them is of a family that serves one of the old gods. And the oldest of that family is always named of the god that they follow. And they are kept alive by those who still remember and leave offerings at the crossroads. And they share it with us in the names of the gods who they descended from.

D: *And by remembering these gods they keep their religion alive.*

K: They have starved because no one or very few leave the offerings that used to be left at the crossroads for them.

D: *They use this to live on?* (Yes*) They're being forgotten.* (Yes) *That's a shame. You said they are named. Do you know some of the names of the gods that they are named after?*

K: (These are phonetic spellings. The tape had noisy background noise and it was difficult to understand.) Like Melvin (Elvin?), and Cur and Mortan. There are hundreds.

** One of the areas Dolores was well known for was her research. She would spend hours upon hours in the library looking up the smallest details. This is where she was as she was working on this book when she passed. So now, it is you the reader that will have to do some research. I know this refers to ancient mythology but am not able to give you the details. **

D: *And they know which god they came from because they carry the same name.* (Yes) *And they let your people live with them sometimes.*

K: We help them when that we are able, and for this it is considered good because the Old Ones, they have smiled upon us too, and know that we mean them no harm.

D: *And there are people who* do *mean you harm in this land.* (Yes)

H: *Can you tell me, have you ever heard of power lines that run across the country? In our country we call them "ley lines."*

K: There is one going across the meadows at which the Giants' Dance runs. It is an intersection of such lines that you speak of. It is where the Earth power *leaks* from the center. And if one goes to these points and opens oneself to this, you can gain much understanding and much power to do great things.

H: *Is there any way of detecting these lines?*

K: Just in making oneself sensitive to certain power forces.

H: *Would you feel it as a force when you were over this point?*

K: Yes. There are those of us who use things to witch, and when we go to witch we can find these lines. The Giants' Dance is on two intersecting lines. This is an extreme power point. There are places in the hills where that there are also power points such as this and they are always honored by the gods. And have come to be known as places of the gods.

D: *You said you can witch to find these places. How do you do that?*

K: You can either use a stick that is from a willow or fruit tree, and by holding it in the hands it will tell you where these lines are. You may also find different things with this.

D: *I've heard you can find water that way.*

K: You can find underground water. You can find different sources of stone, different types of stone … metal. You just learn to focus on what you are looking for.

D: *And use the same kind of a stick?*

K: Many people use a stick all of their lives, the same one. The willow has very good energy lines that run through it, and it is very sensitive to things. And it is also more limber and therefore rides easier.

D: *I've heard it has to be a fresh-cut branch.*

K: Either fresh-cut or one that is kept alive.

So it appears that the art of dowsing is very old, and the technique has not changed much through time.

D: *You possess much knowledge of many things that you can tell us that we don't know.*

H: It's very good of you to share it with us.

D: *Because we won't use it in a bad way or tell anyone.*

H: It is learning, and it is helpful to know these things. Helpful to grow.

D: *We would never tell the ones in the fort or the ones who you fear, because we don't do things like that.*

When Karen awakened, she had no memory of the session, but she was bursting with energy. She had so much, she said it felt like it was shooting out of her. She needed to do something with it. She was very excited. So we put her to work using it as healing energy on us. This releasing of it made her calm down. She didn't know where it came from and why it affected her in this way. She apparently absorbed it when describing and experiencing the ceremony around the altar on the isle.

We did not encounter the Druidess again until we held a session a few weeks later. It was again held at Harriet's house. I had again been going through my procedure and speaking to several entities living their lives in various time periods and locations. We had spoken to two other entities before this portion. We cut them short because Karen had asked at the beginning of the session to be returned to the time of the Druidess. Although she remembered nothing of the session, she enjoyed the exhilarating feeling she had of being able to tap into that tremendous energy field. She hoped to do it again and maybe learn something about directing the energy. We agreed to try it. We could always return to the other entities at another time to gain more information. I moved her backward again to the 700s. At the end of the count she had immediately entered the scene.

K: We are preparing for the ceremony on the island. We're doing the initiation. (That word was pronounced deliberately, as though it was a strange word.)

D: *What is that for?*

K: To bring new ... (Searched for the word) disciples to my Lady.

D: *Do you have new disciples there?*

K: Yes. They will be appraised and then the decision will be made. Whether they will stay or whether they will be sent home.

D: *How do you make a decision like that?*

K: It is not our decision to make. It is up to my Lady.

D: *How do you know what decision she has reached?*

K: The high priestess will know because it will be told unto her.

D: *Can you tell us what is happening? How a new disciple is chosen?*

K: They are first clothed in the white robes and they are placed in the center of the circle. And we begin the focus of energy. It is one by one to each of them. The energy is *pressed* toward them, to be either accepted or repelled. And depending upon how it is either received or not, the ultimate decision lies in that.

D: *You mean everyone in the circle is focusing energy toward the person that stands in the middle?* (Yes) *And how do they react whenever it is accepted or repelled?*

K: If it is repelled, the person will go into ... ah, (She searched for the word.) spasms, where the body will jerk. And it is known that this is too powerful for this person. They may have the ability to be a channel, but this is too powerful, and they cannot accept this.

D: Even though they want to, they can't do it. (Yes) *How do they react if they accept the energy?*

K: They are told if they can feel this, to let it build up. And then they are told to channel it back, just by thought focus, upon the high priestess. And when she feels this energy returning, she will know that this person is accepted.

D: They will be a good one to teach. (Yes) *How do you focus this energy? How do you make it come into your body?*

K: You open yourself. Feel oneself to be very calm. To where all is still.

D: Do you place your hands that way?

She had her hands placed over the solar plexus, with all the fingers and thumbs touching while pointed outward. Almost like the shape of a pyramid.

K: Yes, it is placed over the point of where the energy focuses. Then, when you have opened yourself, it is like listening to music. You feel the vibrations in you and you just draw on them. And you breathe in and out. And with each breath, you bring more in.

D: Breathe slowly?

K: Yes. And then to channel it out, it is almost like the reverse process. You place your hands like this and will it to flow through you. (Put the palms out.) In which it is like the current from the stream that is flowing. And you just let it flow through.

D: And this is the way it's directed? (Yes) *The channeling of energy, can it ever be harmful to the one who channels it?*

K: It can be harmful if they perhaps take more than they are capable. But usually there is the protection because a single person cannot draw in more than they can receive. The only harm in channeling is if many, many people are channeling it *at* you. It could perhaps be harmful.

D: Then when you take it in, do you have to release the energy? It has to go somewhere?

K: Yes. You either return it to my Lady or you give her love and spread it to others who have need of this. In healing or in other methods, yes.

D: *Then you must send it somewhere.*

K: Yes. It is not for your own gain.

D: *When you use this energy this way, can it help you to heal people by focusing it out that way. (Yes) Is that the only way it can be done? Just be calm and to breathe slowly and focus it.*

K: It is one of the ways, yes.

D: *One of the ways. Is this the easiest way? (Yes) We're asking because we hope to learn and want to do this for good. What is the other method? Can you do it by yourself or does it have to be done with other people?*

K: It may be done by one's own.

D: *Can you tell me what that method is?*

K: (Emphatic) No!

I would have to settle for what we had and not press our luck.

D: *Okay. But this method is the easiest one to learn. You would always have to use this energy for good, wouldn't you? (Yes) Now if you generate this energy and focus it out, do you touch the person or place your hands over the person?*

K: Usually you just place them over the person and feel the energy that surrounds them. Everyone has energy that comes into their body, that is surrounding them. And you place it upon this.

She was probably referring to the auric field.

D: *Then you have to place it over the part where they are ill? Or just over their head or what?*

K: Sometimes over the part that is ill. Sometimes just all over the whole body. And putting energy into the whole body, because usually it is not just one point in a person that is having problems, but the whole body suffers.

D: *You would have to move your hands over the whole body?*
(Yes) *Unless there was a spot where they said they hurt.*

K: Then you could put perhaps more energy into that area, but you would also need to go over most of the body.

D: *If you're putting your hands like that, can you tell if someone is hurting in a certain area, without them saying so?*

K: Yes, you can feel the pain through yourself.

D: *Does this bother you?*

K: Sometimes, yes.

D: *How can you get rid of that so it won't bother you?*

K: Then you create a focus again, directing it inward rather than outward. Then it should go away.

D: *You try to, what, wash it out of your body?* (Yes) *Because you don't want it to hurt yourself.*

H: *In your training, do you have any way of recognizing others that have been trained as you have been trained? Even though they have not been trained with you? Others of like beliefs.*

K: Give me your hand.

Harriet gave Karen her hand. Karen held it in both of hers and concentrated.

K: I see a temple of light. There are many, many people there who are studying and learning. It … seems like a long time ago.

D: *Before your time?*

K: It is the study for good and for healing. I see the using of different vibrations. They think of this in terms of colors, but they are the vibrations that *I* use. They are into generating self-healing and that all healing must come from within.

Karen dropped Harriet's hand, and took a deep breath.

D: *Then this person had done this in another time? An earlier time before your time.*

H: *Will this be carried on from generation to generation?*

K: You must open the channel. The ability is there. You must learn to open yourself to what you have learned. And focusing your energy and bringing it and drawing on it, to use for others.

H: But the gift is never lost after you once have it?

K: No. Once it is learned, it is always there. It must perhaps, be uncovered.

D: Brought back again?

K: Yes, or perhaps there are so many things, so much different experiences that have covered it over, that it must be brought to the surface. But it is always there.

H: It's nice to know it's there.

I couldn't resist the opportunity. I asked, "Could you take my hand and see if you can see anything?" Karen took my hand in the same manner, holding it between hers and concentrating.

K: I see a very patient person. You have great curiosity. You love knowledge for knowledge sake. There was ... I see a large open building with many, many books ...

She then shuddered and threw my hand away abruptly.

D: Oh! What's wrong? (She seemed disturbed.) Was it something you didn't like? (No answer) I'm sorry, I didn't mean to disturb you.

K: You must search for knowledge because of those who destroyed that which you felt was yours.

D: Someone destroyed my knowledge or what?

K: The knowledge that you protected. Therefore, you feel that you must search for the knowledge that has been lost.

D: But did you see something that was disturbing? Is that why it bothered you?

K: I saw fire!

D: Oh, I see. Well, I don't want to disturb you. You think this is why I am so interested in these things?

K: Yes, it has a great deal to do with that and the search for what you feel you have lost, and you wish to gain again.

D: *But it's not bad to be curious, is it?* (No) *I feel it can only be bad if you use it in the wrong way. Is that right?*

K: This is true. But you must always watch for those who are using the knowledge that you give them, to make sure that they cannot use it in a wrong and harmful manner.

D: *But sometimes you don't always know how people will use it when you try to show them the way. I guess if I do it in the right way and hope that they will use it right, will that be enough?*

K: If you will place your energies into the work you are doing, and put this energy into protecting it, so that it cannot be abused or mistreated, this will create a protection about it.

D: *I just hope that it will serve the purpose and do the right thing.*

K: You must not *hope*, you must *believe*. Hope has no power or strength but believing does.

** Dolores has spoken many times in her lectures when asked about her own past lives about the life in Alexandria at the Library when it was burned.

To the best of my recollection, she was one of the people who cared for the scrolls that were kept in the Library. She was not one who would write on them or study them but was one who would retrieve the scrolls when requested by a scholar or professor. It was her job to protect them.

When the Romans caused the fire that burned the Library, Dolores, as the person from that time, tried to save as many scrolls as possible. In doing so, she was killed and was not able to complete her mission.

Dolores has stated that because of this, she feels she is now trying to get back the knowledge that was lost. Many people ask, "Do you have to rewrite the whole Library?"

While in Russia, Dolores had a session with a young man who also was in Alexandria at the time of the burning. He was one of the scholars who studied the scrolls and was there when the burning started. He also tried to save as many scrolls as he could but was killed by a falling beam that struck him across the shoulders.

I don't know if Dolores ever found anyone else that was there during this time but to find just one was astonishing. **

H: Do you do anything with the studying of the stars and the planets in your work? Is this helpful in any manner?
K: We watch the movement of the stars for they tell what will be. The compelling of people who are here, on the whole planet, yes.
H: Which is the most important star?
K: You cannot say that one is more important than the other. Because it depends on which emphasis you are trying to receive. Their energy is used for different things and we cannot say that one is more important than the others.
H: Can you tell us a little bit about which ones are important as to, for instance, your energy. (Pause) Is this possible or is this not? (She began to tense up.)

Relax, now, relax.
I was trying to get another tape out of the case. If we were going to discuss the stars I wanted to go on. Otherwise, this one was running out. But apparently, she didn't want to talk about it.

D: I want to thank you for what you've been telling us. Is it all right if we come from time to time and speak with you?
K: I will tell you what I may.
D: Okay, we don't ever want you to tell us anything that you don't want to, or that you will get in trouble for. We're just searching for knowledge too. And we want to use it in the right way. I really do appreciate what you have told us. We enjoy speaking with you. Thank you.
H: Thank you.

Karen had asked us to get the instructions for the healing energy. When she awakened, she was again bursting with energy and wanted to direct it somewhere. She apparently picked it up from the Druidess entity. She went to each of us placing her hands on our aura field, trying to release the energy as a healing force.

We could definitely feel a tingling sensation moving through our bodies.

Since Harriet was out of town, this session was held at my daughter Nancy's house. There was no one else present to act as a witness. By the end of this session, I regretted not having someone else there. What occurred during this session shook me and was the most unsettling experience I have had as a therapist. After encountering another entity on my journey backwards through time, I moved her to the 700s again, and she emerged as the Druidess in a peaceful scene.

K: I'm gathering herbs. They are for preparations to heal the sick.

D: *Is this what you do?*

K: This is part of what I do, yes.

D: *Do you know which herbs to use?* (Yes) *Do you know how to prepare them?*

K: Yes, some are just eaten raw, and others must be brewed into a form that is usable.

D: *I think that would be complicated.*

K: One must just be careful. Some herbs are helpful, if used in the right amounts. But if too much is used, or it has not been steeped long enough, it can be deadly.

D: *So you must be careful to use the right amounts.* (Yes) *What kind of herbs are you gathering? Do you know the names?*

K: There is the nightshade and the foxglove, and also there is the hemlock and sheep's bane** and different things like that.

** Sheep's bane is an herb of Hydrocotyle or the closely related genus Centella. **

D: *Some of those herbs I've heard are poison.*

K: Yes. (She began sneezing.) It is the flowers that die in the air.

D: *Oh, yes, they make things go in the air, don't they, when you*

walk through them? (She cleared her throat.)
K: Also, some of these are the ferns and things, they have the …
(trying to find words) ah, the things that come off the back of
it, the seeds. (She sneezed again.)

She couldn't find the words for the spores that ferns give off,
or the pollen released by plants. This was what was causing the
irritation to her throat and nose.

D: *These are in the air.* (Yes) *I know many herbs, but I don't
know if they're the kind that you use. Like sage? Do you
know that one?*
K: It is not familiar to me.

She sneezed and coughed. I gave suggestions to relieve the
physical discomfort. "It won't bother you. It's just in the things
in the air, it won't bother you at all." She stopped coughing, so
I returned to asking about the herbs. "There are the ones called
rosemary and thyme. These are herbs that I know."

K: I do not know of them.
D: *What about mayapple?*

I was thinking of plants that grow in the woods in the Ozarks
where I live.

K: Describe it to me.
D: *It is very low to the ground. It has a plant with a very big leaf,
usually only one leaf shaped like a hand. And it has a little
round fruit. And it's mostly green.*
K: Is it poison?
D: *I don't think so.*
K: I do not know this.

These were plants that Karen was familiar with because
she had lived in the Ozarks many years, but they were apparently
unknown to the Druidess.

D: *Maybe it doesn't grow where you live. And we have one that is called ginseng. (She frowned.) I was wondering if you used the same herbs that we would use. Some of the herbs I'm speaking of are used in cooking food.*

K: The ones I am gathering are for healing.

D: *There would be a difference. There is one called lambsquarter.*

K: It is for you to eat. (She coughed again.)

Although lambsquarter is considered a weed and a pest to gardeners, it is edible and put into salads in the hills where I live. So she was correct.

D: *Well, you told me that you eat the berries and the nuts.*

K: Yes, and fruit. There are a few herbs that I eat. Some of them gather around the quarter (I think it is quarter. Unclear. Maybe: water. Or was she referring to the phase of the moon?) and different things like that together. But mostly the fruit and the berries and nuts.

D: *What do you eat in the wintertime?*

K: The things that have been stored away. Sometimes people eat the roots of different things and ... (She coughed again and cleared her throat. I again gave suggestions for well-being.)

D: *I know that in the wintertime many plants aren't growing. It's hard to find things to eat.*

K: If it gets very bad, there is always boiled bark.

D: *Oh? Does that taste good?*

K: (Laugh) No! It has a bitter taste. It depends on the bark. Like elms' bark is good for some things that are wrong with the body.

D: *For healing, you mean?*

K: Yes. But oak bark is all right to eat and pine bark is, or fir is also good to eat. If you can get past the taste, yes, it will sustain you.

D: *If there's nothing else to eat. Do you ever do any cooking?*

K: There is not much cooking that is done. Most of the things are eaten in their natural state, except for things like the bark which is boiled. But there are many fruits that will store for long periods of time. The apple will stay good for quite a while, as long as it is kept cool.

She started coughing again, so I decided to move her to relieve the discomfort from the blowing pollen in the air.

D: *Well, it seems like that's bothering you, so let's move ahead then. We'll leave that scene. Let's move ahead to another time. Let's go forward to an important day in your life. A day that you consider to be important as you are growing older. 1, 2, 3, it is an important day in your life as you are older. What are you doing?*

K: I'm at the ceremony. (The coughing stopped immediately.)

D: *Which ceremony is that?*

K: To the Lady.

D: *On the island?* (Yes) *Can you tell me about it? (Pause) Or are you allowed to tell me? (Pause) I don't want to get you in any kind of trouble. Is it a nice ceremony?*

K: Yes. I'm to be one step closer.

D: *This is an important day then. What do you call these steps? Do they have names or positions?*

K: Yes. There is the high lady priestess. That is the highest that you can reach. And then there are the priestesses and then there are just the ladies-in-waiting. And then there are the maidens who are the lower. I am to be made a priestess. I was a lady-in-waiting.

D: *Are there many of you that have reached that position?*

K: No, there are only two among us who have reached this position.

D: *Then it is an honor to have gone that far. How many did you say there were of you?*

K: There are perhaps thirty in all. Maybe a few more.

D: *And there is only the one that is the high priestess. Is she very old?*

K: I don't know. It is hard to judge the age. It is said that the high priestess is ageless, because of the power of the Lady on her. It is only when the hand is taken away that death can occur.

D: *Did you say you have these ceremonies every month?*

K: It is sometimes.

D: *How many days do you stay on the island?*

K: Until we learn different things. Like this month we will stay almost the whole month because there are the ceremonies that must be completed. Herbs also that have been gathered. And we must do this here where we are protected and that there is no possible way for others to come upon us, so that the work may be done.

D: *You said there were people who were trying to find out your secrets?*

K: Yes, there are those who wish to use us against those they do not like, for they know our power is great.

D: *It would be bad if people like that were to use your power, wouldn't it?*

K: It would be an atrocity. We are taught that if we have been caught, if there is no other way, that we must kill ourselves. So that we may not be used.

D: *Do you think they might use the power in a good way?*

K: No. How can something that is base learn to use something purely, when there is nothing but baseness inside themselves?

D: *But still if you were caught, they couldn't make you tell, could they?*

K: It is perhaps, that we are afraid that they have a little knowledge of what we are, and they would be able to use this little knowledge that they have against us, and perhaps make us tell. We are not to take this chance.

D: *You could always fool them. You wouldn't have to tell them the truth. They would never know the difference.*

K: This is the law. If one did not kill herself, she would be killed by those of her circle because she would have lost faith with them.

D: *I can see that's why you don't feel you can tell me some things. I'm not an enemy though, I'm just someone who talks to you. You know that, don't you?* (Yes) *You don't feel that I could hurt you, do you?*

K: I do not feel this, but how can I explain this to others if they questioned?

D: *Yes, I see. It's better not to take the chance then. No, you don't have to tell me anything if you don't feel you can. Even though I can assure you, you are perfectly safe talking to me. Do you just stay away from those people who do mean you harm?*

K: Yes. As much as we possibly can, we stay away from those.

D: *What do they look like? How can you tell these people?*

K: They are tall, and they wear odd clothing. And they have spears and they march. They are men of war.

D: *Do they live near where you live?*

K: We have not seen any here. But within a day's journey, it is said that they have come that far.

D: *What are* they *doing in the land?*

K: The Lady says that they come to conquer.

D: *Then we don't want to let people like that know your secrets.*

She started coughing again. I thought by moving her from the blowing pollen it would alleviate the coughing.

D: *Why are you coughing?*

K: It is something I am working out of ... myself. It is ... let me explain. When one takes and uses the energies to heal, what is in this person you take it upon yourself. And I am just beginning to work it out.

D: *Then you were healing someone, and a part of what was wrong with them you took within. Is that what you mean?* (Yes) *Is there any way to heal without taking part of the sickness?*

K: There are those that are higher than I who have this ability, but this empathy is part of what I am.

D: *I thought maybe you could protect yourself so you wouldn't take on part of their disease.*

K: Eventually, yes. But I'm still learning.

D: *But this is good of you to be willing to take it on yourself. But then you have to work it out. I just wondered why you coughed.*

I thought we had learned enough here, so I moved her ahead in time to another important day in her life. When I finished counting, her face clearly indicated that something was wrong.

K: I was ... sent for to heal. (She seemed frightened.)
D: *Where are you?*
K: In a room ... and they have locked the door!
D: *Who has locked the door?*
K: The people who are here. It was a trick!
D: *Oh? You mean these people are not really ill?* (No) *But you thought it was safe? It was all right to go there?*

She was taking a long time to answer. Fear was evident.

K: It is just a hut. We have been here before. And ... they *killed* them! They killed the people who lived here.
D: *Who are the people who have locked the door?*
K: They are ... they must be strangers. They are speaking together. I can hear them.

I did not know if she was experiencing anything yet, but she was definitely afraid.

D: *What do you think is going to happen?*
K: (Her voice was strained.) I must die! I don't wish to, but I *must!*
D: *Why? What are they talking about?*
K: I don't know. I cannot understand them. They speak in their strange words.

Something unusual began happening here that worried me. She took a deep breath and stopped talking. She seemed to be involved in something I didn't understand. She placed her hands together over her solar plexus. The fingers and thumbs touching and pointed outward, with the arms and base of the hands resting over her solar plexus. The same positions she had shown me before when she was describing how she directed energy toward the initiates. This time it appeared different. Something was not right. She was too intense. It made me uncomfortable. She was concentrating deeply on something and her breathing began to alter. I had a feeling the entity was doing something to herself. She had said that she would have to kill herself in the event of capture. Was the power of the Druids so powerful that they had control over their own life and death? I didn't know and I didn't want to find out. It is said that the subconscious is protecting the person even at this deep state of hypnosis and that the subject is never in any danger. But the intense concentration of her focusing and the altering of her breathing made me feel uneasy. I was afraid maybe the Druidess was powerful enough that she could harm this present-day body structure without really meaning to, as she destroyed her life in the seventh century. Possible? I don't know, but I didn't care to take a chance with messing around with power like that. Last week she had brought forward tremendous energy that she had accumulated from that entity. I thought it would be safer to remove her from the intense concentration and get her out of the situation. Better safe than sorry.

D: *Okay. I will count to three and you can be removed from this situation, and look back on it, and tell me what happened. It will be easier that way, won't it? (No answer) (I insisted.) Will it be easier that way? (Yes) (I had finally broken her concentration.) Okay. I will count to three and it will be over, and you can look back on it and describe it without any involvement. I think that will be much kinder. 1, 2, 3, whatever happened has already happened, and you can look back on it without any emotional involvement. Talk about it objectively.*

I was very relieved when she lowered her hands and began breathing normally once more.

D: *Can you tell me what happened?*

K: It was decided that the best method of which to end this life would be simply to cease to function.

D: *Did you have the power to do such a thing?* (Yes)

I felt chills at the words "cease to function." I think I made the right decision to remove her from the concentration. Others have said that probably nothing would have happened at all, but they were not present. I believe it might have been too risky to find out otherwise. I always try to obey my instincts in these instances. Safety of the subject is the primary concern. Karen and I were the only ones in the house during this session. I did not have the advantage of Harriet's experience or advice to guide me. This was the only time in thirty years' experience that I have encountered a situation that frightened me and caused me to question my ability to handle it. Apparently, the Druidess possessed great power, and I am glad I didn't have to see how far that power could reach. Now that she was out of danger, I relaxed and tried to regain my composure as I continued.

D: *Do you think these were the people that were going to hurt you? To try to use your power?*

K: They wish for knowledge, yes.

D: *But you couldn't understand their language. How could they have made you tell them secrets?*

K: When they first spoke, they spoke in the language of the people. So, they knew how to speak the language, but I was not able to understand them when they spoke among each other.

D: *Do you think they would have done something to make you reveal your secrets?*

K: They would have tried. I had no wish to fail if they had tried, therefore I removed the problem.

D: *You just ceased to function?*

K: Yes. They were very angry. They could not stand the thought that the possibility of having that power had been snatched away from them. They looked for a weapon, and they thought that it possibly was poison that I had taken.

D: *But you had no choice, did you?*

K: I could not face the thought of breaking under the pressure that they would exert. For never could I go and be with my friends and worship my Lady. Therefore, there was no point to continue this existence.

D: *Then you feel that what you did was right to do. Others have done the same thing. (Yes) In that case it was the only thing you could do. Do you see any of your other friends now that you have left the body?*

K: Yes, they are with me.

D: *Oh, that is good. You will get to be with them for a while. Sometimes things happen that we don't really like, that we don't want to do, but these are things we can't control. I think you were a very brave person. A very good person. You had much knowledge. You just didn't want it to be used the wrong way. To fall into the wrong hands.*

K: My people, they strive for knowledge to use for good. And we swear an oath so that this power shall not fall into the hands of those who have greed or malice because this is what brought down the fathers of my people a long time ago. This is what we swear.

D: *Yes, there is no way it can be used in a bad way. You're a very noble person, a very good person.*

I moved Karen away from the scene and moved another hundred years back in time. She then entered the lifetime of the traveling singing minstrel, which will be explored in another chapter. The experience had no lasting effects on her as she left the lifetime of the Druidess behind.

Chapter 2
The Druidess, Part 1 (Bernadine)
(Recorded February 9, 1984)

I had worked with Bernadine on a few occasions to try and find the cause of the disfiguring ailment that she had had since her teenage years. It was a condition that caused her almost constant pain, but she had adjusted marvelously, and had learned to live with it. She knew how to use mind control to manage the pain, and lived a normal life, but also became very adept at metaphysics, as well as being an accomplished astrologer. Later I learned that it was called Scalara (phonetic). We had traced it to a parallel life when she was a German soldier during World War II in Germany.

** As we research Dolores's files, we hope to find the many other stories that she found during her work with these individuals. As you can imagine, there are many! **

During this session we were going to explore other lifetimes hopefully unrelated to the disease. This session was held at her apartment in Fayetteville.

I used a method that I no longer use. I asked her to look through a large photograph album to find a photograph that was taken during this lifetime, and then remember what was occurring at the time the picture was taken. This method works well when regressing during the present life. I believe we might have been searching for the time the disfiguration first appeared.

D: *Twelve years old. A happy day. Can you find a picture like that?* (Uh-huh) *Tell me what it looks like.*

B: Oh, they're taking a picture of the family. And we're outside by the car. And I have my hair in curls up on my head. (Chuckle) It looks like on rollers, only it's just big curls. And I don't really want to have my picture taken.

D: *You're not that happy about it?*

B: I just don't like having pictures taken. But they make me come on anyway. And I lean up on the car ... at the end. Standing on one end, with the rest of the family.

D: *And that's what was happening the day that picture was taken?*

B: Ummm, and we had some relatives visiting. That's why they wanted to take the picture. It's my grandma and grandpa.

D: *But you just weren't happy about it.*

B: I just didn't want to have my picture taken.

D: *Okay. Well, then stop looking at that one. Look through the pages some more and find another picture of you when you were about five years old. On a happy day. Can you find you?* (Uh-huh) *Okay, what does that picture look like?*

B: I'm barefooted. It's at camp meeting. And my hair's cut real short like a ... bob.

D: *Is anyone else in the picture?*

B: Uh-huh. There's a young man. I think he was the preacher, or the preacher's son, or something like that.

D: *About your age or what?*

B: No. He must be twenty or something like that.

D: *Oh. Just the two of you in the picture?* (Uh-huh) *And you said you're barefoot.*

B: Uh-huh. I have a little dress on. It's ... (chuckle) I got bloomers underneath it, Momma made to match the dress.

D: *(Chuckle) I bet you're a cute little girl.*

B: I guess so. Kinda ornery, I think.

D: *(Chuckle) Okay. Let's look at some more pictures. Let's find a picture of you when you were just a baby. There must be baby pictures in the album too. Can you find me a baby picture?* (Yes) *Okay. What does it look like?*

B: Well, like any baby, I think.

D: *Is there anything else in the picture?*

B: My mother. I'm on her lap.

D: *Is she the only other one in the picture?*

B: No, my sister's beside her. Just us three.

D: *An older sister?*

B: Uh-huh. There was just two of us then.

D: *Oh. You were the beginning of a large family, weren't you?*

B: Next to the oldest.

D: *You're just a little baby in the picture then.*

B: Uh-huh. It's funny. It looks like I have dark hair. I don't think I had dark hair.

D: *You think you had light hair?*

B: I guess. I always thought I did.

D: *But in the picture it's dark?*

B: Uh-huh. It's black and white.

D: *But that's a picture of you when you were a little baby.*

B: I kind of look like my daddy.

D: *Well, this picture album has lots and lots of pictures in it. Lots and lots of pages. I want you to turn some more pages. And let's go back to before you were a little baby and see what you can see as we go back further. There are many, many pages and many, many pictures. Find one that is important to you. And as you find that one, stop and look at it. A picture that is important to you. Back before you were a little baby. You may look different. You may not think it is the same. But you'll know when you find it. A picture that is important. Let me know whenever you have found it.*

B: Hummph. The one I keep seeing is a ...

D: *What?*

B: The one I keep seeing is ... my mommy pregnant.

D: *Your mother pregnant?*

B: She's pregnant. I think it's with me. She and daddy and another couple.

D: *You're watching it? Looking at the picture?* (Uh-huh) *Does she look young?*

B: Yes. Pretty.

D: *Okay. I'm going to ask you some questions. And you will know the answers. They will come right into your conscious, and you will know the answers to the questions. Is your mother pregnant with you at this time?* (Yes) *Are you watching or are you inside the body? What do you have a feeling of? (Long pause)*

B: I'm not … It's a body in there, but I'm not in it yet.

D: *Can you see the body, or do you just know it?*

B: Both.

D: *Do you seem to be watching, or what do you have a feeling of?*

B: It's funny. It's like I'm in there and I'm out here too.

D: *Two places at once?* (Uh-huh) *Try and describe what it feels like.*

B: Like I know that's me, but I'm not really there yet. It's like I know that's where I'm gonna be. And yet I want to stay out here too. I'm just not too sure that's what I want to do.

D: *Why aren't you sure?*

B: I don't think I want to be a baby again.

D: *Is the body very developed?*

B: Pretty much. It has fingers and toes. And the heart's beating.

D: *Have you entered that body at all, or have you been watching the whole time?*

B: Oh, I've been there. I just don't want to stay. It's all closed up. It's like prison.

D: *I can understand that.*

B: I like to know what's going on outside.

D: *What do you plan to do?*

B: I have to go in and stay pretty soon.

D: *Is it all right to stay outside like this and watch?*

B: Not too long. I think they want me to go in and stay.

D: *Who wants you to?*

B: They. The others that sent me.

D: *Do you know who they are?*

B: The wise ones.

D: *You said they sent you. Do you have anything to say about it?*

B: Not now. It's already decided.

D: *Before did you have anything to say about it?*

B: I think so. I think I decided it was time. I just didn't want to be a girl this time.

D: *Oh. Why not?*

B: I just didn't. I would rather have been a boy.

D: *Does someone make that decision for you?*

B: They told me it's because I need to.

D: *Is there something you have to learn by being a girl this time?*

B: Yes. I still don't want to do it.

D: *Did they tell you you have to? There's no way out, or what?*

B: It's what I have to do.

D: *Do you have any idea what it is that you're coming back for?*

B: Learn some lessons that I still haven't learned. To care about other people. To take care.

D: *Do you think that's something you didn't do last time?* (Yes) *Do you think that's the main lesson, or are there others?*

B: Oh, there's more. But that's especially what I need to learn.

D: *Uh-huh. What are you doing right now?*

B: (Pause) Going into the body. It's so cramped. I don't like being bound up.

She was breathing heavily.

D: *Is it almost time to be born?*

B: I don't think so yet.

D: *But they told you you have to be inside?*

B: (Discomfort) Yes, I'm supposed to stay.

D: *It's something they want you to experience.*

B: Yes. (Emotional) I want to run away. That's one thing I have to learn, is not run away.

D: *To stay with a situation?* (Uh-huh) *How does your mother feel about all this? Do you know?*

B: She's not too sure sometimes.

D: *Can you tell what she thinks and feels?*

B: She wants me, but she's uncertain about something.

D: *Do you know what it is? (Long pause, no answer.) Is it important to know how she feels?*

B: I think so.

D: *How does your father feel? Do you know?*
B: He wants me to be a boy.
D: *Has he other children?*
B: Yes. He already has a girl. And then they had another one that died.
D: *Between you and the other girl?*
B: Uh-huh. That's something that bothers my mother.
D: *Oh. Maybe she's a little worried about that.*
B: I think so.
D: *Uh-huh. Well, you know how men are. They always want boys.* (Uh-huh) *You can't take that personally, can you?*
B: I want to be a boy too!

I decided to move her forward to the time of the birth so she wouldn't have to experience too much of the cramped uncomfortable feeling. I also gave her the option of watching the birth rather than experiencing it. I have had subjects go through the actual birth in other sessions, and it can be a very traumatic experience. They feel pain around the head and shoulders and are fighting to breathe. There is often the distinct feeling of choking and gasping for air. This is not only uncomfortable for the subject, but also for the hypnotist. At such times I remind myself that they will not be harmed by the experience, because they actually were born, they got here okay. I try to alleviate any discomfort the best way I can. I have found that it is the choice of the incoming soul whether they want to experience the actual birth or wait in the room until the baby is born and enter then. Either way it is a lesson that the soul chooses to experience. The only rule is that the soul must enter when the baby is separated from the life force of the mother, when the baby takes its first breath, or the child will be stillborn.

D: *I will count to three, and on the count of three you will be at the time of your birth. The time that you are being born. And you can experience it without any discomfort. 1, 2, 3, you're at the time of your birth. Can you tell me what's happening?*
B: It's in a car. And we're going to the hospital. It's a long way.

D: *It's your mother and father in the car?* (Yes) *Who is driving?*

B: My father.

D: *How does your mother feel?*

B: She's glad it's time. She wants to get it over with. So, do I!

D: *Is it very much farther to go now?*

B: (Pause) A little ways yet.

D: *Can you tell me what you're experiencing? What you're feeling? Can you give me an idea what it's like?*

B: I wanna ... I wanna get out! I still don't want to be born this time.

D: *It's hard to have it both ways, isn't it?*

B: It's like I ... feel pulled in two.

D: *Okay. Let's move ahead till we're at the hospital. Does she make it to the hospital?* (Uh-huh) *Tell me what's happening.*

B: Going someplace. Taking her. It's getting hard.

D: *Do you have the same feeling of being in two places at once?*

B: (Heavy breathing) No. I'm here.

D: *You're born now?*

B: No. I'm still ... it's happening. It hurts.

D: *It won't really bother you. Just relax. You will not really feel anything. You can talk about it. It's good to talk about things. (Heavy breathing) Where is she ... where are you being born at?*

B: We're in the delivery room, I guess. It's ... lots of noise. And bright lights.

D: *Are you out now?*

B: Uh-huh. (A big breath.)

D: *That's a relief, isn't it?*

B: I don't like it! (Pause, as she breathes heavily.) It's cold! It hurts!

D: *What hurts? You're born now, aren't you?*

B: I think so.

D: *Why does it hurt?*

B: All over. My head, it hurts.

I gave soothing suggestions to alleviate any physical discomfort.

B: The doctor had to do something. I was stuck.

D: *And that was what caused the discomfort?*

B: Partly.

D: *Does it feel better now?*

B: Uh-huh. It's still cold! I wish they'd leave me alone!

D: *What are they doing?*

B: They held me upside down. They slapped me. And they … just won't leave me alone.

D: *Are they going to make it so you're not cold?*

B: I hope so. They took me away from my mother. I don't like that.

D: *Where is your mother?*

B: She's over there on the table.

D: *Does she know what's going on?*

B: I don't think so. (Mumbling, couldn't understand.)

D: *Well, they'll probably bring you back to your mother. There's all these things they have to do first, aren't there?*

B: I don't like being born. I want to go back!

D: *Go back where?*

B: Not here!

D: *Where do you want to go back to?*

B: With the others.

D: *Did you like it there?* (Yes) *But this was something you had to do, wasn't it?*

B: Uh-huh. I'm watching now.

D: *What are you watching?*

B: Me and my mother.

D: *What's happening?*

B: Oh, they're still fooling with me. But I … left for a while. I have to go back though.

D: *Where is your mother now?*

B: They're doing things to her. And she's glad it's over. It's all right with her. It's good I'm a girl.

D: *She doesn't mind, does she?*

B: She's just glad I'm here. I still can't get used to it.

D: *Do you like it better when you can watch it? Instead of being in the baby?* (Uh-huh) *These people that you're being born to, have you known them before?* (Yes) *Your mother and your father?*

B: Both of them.

D: *Do you know what karma is?*

B: Why I came?

D: *Is there something, like karma, you think is the reason why you came to these people?* (Yes) *Do you think you can tell me about it? Explain it if you can? (Pause, no answer. She was very relaxed. Perhaps tired from being born.) I mean, with these people, was there a reason?* (Yes) *Tell me what it was. (Pause) You see, it's all right to talk about it now. But as you grow older you may forget. And you can tell me now before the memory is erased.*

B: (Pause) Hmmm. I'm seeing my grandmother.

D: *Is she there?*

B: She's involved. It's my daddy's mother. I see her. She's ... she was my mother one time. And he was my brother. And he ... he did something to me. (Pause) Something bad.

D: *Oh? Well, it won't bother you to think about it. Sometimes it's better to understand. Your father was your brother in another life?*

B: Uh-huh. Something else too. (Softly) He has to take care of me.

D: *Is that how he's going to pay back what he did before?*

B: Partly. He takes care of a lot of other people too, this time. And I ... I am supposed to observe this. Learn this from him.

Bernadine's father was a Protestant minister in this life.

D: *Then you think it's more his karma than yours?*

B: I believe so. I believe so.

D: *What about your mother? Was she involved in the same situation?*

B: Something else.

D: *Can you see what it was with your mother?*

B: (Pause) It was decided on the other side. I agreed to share this life with her. She's supposed to teach me. And help me with what I have to do. It goes *way* back. Way back. I see us wearing long robes. (Her voice was so soft I had difficulty hearing her.) It's a group of women. We all wear white robes. We deal with things that other people don't understand.

D: *What do you mean, other people don't understand?*

B: Some people call it "religious practices." But it's just the natural laws that they don't understand. They have forgotten. She is the priestess. She is the wise one. She teaches the rest of us.

D: *Where are you? In a building or what?*

B: Mostly outdoors. We are on an island.

D: *Do you have a name for the kind of people that you are?*

B: (Pause) We are called … (She had difficulty saying the name.) Drue … Drue … (She was obviously trying to say: Druid or Druidess.)

I had the uncanny feeling she was talking about the same group that Karen had talked about the year before. Now how could I ask questions and get verification without leading her? I would have to proceed carefully. Bernadine and Karen knew each other, but Bernadine was much older, my age.

D: *Are you always on the island?*

B: No. Not always.

D: *Why do you come to the island?*

B: It is our sacred place.

D: *What do you do when you're on the island?*

B: We have ceremonies. And she has contact with the masters.

D: *Do you have any certain—oh, should I say "person," or "god" that you worship? Would that be the right word? (Pause) When you have your ceremonies?*

B: It is all.

D: *It is what?*

B: The All.

D: *Do you like it there with her and the others?*

B: Oh, yes.

D: *Have you been there very long?*

B: Not *me*. The others, some of them have. I'm new, young, compared to some of the others. I'm just learning.

D: *Where did you come from? How did you get with this group?*

B: They found me.

D: *Didn't you have a family?*

B: Once.

D: *What do you mean, they found you?*

B: My mother and father were killed.

D: *And they took you then?* (Yes) *Well, when you're not on the island, where do you live?*

B: Different places.

D: *You have no permanent place?*

B: No. There are several places where we go. We go where the things grow that we use. Sometimes we have to go and hide, because there are people who don't like us.

D: *Who are the people who don't like you?*

B: The magistrates.

D: *Where do these people live?*

B: In the towns. We stay away from the towns.

D: *Why don't they like you?*

B: They say we use magic.

D: *They're ignorant, aren't they?* (Yes) *They just don't understand. Are there any men in your group?* (No) *I've heard there are some men that are Druids.*

B: There are some other groups. But there aren't any in our group.

D: *Only women?*

B: Yes, in the one I'm in.

D: *Are there many of you in this group?*

B: It changes. Sometimes there are just a few of us. Sometimes more. Some of them go to other places. Some of them stay on the island longer.

D: *How do you get to the island?*

B: There is a way. Not always. When we go, there is a way.

D: *Do you go in a boat? (I asked this purposely so I would not lead.)*

B: Sometimes they have to come in a boat. But we go when there's … I want to say we walk across sometimes. Sometimes there's water there and you can't walk there.

D: *You mean the water is not always there?*

B: No. It's not always an island. You have to know when and where to go.

Somewhere in here her voice changed, and the way she arranged the order of the words. It was obvious she had entered totally the personality of the other entity.

D: *Sometimes the water covers the way you have to go?*

B: Yes. Many times.

D: *How do you know when it's all right to cross?*

B: The head priestess always knows. I have not learned these things yet.

D: *Do you like it there?*

B: Yes. There is much to learn.

D: *Do you like the other women that are with you?*

B: Of course. Why should I not?

D: *Well, I just wondered. Are there any of the women that you have made friends with? (Yes) Do you know any of their names? The ones that you have been particularly friendly with? Who have been helpful to you? (Pause, had difficulty.) Or can you think of their names?*

I was looking for some verification of Karen. Of course, even if this was the same group it may have been before or after Karen was there. We have no way of knowing how long the group functioned. It is still remarkable that they were apparently describing the same time and place.

B: (Pause, had difficulty.) Lureen (phonetic).

D: *What is* your *name? (Pause) Can you think of it?*

B: (Had difficulty understanding, and had her repeat several times.) Liena (phonetic: Li-en-a).

D: *See, sometimes it's hard to think of names.*

B: I thank you.

D: *That's okay. Where you have your ceremonies on the island, is there an altar?* (Yes) *What does the altar look like?*

B: It is stone.

D: *Is it a certain color?*

B: White.

D: *Is there anything different about it?*

B: I know not. Different from what?

D: *Well, I don't know. Than ordinary stones that are found in the fields. In the countryside.*

B: It is white.

D: *Do you use this altar in your ceremonies?*

B: The high priestess does.

D: *Do you wear any type of ... oh, I want to say "jewelry," or any type of religious objects on your body?*

B: A belt. What I wear is different from what the priestesses wear. The high priestess wears a chain around her neck. It is quite large. It has ... I don't know what you call it.

D: *What does it look like?*

B: A jewel.

D: *Oh. I bet it's beautiful.*

B: It is.

D: *Do any of the others have things like that on their necks?*

B: Not like hers.

D: *That's a nice place, isn't it?* (Yes) *Those are nice people too, aren't they?*

B: Yes, they are.

D: *Would it be all right if I come back and speak to you again sometime?*

B: I think so.

D: *You would not have any objection to it?* (No) *I'm just curious and I like to ask questions. I mean no harm at all. Okay. Let's leave that scene now.*

(Subject brought back up and oriented to the present day. When Bernadine awakened, she did not remember anything about the session. We discussed it and she could see the connection between her mother, and also the closeness she felt for Karen. She seemed to think the belts the people wore were different colors, each color denoting their rank, etc.)

Chapter 3
The Druidess, Part 2 (Bernadine)
(Recorded April 4, 1985)

It was over a year before we could return to the story of the Druidess, which I was trying to correlate to Karen's similar story. On the day we had this session the primary reason was to relieve Bernadine of pain. Although she was very accustomed to dealing with and handling her pain, there were days when it became unbearable, and the only solution was to go to bed. The pain would center in her left eye and that side of the head. At these times she could not tolerate any light and would put on an eye shade or eye mask, close off all light to the bedroom and go to bed. This day we wanted to try hypnosis to give her relief. While she was under, we wanted to attempt to contact the other entity as well. So, my first concern and suggestions were to relieve the pain. After I used her keyword, I gave suggestions that it would feel as though her eye was being bathed in cool water, a very soothing sensation. I had to monitor her carefully to be sure that the discomfort did not return while we were having the session. If it did, I reinforced the soothing and pain-relieving suggestions. It was difficult to completely monitor her body signs, because of the eye mask I couldn't see the REMs, or eye movements. I had to rely on other signs.

D: *Now I am going to count to three, and we will journey back through time and space.*

I did not need to tell her where to go. At the end of the count, she was back in another time. Maybe she went eagerly in order to completely escape the discomfort her body was experiencing. At any rate she immediately immersed into the other personality. I asked her what she was doing and what she saw.

B: A tree. A small tree. It must be a sapling. Not very large. Taller than I am. It doesn't have leaves yet. It has a few small branches.

D: *Where is this sapling?*

B: Hummph. It's out here by itself. I'm not sure where.

D: *What is significant about the sapling?*

B: It has medicinal qualities. The twigs we take and crush them. And use what is the product of the crushing in our cures.

Her voice was strangely slow and methodical, as though the language she was speaking and the words she was using were unfamiliar to her. She was speaking very purposely.

D: *What type of cure would this provide?*

B: It is combined with other potions for the ache ... the fevers.

D: *What type of a sapling is it? Does it have a name? A type of tree?*

B: (Slowly and purposely) I am still ignorant in many things. This has been shown to me. I do not know if it has a name.

Her vocal cords and mouth seemed to have difficulty forming these words. They were definitely foreign to her.

D: *Who is showing you these things?*

B: The other sisters. The older sisters.

D: *They pass the knowledge down?* (Yes) *Then you haven't been doing this very long?*

B: I am new in training. I have much to learn.

D: *It must take a long time to learn all these things.*

B: I hope to be wise as they are someday.

D: *Have you already had your initiation?*

B: No. Not the final. I have been given the beginners' initiation. It is only the pledge. The making me an apprentice, so to

59

speak. (That word was difficult for her to pronounce.)

D: *Where was the beginners' initiation held?*

B: On the island.

D: *Were there many people there?*

B: All of the sisters.

D: *Were there many who wanted to become sisters?*

B: Only those who have already been approved are allowed to go to the island.

D: *It's not easy to become a sister? Is that what you mean?*

B: Yes. It is not a well-known accepted thing in our arts.

D: *Where did you come from before you joined the sisters?*

B: A village. Just a few families.

D: *Were you very old when you left there?*

B: When I joined the sisters? (Yes) No. Well ... how old is old? I was fourteen summers.

D: *What did your parents think about you leaving?*

B: I have no parents.

D: *Who did you live with in the village?*

B: Another family who took me in. Me parents be dead.

D: *What of the other family? What did they think when you left?*

B: 'Twas one less mouth to feed.

D: *Then it didn't bother them then.*

B: They had no say, not being my true family.

D: *How did it happen that you left? How did you know of the sisters?*

B: I met one in the glen, when I be wandering. I always be a wanderer. And talk to the wee folk.

D: *Oh, I've heard of them. Can you see them?*

B: Can not ye?

D: *(I tried to gain her confidence.) I think so, sometimes.* (Aye) *I've talked to other people who can.*

B: I talk with them. And some folk say I be daffy.

D: *Oh, I've also heard that too. Any time we do things that are different, this is what they call us, isn't it?* (Aye) *But we know better, don't we?* (Aye) *But you met a lady?*

B: Aye. 'Twas one of the sisters. And she talk with me. And she also be friend of the wee folk. And she know me. E'en better than me maw, when she be live.

Her accent was becoming more pronounced as she spoke the words the way she was accustomed to. It at times sounded a bit Irish, but not quite. This was definitely not Bernadine speaking, but the other entity. This is the manner in which they convert English into their own language, by putting words into an unusual order. It always sounds as though they are translating in their head from one language to another, because the words are in a different order. This is the sign of a true somnambulist. They truly become the other personality.

D: Do you think some of the knowledge comes from the wee folk?
B: Aye. 'Tis sure.
D: That the wee folk tell the sisters some of this knowledge.
B: 'Tis what they be for doing.
D: What is your name? What can I call you? (Long pause. No answer.) Is there something I can call you?
B: Be called Linel. (She seemed unsure.)
D: Linel (phonetic: Lin nel). Am I saying that right? (Aye) *Okay. How are you dressed?*
B: 'Tis but a dress of rough material. 'Tis very plain. And I long sleeves. And nay much color.
D: Does it just hang loose or what?
B: Aye. Today that is how I be.
D: On other days do you wear it differently?
B: Sometimes I wear the belt. The rope.
D: Is there anything significant about wearing the belt?
B: Aye. 'Tis mark of the sisters.
D: That is how you will know each other. Is that what you mean?
B: Aye. That is one of the marks.
D: What is different about the belt, that you can recognize each other?
B: 'Tis sometimes how 'tis tied. Sometimes what is on the belt. For to know those who are at different levels.
D: You mean an ornament on the belt or something?
B: Aye. It could so be called.

D: *If you are a beginner, what type of ornament is on yours? How is yours different?*

B: I no wear the ornament (carefully pronounced), as you call. 'Tis earned when one passes the test.

D: *Oh. Then yours is just the belt?* (Aye) *What does the ornament look like, once you have passed the test?*

B: 'Tis more than one.

D: *I would really like to know, to learn, myself. What is it that designates the different levels?*

B: That I nay can tell thee.

D: *But you know I don't tell things.*

B: 'Tis only for initiates to know.

D: *Well, I don't want to get you into any trouble. But you know you can tell me things you would never tell anyone else.*

B: I be sworn. I nay can break my word.

D: *I respect that. I really do. But I do want you to feel safe with me. You can feel that, can't you?*

B: It nay I trust thee not. 'Tis but I gave my word.

D: *That's all right. I will never ask you to break your word. If I ask you a question and you cannot tell me, just say so. I will respect that. I only want what is good for you. If you cannot tell me, just let me know. That's all right. Are you happy with your life there?*

B: Aye. 'Tis so much better than when I be a spare mouth in another family where I do not belong.

D: *You felt out of place there. Is that what you mean?*

B: Aye. They be kind, but I nay be their family.

D: *You feel more like a family with the sisters?*

B: Aye. 'Tis my family now.

D: *Do you have a leader, so to speak?*

B: Aye. There be different leaders. We have our head sister, and they be the mistress over her, when the groups join together.

D: *There are various other groups too then?*

B: Oh, aye. We nay live all the same place. For we be moving much. Not to be known by those who pursue us.

D: *Why do people pursue you? I would think you were doing no harm.*

B: They nay understand. They nay … some think we be witches. Some think we be … bad, because they nay understand what we do.

D: *Do you do bad things?*

B: (Emphatic) Nay! Nay!

D: *Do you help other people?*

B: Aye, 'tis what our work be. For healing and working with nature and the wee folk. And we gain knowledge. And 'tis much secret. Which be what they nay like. For they wish to know where we gain our power.

D: *Why do you think they wish to know these things?*

B: For they nay have control if we have power they nay understand. And they fear us for that.

D: *Are these a certain kind of people, or just everyone?*

B: Oh, nay everyone. Is many to whom we bring healing, and many seek us out and protect us. And sometimes provide for us. But they nay let the magistrates know of this. For they do think their job be to catch us, to trap us. And find us practicing the magic, as they call.

D: *Then it is like the officials? Is that what you mean?* (Aye) *How do you stay away from these people?*

B: We be warned by many of the people when they know them to be about. And we keep to the woods and the glens, and away from the roads. And only go to the villages when we are informed that 'tis clear. Sometimes there are those who are dishonest and betray us. So, we must be very cautious.

D: *Where do you live then if you have to move so much?*

B: Aye. We live with Mother Nature (had difficulty with the word "mother"). With the hills and the caves, and the forest. And our friends. Be the elementals. And they sometimes guide us. And we have our secret hideaways.

D: *Do you know the Old Ones? (No answer.) Have you ever heard of that term?*

B: (Cautiously) I be not to speak of such.

D: *For I have heard of them. I wondered if you had.*

B: I have heard. What know you of them?

It was interesting that she had been using the familiar noun "ye." Now that she was suspicious, she changed to the subjective noun "you." This was a difficult question to answer without leading. Maybe if it was done correctly, I could gain her confidence.

D: *Well, I know they live in the hills and the caves. And they practice the old religions of many, many years ago. And they are friends with the sisters. I do know that. Is that correct?*
B: Where be ye from?
D: *Oh, you might say I am one with nature also.*
B: Only those among us know such things. 'Tis dangerous knowledge.
D: *I know. That's why I told you you could trust me. For I know many things. And I would never think of hurting you. I have heard the Old Ones do practice the old religion of the old gods. And there were not many left. Is that correct?*
B: 'Tis ... I know not if I be free to speak to one who has such knowledge already. I do not wish to break my vows. And ... (I could see she was in turmoil, being pulled two ways.)
D: *That's all right. I respect that.*
B: To one who knows of the Old Ones, ye must be friend or would not have survived to this time.
D: *Yes, that's true. I've had to be very careful also.*
B: Ye know the Old Ones yourself?
D: *No, I've only heard of them. I've never been allowed to meet them. But I do know they exist.*
B: Only those initiated are allowed to meet them. I have not had such privilege yet.
D: *Someday you might though.*
B: Aye, I hope so.
D: *I've also heard the Old Ones help provide the sisters with food.*
B: 'Tis much which they provide. And we be much beholden to them.
D: *Oh, they are very kind people.*
B: Aye. 'Tis sad that there be those who wish to destroy them.

D: *Those are the people who don't understand. They aren't like us.* (Aye) *Do you go to the island very often?*

B: Only at special times of the year. Some go more often. Every moon there are those who go, but not all.

D: *It's safe there.*

B: Aye. I should like to spend more time there. But I be having work to do and training, which must be done in other places.

D: *The island is one place where the bad people cannot follow.*

B: Aye, they know not. (Surprised) How ye know this?

D: *I told you, I know many things. I have much knowledge of your ways. That's why I will not betray you.*

B: For 'tis secret.

D: *Yes. I know of the land bridge.*

B: Ye know? *(Yes)* Hay ye crossed?

D: *No, I have not been allowed, for I am not a sister. But I'm very close unto you sisters.*

B: Aye, 'tis a special journey to be made.

D: *I know that it is not there all the time.*

B: No, 'tis this which is our protection.

D: *This is what keeps the others from following. They never know of that.*

B: Aye. We hope that none of our pursuers know of this.

D: *I don't think they do. I have never spoke of it to anyone else.*

B: 'Tis shrouded, as you know, in mist. So only the few know it ever exists.

D: *Yes, they can't see it, for it's underwater, isn't it, most of the time?* (Aye) *This is very good. Is it a long bridge from the land to the island?*

B: Oh, 'tis ... maybe ... (Uncertain) I count the steps to ... I know not how else to give example. Perhaps thirty ... or so.

D: *Steps? From the shore to the island?* (Aye) *Then it's not very far.*

B: No. Only ... one has to know the way to be at that particular spot. And this be much longer journey.

D: *But couldn't the pursuers come in a boat?*

B: Perhaps, if they knew of the gatherings. But we hope that none know.

D: *They don't know you're there then.*

B: We should hope not.

D: *Is there only the one island?*

B: On which we meet, you mean?

D: *But are there other islands around there?*

B: Aye. But this be part of our safety. For if they learn, they know not which island.

D: *That's good. If there was only one island, it would be easier to find. But if there are many, they don't know that you're even there.*

B: Aye. 'Tis easy to be confused. Especially in the mists. For everything looks the same in the mists.

D: *Are the mists always there?*

B: I know not, when I be not there. When I be there, they have been. Some say that our Lady creates the mist for our safety. I know not if this be true.

D: *It could be. It's possible.*

B: Aye. I think perhaps 'tis true, for she be powerful.

D: *I've heard of her power. Have you ever been allowed to see her?*

B: (Pause) Not her face. I hay seen her in her light. But I do not know if one can see her face after initiation. For we are not informed of all such things.

D: *You have much to learn then yet, don't you?* (Aye) *Do you have any close friends among the sisters?*

B: They be all my friends. 'Tis very good to have so many friends.

D: *That is good. Many people go their whole life and never have a real friend.* (Aye) *Then they are like family, aren't they?*

B: We be blessed to have such family.

D: *Yes, that's very good. All right. Have you ever heard of the Druids? Does that name mean anything to you?*

B: We be sometimes called such by some folks. 'Tis not what we call ourselves.

D: *What do you call yourselves?*

B: (Long pause) I be not free to say secret things. But "sisters" be what we call each other.

66

D: *I didn't know if it was a secret. But I have heard that the Druids were mostly men.*

B: Aye. 'Tis not the same as we be. But there are those who also call us this. For we have secret ceremony, and much of the ancient teaching, which be common to the other sect.

D: *Then you have no men in your sect?*

B: No. We be sisters only.

D: *Do the men have different beliefs than you do?*

B: Aye. Some. I know not meself much of them, except they … some be used for purposes which we nay use. We nay approve of some uses which they have.

D: *Oh, then they do have different beliefs.*

B: For my understanding, they use some of same ancient teachings which we learn. But they hay turned them to uses not approved by the spirits. This be my knowledge only. I know not if I know correctly.

D: *But you think they abuse the knowledge the wrong way then.*

B: 'Tis said among the sisters that this is so.

D: *Would this be why they don't mix the two sects?*

B: This be why we no …

D: *Associate with each other.*

B: Aye. For our purposes be to bring healing and love and harmony with our world. And this be our purposes.

D: *Yes, that is what I have for a purpose too. I want to bring knowledge to people who seek knowledge. I want to do it in the right way. So, see, we do think alike, don't we?*

B: Ye be strange to not be a sister. Not many there be, ordinary folk, who know such as ye know.

D: *Maybe someday they will allow me to be a sister. Who knows?*

B: Ye wish to be a sister?

D: *Possibly.*

B: 'Tis a good life if ye be strong, and nay mind living outdoors and depending on the good folk, as well as the countryside.

D: *Do you think they might consider me, if I talked to someone about joining?*

B: I nay know myself, but the elder sister perhaps could tell you. She be very kind, and wise. And I nay know with how … if they bring ladies into the group. I only know most of us begin as novice, young ones.

D: *Do you think I am older? That they might not let me in?*

B: I nay know. Ye might inquire.

D: *But I would like to be a friend.*

B: 'Tis no cause, I see, to nay be friends.

D: *I can help protect. That is good.*

B: Ye be one who knows of the coming of our pursuers?

D: *That would be a good idea, wouldn't it? I could warn you.*

B: We be always grateful for this, for on this our survival depends.

D: *I respect what you're doing, and I would help you in any way I could.*

B: 'Tis good. For those who know of the good we do.

D: *But you see, I have a great curiosity. That's why I ask many questions.*

B: Curiosity?

D: *Do you know what that means?*

B: 'Tis a strange word.

D: *It means I want to know many things, so I ask many questions.*

B: Aye! That ye do!

D: *(Chuckle) But not to get you into trouble. It just means I want to know many things.*

B: Oh! Myself also wishes to know many things.

D: *That's what the word "curiosity" means.* (Oh?) *You want to know.*

B: Sure. I be curious also then.

D: *That's why if you can't tell me, just let me know. Because I have no way of knowing if it is a secret. I just ask questions.*

B: I answer if I be able.

D: *That's all I would expect. Are there any of the large stones near where you live?*

B: Where I live be many places. Ye refer to the markers?

D: *Well, I've heard there are some places where there are many stones together. Is that what you mean?*

B: Aye. 'Tis those placed by the ancients. They be very special places for energy and wisdom. And much there be I know not yet. But there be those who know much of these things.

D: *Are there any of these large markers near where you live?*

B: Those that be together in the large place be some distance from where we be at present. But 'tis walking perhaps ... depends on how fast you walk. But I could reach in ... a day, and perhaps half of another day.

D: *Oh, then it is not really close.*

B: Not to right here.

D: *Is this the large one?*

B: This be the grouping I speak of.

D: *Yes. I've heard there was one that had a large circle. Is that the one?*

B: Aye, 'tis this I think you be referring to. For 'tis known by many. And many nay understand what it's purpose be.

D: *There are also smaller ones?*

B: Aye. They be individual ones in various places.

D: *Do you have a name for the large one, that you call it in your country?*

B: I nay know what others call. I nay know if I be allowed to speak of this. Again, I hay not been told if this be secret.

D: *It may not be. Especially if it is a well-known place, it may not be a secret. (She was confused.) Can you tell me what the people call that large one?*

B: To some 'tis known as the Magic Circle. 'Tis this to some of the folk. And ... I nay be able to speak of our own language. For 'tis part of our ... I nay know if I should speak of this.

D: *That's all right. If you don't feel comfortable with it, it's okay.*

B: I nay want to break my word.

D: *That's all right. I don't think it's true, but I have heard it said that the Druids built the large circle.*

B: 'Twas the ancient ones. If they be known as Druids. The term is used different ways by different people. And we nay wish to refer to Druids, as they be in these days, as same who placed the magic stones.

D: *I always thought it was much older and had been there much longer.*

B: Sure, longer than the Druids of today. And I nay know for sure if ancient ones who placed them be Druids or not. For 'tis a name misused.

D: *Many people don't know what the real name Druid means, in other words.* (Aye) *Well, do you ever go to the large circle for any special occasions?*

B: Aye. I have been there twice. And should like to go again. For 'tis much ... I know not how to explain. Much happens there when one is in the surrounding area, and the power is increased. And some of our group go there at certain times for ceremony. But I know not what this consists of. For 'tis part of only the high initiates who do so.

D: *On the times you went there, was it a special occasion?*

B: Aye. 'Twas a gathering. But we were not allowed to take part in what the high initiates were doing.

D: *Because you were new?* (Aye) *But you got to watch. Was it a special day?*

B: 'Twas word sent to us from other groups. And I know not if it be some special time for repeating, as in going to the island. I think perhaps it be called by one of the mistresses.

D: *I thought maybe on certain days they might go.*

B: Perhaps that be the purpose. If so, I did not learn so myself. There is much of which I still know not.

D: *Yes, there's so much knowledge to be learned. Have you ever heard of a place I've heard of, called the Giants' Dance? Have you ever heard that term associated with the rocks and the stones?*

B: 'Tis strange ... strange saying. Giants' Dance?

D: *Uh-huh. I've heard there was a circle that was called that.*

B: Ye mean the place be called that?

D: *Yes. It may not be in your part of the country.*

B: I know not of such a place. The stories be that many strange happenings take place at the circle. And not only the wee folk, but other creatures often unknown to the average person, appear. And I know not if that includes giants, but 'tis possible.

D: *Anything is possible. I believe the man that told me of this was in Erin. Do you know that country?*

B: Erin? Aye, 'tis across the sea.

I was referring to information given to me by the wandering minstrel in another chapter.

D: *Oh, that would be why you had not seen that place then. Do you have a name for your country? (Pause, no answer) Where you live?*

B: (Confused) Be country? Village?

D: *It has no name that people call it?*

B: Some villages have names. We have no home and live in many places.

D: *I just wondered. But Erin is across the sea.*

B: So I be told.

D: *All right. I have to go now. Would it be all right if I come again and speak with you? (Aye) For you see I mean no harm.*

B: I think ye do not. I do not wish to be rude, but I answer as I feel I can.

D: *That's perfectly all right. That is all I ask. So if I can come again some time, I would really appreciate it. And we can speak again.*

B: Aye. Perhaps you wish to speak to the elder sister about becoming a sister.

D: *That's possible. I will think about it. (Aye) But I've enjoyed speaking with you. You have helped my curiosity.*

B: Aye, 'tis a good word.

D: *It's a strange word, isn't it? (Aye) All right. Well, thank you for speaking with me. Let us leave that scene now.*

I oriented Bernadine back to the present day. I continued with pain control before she was awakened. Upon awakening she felt greatly relieved, and she had no memory of the session at all. This proved my conclusion that she was a somnambulist.

Time went by and our lives went in different directions. I was never able to have another session with Bernadine, so we don't know if she met the same fate as Karen. She helped later on the astrological data for *Nostradamus Volume II.* We remained friends, but never found time to have another session. Bernadine died just after Christmas 1995, and that in itself was a strange story related to her pain. I don't know if it should be included in any book that I write using this material.

Section 2
Brenda's Story as Astelle

Introduction
Astelle

When I first met Brenda, she was curious about whether she had past lives and if she could be hypnotized. That is the wonder of many clients. But it is a very natural state of the body, so I had no concerns. I was curious to see where she would go and the kind of life we would find. I ended up working with Brenda for quite some time because she proved to be such a good subject and very willing to see what was "back there." When I worked with Brenda, it was in the early days of my practice, and I did not use the method I currently use of having the client go to the "most appropriate time and place." This is very effective to see where some issues in this current life may be coming from. I was still learning ways of doing this work. What I had been doing with Brenda was going back in time by roughly one-hundred-year segments to see who and where she was. I later found I could just instruct my clients to go to the most appropriate time and place.

Because I worked with Brenda with the intent of finding out about all of her lives over a period of many sessions, we used a keyword to be able to go into the deep level of trance very easily and quickly. A keyword is used any time I think I might work with someone again as in this case. I would use her keyword and count her back.

A Note from Dolores

In the beginning of this story when she was describing the horrors of the Inquisition and the callousness of the church, I told her after the session. "Brenda, what are you trying to do to me? There's no way I can write about this. They will hang me from the highest tree if I try to tell about the horrible things the church did in those days. They will never stand for hearing such things about their church fathers." This is the way I still feel. There is too much explosive material contained within this story. It is probably the truth about the way the church really behaved, but I feel I must wait a while before I dare write it. I will receive enough ridicule from my other stories as it is. I am not quite ready to go out on a limb with this one.

****

Before Dolores passed, she was working on this book. I think she knew the information needed to be told and the time was right.

I put these chapters in the order of when they were recorded so you could receive the information the same way Dolores did.

~Nancy

Chapter 4
A Follower of the "Old Ways"
(Recorded April 29, 1986)

I had been working with Brenda for quite a while going through many different lives. Because she was so comfortable in the somnambulistic state and had access to a great deal of information while in that state, I spent months exploring many possibilities. At this time in my research in 1986 I was still discovering what was capable of being accomplished through deep-trance hypnosis. Since there were no instruction books on the subject, I was developing my own rules as I went along.

During this year of 1986 I made my first contact with Nostradamus, and Brenda was to be essential and instrumental to that contact. But at this time before that project began, we were still discovering what it was possible to do. I had already taken her through several different lifetimes, and during the in-between state we call "death" her subconscious told me that I should explore a lifetime a long time ago when Brenda was known as Astelle. I was told that this lifetime would be important for Brenda to understand relationships in her present life.

So after she had entered the deep-trance state I instructed her to travel back through time to locate the lifetime of Astelle. I had no idea of the time period we would find ourselves in, but I had no doubt that such a life existed. The subconscious would not have suggested that we locate it if it were not a reality.

When I completed counting, I asked her what she was doing. She responded that she was preparing some food in a kitchen. Her name was indeed Astelle (phonetic with the accent on the first syllable).

D: *What country are we in?*

B: (Hesitated.) Ah ... it's a duchy.** This part is run by the duke. And he has allied himself with the Flanders.

D: *I was wondering if you had ever heard it called a name.*

B: It's just a duchy. There is a name for it that the nobles use. But it's not important to everyday living, so I really don't know.

** A duchy is the territory of a duke or duchess, a dukedom. **

D: *You said you're in the kitchen. Is this where you live?*

B: Yes. I work under here ... for one of the nobles here in the duke's ... place. I am a kitchen maid ... scullery maid? I'm not sure what it would be called. I work in the kitchen mostly.

D: *Can you tell me something about this place? What it looks like?*

B: The kitchen?

D: *Well, that or ... is it a house? Or is it larger than a house?*

B: If the house you mean is the dwelling that the ordinary folk live in, yes, it is much larger than that. It has many rooms. It's mostly two stories high, but part of it is three stories high. It's made out of stone, and most of the houses are usually made out of wattle.

D: *(I didn't understand.) Out of what?*

B: Wattle. You get straw and some sort of clay, and you build a light framework, and you spread the straw on the framework, and you put clay on it to hold it in place. And it dries into a hard wall.

D: *Oh? If it is straw, what happens when it's raining? Wouldn't it just dissolve?*

B: Oh, you know, whenever clay gets wet it seals openings. And when the clay dries sometimes it will come up with a leak. And you get more clay and you dab it over, wherever the leaks are.

D: *What are the roofs made out of on those kinds of houses?*

B: The same thing. And usually in the summertime the roofs will be fresher straw. And the door is usually either made out of wood, if you're well-off, or some sort of animal skin hung across the door.

Encyclopedia: Architecture. Wattle and Daub: A form of construction relying on interlaced green twigs (or withes) through whose interstices clay is forced and matted. In medieval half-timbered buildings, the nogging or fill between the timbers was often composed in this way.

When I first heard about this type of construction in 1986, I thought it would be very flimsy and definitely not durable. Since that time, I have made many trips to Europe, especially to England, and I discovered that I was wrong to jump to such a conclusion. I have a good friend who has an advertising company in a very old building in the small town of Ringwood in the south of England. In America we are free to do what we wish with property, but in England the authenticity of the original structure must be maintained. If a building is rebuilt or remodeled it must be built in the exact style of the original. My friend had remodeled the three-story building, but she showed me something very interesting on the second floor. The wall of one of the offices had been left exposed and covered with a sheet of glass. She said as she pointed to the intertwined small branches and plaster in the wall, "That is what's holding this building up!" It was the wattle-and-daub construction, and the clay, plaster or whatever was used had hardened to a cement consistency. It was strong enough to last through four hundred years, and except for some settling and shifting, the building was still standing. So, I discovered that this old form of construction was quite practical, economical and durable. Probably many of the old walls in Europe contain wattle-and-daub construction.

D: *Is that the kind of a home that you lived in before you came to this place?*
B: I don't remember. I've been here all my life. I think I was

born to somebody here in the house. I'm not sure.

D: *Would this place be called a "castle"? Or do you know that word?*

B: (Slowly) I don't ... know that ... word. I don't think it would apply. I've never heard it.

The trait of a true somnambulist is that they do not recognize words that do not exist in their time period, even though they are quite familiar with them in their present lifetime. It is a sign of true time travel and being in the other time period totally.

D: *This is just a large house then.*

B: A large ... I'm trying to think of the word that it is called. I can't find the word. But I'll tell you how it looks, and maybe you will know a word for it.

D: *Okay, because I know many words.*

B: In the kitchen where I do most of my work, it is high-ceilinged. It has beams going across the ceiling. The beams are black from the smoke. And there's a large walk-in fireplace where we do the cooking. And there are all kinds of pots and pans and utensils hanging on the wall. And there's a large ... or rather, a long table. It goes down the length of the room. And this is where we prepare the food and everything, is on this table. We cut up the food and everything here and put it in the pots. And put the pots near or over the fire, depending on how we're fixing the food. The floor is also made out of stone, but flat stones. It has to be made out of stone because wood floors don't last very long with the food scraps and everything.

D: *That makes sense. Are there many of you in the kitchen to do the work?*

B: Well, there's ... let me see ... (She appeared to be looking around and counting.) There's the main cook ... and there's the two others that also cover the main cook's duties. And then there are a handful of us that do the cutting and the peeling and such as that. And there are the two dogs, too.

D: *Are the dogs always in the kitchen?*

B: Yes. They help keep the floor from getting too piled up.

D: *Oh. You mean whenever you're cooking, you just throw things on the floor?*

B: Yes, in amongst the straw.

D: *Oh, there's straw on the floor on top of the stone?*

B: Yes, stone would be too cold, particularly in the wintertime. So, we put straw on the stone so it won't be so cold. We're just servants so we don't have foot coverings.

D: *And then you just throw the food scraps on the floor with the straw?*

B: Yes. It's done that way in the dining room, too, when the nobles are eating. The bones and such are thrown on the floor, and the nobles' dogs eat those scraps, too.

D: *Then there's also straw on the floor in the dining room. Ummm, there must be many dogs in the house.*

B: Just the usual number for a house this size.

D: *What would the usual number be?*

B: I've not thought about it. I'd say eight or ten.

She continued with the description of the house, "And there are the hallways that branch off from the dining room that go to the other parts of the ... place. And they don't have straw on their floors, because people don't *use* the hallways. You just go down the hallways to get to another part of the place. I've heard tell from the maids who work in the bedrooms, that the bedrooms look really fine, with tapestries and such. And there are rugs on the floor."

D: *I have heard that the tapestries are to help make the house warmer. Is that true?*

B: Yes, that is true, because there are drafts. Plus, even if there are no drafts, the cold from the walls, since the walls are made out of stone, the cold kind of radiates—is that the word?— inward. It gets to your bones. And the tapestries help hold it back some.

D: *Are there windows in this house?*

B: Windows are openings in the walls that are not doors? *(Yes)* They are usually long and narrow. And they have shutters over them. Mainly they're for in the summer to help with ventilation. And they're made to where it would be convenient for the archers.

D: *I was thinking you would need some way to close them, otherwise it would get cold.*

B: Yes, the shutters do that.

D: *Then the archers have to be able to shoot through them, you said?* (Yes) *Why? Is there danger sometimes?* (Yes) *Are there more fireplaces throughout the house?*

B: Of course. Every room has at least one fireplace. The dining room has two. In the kitchen the fireplace is so large that a second one is not needed. But all the other rooms have fireplaces. ... Except for the room at the top of the tower. I hear tell it has this wondrous metal shield that a fire is kept going in. I've never been there. It's only what I have heard from other servants.

D: *You mean it is a container that fire is put in?*

B: It's called a shield, and I hear that it is like a very shallow bowl, but very large. Very gradually curved and very large and round. And in the center of this a small fire is built and kept. And I heard a wondrous thing, that it was suspended from the ceiling by chains. I suspect that the master is involved with unholy things in that room. It is said that he calls up the spirits with that. But that is not talked about.

D: *I can see why. But that sounds like such a wondrous way to heat, that there would be more in the house.*

B: It's not effective for large rooms, I hear. It's good for small rooms. But even at that, you have to have one of your windows partially unshuttered so that the smoke may escape.

D: *Oh, yes. The fireplaces would have the chimneys, wouldn't they?* (Yes) *But you said you have never been in that room?*

B: No. I really don't know of anyone who can truthfully say they have. What I've heard is just hearsay. Or perhaps one or two servants have been in there to clean it upon occasion. At which times the master would have his unholy implements well packed away, I'm sure. But they said it was a most unusual room.

D: *Well, you never know if some of the things you hear are true or not. It may just be talk.*

B: Perhaps. But everyone does know that there is no chimney in that room, so there must be some way of heating it. If indeed it is heated.

D: *Does he spend a lot of time in there?*

B: I know not. I think that he does spend several evenings there. It is said that there are several parchments in there. What the nobles use, you know, to write on. And it could be that he has some knowledge stored there.

D: *Do you know how to read?*

B: (Emphatic) No! That is the thing the nobles do. I cannot count very far either. But I did need to know some counting to help with the cooking.

D: *Then only the nobles would be able to read any parchments he would have.* (Yes) *About how old are you? Do you know?*

B: Ah ... (thinking) it is said that I have been here for ... (Unsure) fifteen years? Maybe sixteen.

D: *Then you are a young woman.*

B: I'm of marrying age.

D: *But you think you were born there?*

B: I think so. I don't remember anything else.

D: *Do you know your mother or father?*

B: I have a dim recollection of my mother. I don't know my father.

D: *Is your mother living?*

B: She died when I was young.

D: *Is that why you stayed there?*

B: I would have stayed here anyway. This is where I belong.

D: *Then you were taken care of by the other people in the house?*

B: I suppose.

D: *But is that all you remember, just working in that kitchen?*

B: That's what I do when I'm working. But when it's in between meals or on a holiday, I go outside in the fields.

D: *You mean you help in the fields?*

B: No, no, just outside. Enjoying being out with other people of my class.

D: *Well, in the house, do you have a place that you sleep?*

B: Yes. There's a place near the kitchen, off of a … see, different ones of us sleep in different places according to where we find to sleep. The place where I sleep is a … there's a nook underneath a flight of stairs. It's rather like a closet. And I claimed that place. The other servants do not consider it desirable because it's just a small closet, and there's no windows or anything. But they do not realize that the back wall of the closet is very close to the back wall of the fireplace, so it's always warm in the winter.

D: *Then you knew what you were doing when you asked for that place. (Laugh)*

B: Yes. So, if I want fresh air, I can get it in the day, but at night I need to stay warm.

D: *Do you have a bed or anything that you sleep on in that little room?*

B: I sleep on the floor. Sometimes when the master discards a cloak, I get it and I put it on the floor.

D: *And it's warm that way.* (Yes) *What kind of clothes do you have on? What do you wear?*

B: I have on a skirt and a blouse with a bodice, and a kerchief.

D: *What colors are they?*

B: Not really any color. They're just of an acorn dye. I guess you'd call them a grayish-brown color. My skirt is a light brown color, and my blouse is kind of a dark cream color. It was never dyed. My bodice is dark brown. And my kerchief … I wear my kerchief around my waist. It used to be blue, but it has faded to gray.

D: *From the washings?* (Yes) *Do you wear anything on your head?*

B: No. Sometimes in the summer I'll wear my kerchief on my head.

D: *What color is your hair?*

B: It's in between gold and red.

D: *Do you wear it any certain way?*

B: No. I just braid it.

D: *I was just wondering if your people wore bright colors in their clothes.*

B: The servants don't. It would not be seemly.

D: *Only the noblemen would wear bright colors?*

B: It's not really bright colors, but *pure* colors, whereas our colors are always faded. And they wear pure colors that are kind of dark. Wine-colored. Maroon, burgundy, blue, gold, black. You know, pure colors. Whereas my clothes are kind of grayish-brown. You know, in-between colors.

D: *But the rest of the servants all dress the same way with the same kind of colors?* (Yes) *Do the men dress differently?*

B: Yes. It depends on whether you are a noble or a servant. The servants, out of practicality, wear britches. They go down to the calves. And a shirt and a vest. And usually a cap of some sort. And the women servants wear like me, a skirt and a blouse and a bodice and a kerchief. Most of them wear their kerchiefs on their heads. I wear mine around my waist because I'm thin enough to where I can tie it around my waist. And also, because there's another woman in the house who is quite homely. She's very jealous of my hair, so I refuse to cover it up. (She was smiling, and I laughed.) And the noblemen wear robes that go down to the floor, and headgear in various fine colors, according to their station in life. The women wear long dresses with long sleeves, of various colors.

D: *What kind of headgear do they wear?*

B: It depends upon their station. Various shapes of hats and caps. Sometimes with veils and such attached, sometimes not. The hats come in different shapes. Sometimes they fit close to the head and are wrapped around like a turban. Sometimes they have brims and crowns and such. And the different shapes mean different things.

D: *Do you know what they mean?*

B: Only the ones I've seen. The clergymen, the priests, wear different shapes of hats according to how high they are in the priesthood. And the nobleman who is involved with law wears one kind of hat. And a nobleman who is involved with … legislature—is that the word?—wears another kind of hat.

D: *Legislature would be a kind of law. It would be more*

complicated, I think.

B: One interprets the law as it already is, and the other one helps create new laws when new laws are needed.

D: *That's the right word then.*

B: And some noblemen who are just involved with the land have another type of hat. And some noblemen are involved with trade, and so they would have another type of hat.

D: *And you can recognize them by what they wear.* (Yes) *What about the master of the house? Does he have a certain kind of a hat?*

B: He's involved with the land, so he wears that type of hat. It has a low crown. And it has a generous brim, and the brim is shaped. I don't know how to describe it any better than that. And it is usually black.

D: *What do you call the master of the house? Does he have a title?*

B: We call him "my lord."

D: *The lord?*

B: *My* lord. Or "master." He's a duke.

D: *Do you know his name? Is there another name besides that?*

B: Ummm, one of his names is Paul. (Pause) I don't know beyond that. There is some family names involved, I'm sure. But I never can remember them, so I don't bother with it. Sometimes my memory is not good.

D: *But you only have one name?*

B: Yes. I'm Astelle. (I pronounced it and she corrected me, putting a definite accent on the first syllable.)

D: *Then servants don't usually have two names?*

B: No. Sometimes craftsmen in the village, like the blacksmith or what-have-you, will have a label describing what they do. Like John the blacksmith. But it's not a name, it's just a description.

D: *That's because there might be more than one John.* (Yes) *I'm thinking, Astelle is not a common name to me.*

B: It's not here either. I don't know why my mother named me that. I've heard tell that the meaning of the name has something to do with the stars. But I'm not sure, unless it's because of the color of my hair.

D: *The red and gold?* (Uh-huh) *Are you happy there?*

B: I guess. I don't know. What's happiness? What's unhappiness? I just live from day to day.

D: *Oh, they say happiness is a state of mind. But at least you're not miserable, are you? If you know what that word means.*

B: I know what that word means. I get to eat and I have a place to sleep.

D: *Well, I guess if someone wasn't happy they would want to be somewhere else.*

B: I've often wondered what is beyond where I can see. But it is not my place to travel.

D: *Then if you had a chance you wouldn't go anywhere anyway. Is that right?*

B: No. I would travel. But it's not my place to just up and travel for no reason. If my master sent me to a place, I would go.

D: *But if you're not really happy, at least you're content. Would that be a good word? (She seemed confused.) Things are all right.*

B: Things are all right.

D: *You're not badly treated then.*

B: (Laugh) Only by the noblewoman who is jealous of my hair. She likes to beat me.

D: *She does? What would she beat you for?*

B: Because she's ugly and I'm not.

D: *I don't think that gives her a reason.*

B: Well, she's a noblewoman and I'm a servant. It gives her a reason. If she wants to beat me, she can.

D: *Is she like the lady of the house?*

B: No. She's a cousin of some sort to the lady of the house.

D: *Then she lives there.* (Yes) *What do you call her? Does she have a name?*

B: She's the Lady Joslyn.

D: *Do you try to stay out of her way?*

B: I just stay here in the kitchen and work. But she occasionally comes down. Whenever she's feeling angry about something, she'll come down here to beat me.

D: *She takes it out on you, and you haven't got anything to do with it.*

B: Well, that's her prerogative. She's a noblewoman.

D: *Do you resent her for that? If you know what that means?*

B: I know what that means. Ah ... I just kind of expect it to happen. I don't resent *her*, but I feel that she resents *me*. Because there is something else. There is a young nobleman who was sent here as a page. And he has attained the status of valet, and soon he will become a knight. She has become interested in him, but he does not return her interest. And she cannot figure out why. Because she does not know that ... he and I are lovers.

D: *Oh? How did that happen?*

B: On days that are good the valets and pages and knights are out in the practice yard practicing their skills. And sometimes they request to have some food brought out there, so they won't have to interrupt what they're doing. And it's usually my job and a couple of others to carry the food out there to them.

D: *And this was how you met him?* (Yes) *Wouldn't he be a different ... status?*

B: Yes. That's why we cannot get married. But he claims that he loves me truly. I know that I love him truly. I do not worry about it. One thing I have learned, that you must take each moment as it comes. And don't worry about the consequences because what's going to happen is going to happen, so you get what good you can when it comes.

D: *What is his name?*

(I had difficulty understanding and trying to pronounce the name she used. She had to repeat it several times. It sounded like: Thoroff, phonetic.)

D: *What does he look like?*

B: (Spoken with love) He's tall and fair. He's strong. He has hair that's like flax, it's very light colored. And it turns white when he's in the sun a lot. And his skin turns golden colored when he's in the sun. He is very fair to look upon. His eyes are as blue as the sky.

D: *Have you been seeing him as a lover for very long?*

B: For about a year now.

D: *Well, do you meet somewhere? Because he couldn't come into the kitchen, could he?*

B: No, he couldn't. Sometimes he'll come to my closet. Sometimes we meet outside. There's a certain place in the grove of trees that we go when the weather is warm. And when the weather is cold, we meet in the stables. We can't meet where he stays because all the knights and valets and such stay together in large rooms. They sleep together in groups. So, we can't go there.

D: *Do you think you'll still be able to continue to meet when he becomes a knight? He will have a high status then.*

B: Yes. We'll continue to meet as long as he is here at this place. The Lady Joslyn is trying to make life difficult for us. She's always calling upon him to attend her. (Laugh) Sometimes she tries to call upon him to attend her at inappropriate times of the day. And the Lord Duke has been being somewhat scandalized by this. He does not blame Roff for he knows how the Lady Joslyn is. But for the Lady Joslyn, she is somewhat desperate to get a husband. She's not pretty. She has an unpleasant voice. And she thinks only of herself. She's not pleasant to be around.

D: *Is she getting older? Is that why she's getting desperate?*

B: Yes, she is an old maid.

D: *How old is old?*

B: She's ... twenty-four, twenty-five?

D: *Oh, are they usually married by that time?*

B: Oh, yes.

D: *You said she calls upon him at inappropriate times of the day. What do you mean?*

B: She'll call upon him to attend her, like ... somewhat after the dinner hour. And she'll try to keep him into the wee hours of the night, so as she's trying to get him compromised. And she will try to claim to be with child, so that they will have to become united.

D: *Oh, then he would have to marry her. Is that the way it goes?*

B: In her case, yes. But he has told me that her schemes will not work. (Smiling) He said that she's so hideous that he can't get it up.

D: *(Laugh) But that's why she keeps calling him to her room?*

B: Yes. And all the ladies know that she is not pregnant, and she is not apt to get that way.

D: *But you said the duke is scandalized by it?* (Yes) *He doesn't really know for sure that nothing is happening, does he?*

B: His lady tells him that nothing is happening. But the reason why he is scandalized is because the Lady Joslyn is behaving inappropriately. And he is threatening to send her away.

D: *(Laugh) You wouldn't mind that, would you?*

B: No, I would not.

D: *This is the reason why she beats you, because she's jealous?*

B: Yes. I am told that I am pretty. I have never seen myself. I don't know. I like the color of my hair. Roff says I'm beautiful, but Roff is not objective.

D: *(Laugh) Have you ever heard of what is called a "mirror"?*

B: The ladies of the house, they have pieces of polished metal that they can see their reflections in. When they are getting ready for dinner or a dance or something like that, their personal servants hold these for them so they can see themselves. But faintly.

D: *But you have never seen yourself in a mirror like that?* (No) *Well, it sounds like whenever she gets angry about anything, she takes it out on you. Is that right?*

B: Yes. After she takes it out on her personal servants.

D: *She must have quite a temper.*

B: Yes, that is one reason why she is not very popular. The temper goes along with her voice. It screeches. *(I laughed.)*

D: *Then does the duke have a large family living there with him?*

B: Oh, yes. A large family and a large retinue.

D: *Does he have children?*

B: Yes. It is said that he has many illegitimate children as well amongst the servants. I suspect that he might be my father.

But of course, I'm not allowed to speak of this.

D: *Is he old enough that he could be?*

B: Oh, yes, he's in his forties.

D: *But at least he takes care of his children if he knows who the children are. Is that right?*

B: Yes. He allows them to stay here and have a place to live and work. And his lady, the Lady Evelyn, she takes it in hand. It has been said that my mother was very beautiful. And it was no wonder that the duke seduced her.

D: *This is common among the servants?*

B: What?

D: *To mix with the royalty in this way?*

B: It is the duke's prerogative. If he wants to sleep with one of his servants, then he may do so.

D: *They don't have anything to say about it?*

B: No, it is considered to be an honor to be chosen by the duke to sleep with him. But it is noticed that there are certain ones that regardless of how fair they are, he chooses not to sleep with them. But he is still kindly towards them. And it is suspected that those of us that he treats that way, that we are his children.

D: *Oh. That's very possible. You never know.—Do you know what a religion is?*

B: Religion? That is like the church?

D: *Yes. Is there any certain kind of religion in the place where you live?*

B: There is the holy Roman church.

D: *This is what the people believe?*

B: It is what the royalty believes. The nobles. Those of us who are servants, we have other sources of belief. But this is not generally known outside our own circles.

D: *Can you tell me about it?*

B: If you wish. You must not tell the royalty, because we would be punished by the most drastic means.

D: *You can always trust me because I don't tell anyone.*

B: You're not from the Inquisition?

D: *Oh, no. No, I'm just like a friend that you can tell anything to.*

B: Me thinks that you do have that of the familiar spirit about you.

D: *What do you mean? (I had not understood.) What is an unfamiliar spirit?*

B: A familiar spirit, not unfamiliar spirit.

D: *Oh, I thought you said unfamiliar. (Laugh) A familiar spirit, would that be something that you recognize, or that you feel comfortable with?*

B: There are ways of recognizing familiar spirits. You see, the duke once studied part of our religion, but he twisted it around and he uses it to his own means. There are those of us amongst the servants that follow the old way. And the church is trying to stamp this out.

D: *Is this the Inquisition that you were talking about?* (Yes) *What does the Inquisition do?*

B: The Inquisition questions you and tortures you, and then executes you.

D: *Do they look for people who believe in things that are different? Or how do they know?*

B: They don't. They just look for people to take out their sick pleasures on. Anybody who dares think differently. Anybody who dares to look up from their place and see something more, regardless if they be Christian or non-Christian. Anybody who acts a little bit different. Anybody who looks a little bit different.

D: *It doesn't sound religious if they do things like that.*

B: No. That is why I was not raised up in the church.

D: *Well, you said you think that the duke has taken some of the ways and twisted them.* (Yes) *Do you think this is what he does in the tower room?*

B: Yes, he calls upon the evil side of things. But the Inquisition durst not touch him, for he is too powerful. So, they take it out of those of us who cannot fight back.

D: *So, you do have to be careful. I've heard a little bit about the old ways. Can you tell me a little more about what that means?*

B: We follow the cycles of the Earth. There are powers in the

Earth and the moon that the goddess reveals herself through. And if you work in harmony with these powers, wondrous things can happen in your life. That is one reason why I do not worry about Roff and the Lady Joslyn. For the grove of trees that I take him to, when we go outside at night, is a special place of power. And every time we go there it strengthens the bonds between us.

D: *Why is it a special place of power?*

B: It is a grove to the goddess. It is a group of thirteen oak trees.

D: *Do you have meetings there or rituals?*

B: Yes. But I'm not allowed to speak of this.

D: *That's all right. But I do want you to realize that you can trust me. When you're ready, someday you might tell me. For you know I will always listen to you.—But does the goddess have a name? Or is she just called the goddess?*

B: We just call her the goddess. It is said that she has many names in relation to her many faces. For the goddess is always changing with the seasons and the phases of the moon. So she has many names to relate to *all* of this. It's very complex to keep up with all the names. And so we refer to her as the goddess or the Earth mother.

D: *That makes it much easier. Then you just call your religion the "old ways"?* (Yes) *It has no other name?*

B: Not that I know of. That's just what we call it.

D: *Okay. But it sounds like you have problems though with Lady Joslyn.*

B: That is all right. We know that everything has to balance out sooner or later. And she's pushing her end on the balance too far. And then when it returns to where it should be in balance, she will be destroyed in the process.

D: *This is the way it works?*

B: Yes. That's why you must stay in harmony, so you won't be destroyed by getting things out of balance.

D: *Have you ever had any other lovers in the house?*

B: No. There have been some young noblemen who have tried to have their way with me, but Roff would prevent them.

D: *Then he has mostly been the only one.*

B: He *is* the only one.

D: *Well, what does a page do in the house? Do they have certain duties?*

B: Yes. When a boy first comes here for training, he is a page. And he does many of the things that the servants do, but he does it in order to learn the inner workings of the system. He waits on the knights or lords. And he's with them all the time. He helps them dress. He brings them food and drink to their rooms when they want it. And delivers messages for them. And when he becomes older, he becomes a valet. At which time he helps the knight or lord with his weapons. Helps them polish them and take care of them. And helps him dress for battle or for affairs of state, such as that. And he acts as his aide. Meanwhile he is undergoing weapons training himself from the weapons masters. And then when he reaches a certain point of development, he starts doing the things that knights do so he may become trained, so that someday he may become a knight.

D: *They must go through all these different stages before they can become a knight.* (Yes) *Was he born in this house also?*

B: Roff? *(Yes)* No. The sons of the household are always sent to another household to be trained, to be sure that they are trained properly.

D: *Then he came from somewhere else. And a knight, would that be as high as he can go then?*

B: No. It's just that that would be as high as his *training* goes. He will have completed his training that he needs to know to take a station in life.

D: *What would the duties of a knight be?*

B: A knight defends and fights. A knight also escorts important people and keeps them safe from thieves and highwaymen. Also if the duke needs to have an important message delivered to another place far away, the knight delivers the message and brings back the answer, and makes sure that he is not stopped by anybody along the way.

D: *We have a word for a person called a "soldier." I thought maybe he might be like that. You said he defends.*

B: I don't know that word.

D: *It would be very similar. They would have weapons and defend.*

B: And often in times of peace when the knights have not been doing much fighting, they have contests done in fun to help them keep their skills up, so they may continue to be in top form for defending.

D: *I've heard of these things. Do you get to watch them?*

B: Oh, yes. It's always a big holiday and everybody gets to watch. The servants have to stay in their place, of course, and cannot mix with the noblemen. But still it's fun to watch and I always cheer for Roff.

D: *What kind of a holiday would you mostly have these things?*

B: What do you mean?

D: *You said it was mostly on a holiday?*

B: Yes. Whenever there's going to be a joust everyone ...

D: *Oh, they* make *it a holiday.* (Yes) *Oh, I thought it was on a certain holiday.*

B: Well, Mayday is always a big day for a joust.

D: *Why is Mayday important?*

B: Well, we know the real reason even though the church would not admit it. It is an important day in the old ways. And thus it is the beginning of spring and new life for the Earth.

D: *I thought spring was earlier.*

B: It is actually. And those of us with the old ways know this. And we celebrate it earlier. But those who are not of the old ways that are involved with the church instead, are not aware of this. And so they celebrate it on Mayday.

D: *Why does the church celebrate it on Mayday?*

B: The church has its reason. I have no idea. There must be some saint or another in the past that did something on Mayday.

D: *Then they can use that for an excuse to celebrate?* (Yes) *Well, this has all been very interesting. I appreciate you telling me these things. May I come again and speak with you on these things?* (Yes) *And visit with you like this?* (Yes) *For you realize that I mean you no harm, don't you?*

B: You have the feel of a familiar spirit. But I must bide a bit and make sure that you pass the test.

D: Oh? What kind of a test?

B: You will know when it comes.

D: Hmmm. That's interesting. Are you going to test me?

B: Perhaps. Or it might be someone else.

D: What would happen if I didn't pass the test?

B: Then I would banish you and would not speak to you anymore.

D: Well, I'm not worried. Because I know that I mean you no harm.

B: That will serve you well then in the test.

D: I'm just curious and want to know many things. That's why I ask so many questions. But I would never hurt you in any way.

B: That is good, for you would not be allowed to.

D: But I just like to come and visit you. If you have anything you want to tell someone and don't want anyone else to know, I am always available.

B: Very well.

D: Everyone needs something like that. (Yes)

That was all Astelle would tell me about the mysterious "test" that would be performed. I brought Brenda back to full consciousness and did not tell her about my curiosity of what the test would entail, and when and how it would be done. Would I be aware of it? I had no idea what Astelle had in store for me. But I knew I would have to gain her confidence if she was to continue sharing information with me. I especially wanted to know more about the practice of the "old ways."

Chapter 5
The Test
(Recorded May 6, 1986)

Used keyword and counted her back to the life of Astelle.

D: We have gone back to the time when Astelle was living. What are you doing?

B: I'm in the kitchen. I'm at the table that's in the middle of the room. I'm helping to prepare food. There is going to be a banquet tonight.

D: What kind of food are you preparing?

B: I'm mostly preparing vegetables. Getting them ready. I have been making various kinds of stuffing for the roasts. And that includes cutting up the vegetables and everything and adding the spices. There is a young pig to be stuffed. And there is going to be a lamb roast. And some deer.

D: Where do the vegetables come from?

B: From the farmers. There's fields of vegetables around the place. This place has grounds for the lords and ladies to cavort in. But beyond that there are fields of vegetables. And the farmers bring to here a certain portion of their crop to go towards their taxes.

D: Oh? They have to pay taxes to the lord? (Yes) Will you be allowed to eat any of this food?

B: After the noblemen are through. Whatever is left over that the dogs don't get. However, here in the kitchen it's easy to get some food. You have to make sure it tastes good before it's brought to the table.

D: *Oh, you have to sample it?* (Yes) *What is the occasion for the banquet?*

B: Some of the lord's family from away off have come here to visit from another place. They have come here to help ... I'm not sure of all the ramifications. I think they're wanting to arrange some marriages while they're here. Plus, they're wanting to agree about helping each other in time of war and such, too. And so they've come here to feast and banquet and make these various contracts and arrangements.

D: *You said they've come from a long way?*

B: Yes, several days journey away.

D: *Are these people who have come been here before?*

B: Yes, but it's been a long time. I was a little girl then.

D: *You spoke of war. Do you think there will be a war?*

B: One never knows. There's always various squabbles and disagreements. It's always good to have some agreements and contracts on hand just in case the situation comes up.

D: *Do they come from a different country, or a different part of this country?*

B: They come from east of here. From France.

D: *Before you didn't tell me what the name of your country was that you're living in. Do you know what it is?*

B: I've heard it called various things. The tradesmen call it Flanders. I think some of the other names I've heard are things that people of foreign countries call it. And they're words I couldn't pronounce.

D: *And you said they're going to arrange marriages? What kind of marriages?*

B: A marriage is a marriage.

D: *(Laugh) I meant, between people that live in the house or what?*

B: Yes. Between the people that live in the house and people that they have connections with. As well as perhaps people in their entourage.

D: *Is there anyone in particular in the house that wants to get married? (I was naturally thinking of the Lady Joslyn.)*

B: (Smiling) Yes, but she has her hat set for Roff.

D: *(Laugh) I was thinking of Joslyn. Do you think they might try to arrange a marriage between Joslyn and someone else?*

B: Yes, because it would be a more suitable marriage for her. Roff is a valet soon to reach his knighthood. But still he is not of as high born of a family as the Lady Joslyn.

D: *Would she be able to marry him if she wanted to?*

B: Yes, but she does not have clear sight in this matter. And so
...

D: *You mean she doesn't have anything to say about who she marries?*

B: Oh, she could. It's just that the lord knows it would be better if she married someone else. And so he seemingly is going to insist upon it.

D: *How do you feel about that? If she leaves or marries someone else?*

B: Oh, I'd like that. It would make life very nice for me.

D: *Does she still treat you the same way?*

B: Yes. Worst, it seems like sometimes. Because it's apparent to all that I'm prettier than she is. I just work in the kitchen and I have to wear the same thing every day—it's all I have—and I don't have the fine jewels that she has, or the powders and such that she puts on her face. And I've heard tell that people agree that I'm the prettier of the two even though I don't have powders on my face, or jewels or anything like that. She doesn't care for that. And she gets particularly angry whenever she hears me sing.

D: *Do you like to sing?*

B: It helps the day to go.

D: *What kind of songs do you sing?*

B: Just ordinary songs. Usually I just hum things that I make up while I'm working. I don't really listen to what I'm singing, so people say, "Sing that again." And I say, "Well, what was I singing?" Because I don't really listen. People say my voice sounds pleasing. But the Lady Joslyn's voice (Smiling. I laughed.) ... that sounds much like a rusty door hinge.

D: *(Laugh) That doesn't sound very complimentary. Well, do you ever sing any songs that are sung by the other people?*

I was trying to get her to sing something for me that I would be able to check out later. This had happened in the past with the other subject who was a minstrel in another life.

B: I don't know. I just sing here in the kitchen. And usually just to myself because I don't want to bother anyone else. So forget that I mentioned the singing.

D: *I'm just curious because I like music. And I was wondering if there were some songs that were always sung, that you might have been repeating.*

B: I don't know. I don't get to mix with the people much. I'm always here in the kitchen. I don't get to go to any of their celebrations.

D: *Okay. But I like music, that's why I was wondering about it.—But you told me once that sometimes Joslyn beats you. Is that true?*

B: Yes. With her hairbrush.

D: *Is it a large one?*

B: It's ... it's two handspans.

D: *That would be a big one. The brushes that I'm used to are small. I didn't think they would hurt very much.*

B: I keep trying to tell her that ... See, brushes are rare and hard to come by, and difficult to make. Most people use combs. And I try to tell her that she's going to ruin her brush, and she won't have one then. But she'd still have the handle, and that's what she beats me with.

D: *(Laugh) She doesn't care.*

B: No, she never has.

D: *Was she ever successful in seducing Roff?*

B: No. For there is that one part of the mind that must cooperate, and if it does not cooperate, all the seduction does not work. And she screams at him and scratches his face, and slaps him, because she says he is totally smitten by me.

D: *She just doesn't understand, does she?*

B: No. Or maybe she understands all too well and she doesn't like it.

D: *Could be. You know, one time I was talking to you about your religion. I am curious about that.*

B: It's in harmony with the Earth.

D: *Are there many of you there that practice the old ways?*

B: More than what the church suspects. ... And we ... we devised a test for testing you.

D: *You did? Well, I'm curious.*

B: And ... we have tested you. You are who you say you are. And you're not part of the Inquisition. Therefore, I will answer your questions.

D: *When did you test me? Was I aware of it?*

B: No. We did not want you to be aware, because you would be self-conscious then.

D: *Who is we?*

B: I and some others here in this place. There must be a word for this place. I know a word in my language. But this language that I seem to be using, ah ...

D: *What is the word in your language that you would call it?*

B: Just a moment. Don't confuse me. There is the word "castle," but that doesn't fit. Neither does "mansion" fit. I'm finding these words. I'm trying to see what fits. Keep! Keep. In this keep.

D: *But is that what you call it in your language? You said there was another word.*

B: No, this is in the language ... in *your* language. It's much nicer than an ordinary keep. It's kind of in between a keep and a mansion.

D: *Yes. A mansion is a very large house. And a castle is also very large.*

B: Yes. A keep** is more of a strategic military location, it seems. And this is located strategically. It's fortified, but not as heavily as a castle. It's kind of like a fortified mansion.

** English term corresponding to the French donjon for the strongest portion of the fortification of a castle, the place of last resort in case of siege or attack. The keep was either a single tower or a larger fortified enclosure. **

D: *Oh, that is why the name would have to be different then. I see.—Well, did you tell these other people that I had come and spoke with you?* (Yes) *They did not find it odd?*

B: No. We speak with disembodied voices fairly often. That's part of our religion. The church would have it that that would be demons, but it is not.

D: *But you had to devise a test before you would be allowed to speak with me again?*

B: Not necessarily being *allowed* to speak to you. We had to devise a test to make sure it was safe, so it would not bring disaster down upon us.

D: *Oh? Could that happen?*

B: Oh, yes. You could have been a trick, a spy sent from the church. Someone who could throw their voice. And that would be disastrous if I said anything that the Inquisition could use.

D: *Yes, and now you know that I will not cause any disaster.*

B: No. You are ... it's hard to describe, but the test ... we tested you. You are from another place and from another time. Somehow you are able to project your voice to us. But you have no connection with the church at all. And there's no way ... even if you were to give all the information to the church, the church would think you were a demon and would not listen.

D: *They wouldn't believe me. That is true. Even in our time they would not believe me. It's for my own curiosity.*

B: Be you careful of the church then?

D: *I don't think the church is ever going to change.*

B: No, it will not. However, there are always followers of the craft, of the religion. There are always those of us who respect our Earth mother. The great mother. She has many names. And as long as there is so much as one person who respects the great mother, things will be all right. The more people who respect the great mother, the more there is harmony. Someday the church will wane and wither up and dry away. That is the natural cycle of everything that is not in harmony with the great mother. It waxes, it wanes, it withers up and dries away. And the church, it waxed. And it appears to now be at its greatest and is merely staying the same. Then it will wane, wither up and dry away. And the great mother will still be there.

D: *Yes. You were talking about this Inquisition. That doesn't sound to me like that is a good part of religion.*

B: No. When a religion or anything of that sort has to resort to force and violence to hold their own, that means they have begun to wane. And realize that the end for them is coming. And they do not wish for it to happen. The end may be many hundreds of years away, but still ... (She yawned and it was hard to understand.) things such as that are part of the end.

D: *I think it makes them seem more insecure if they have to do things like that.*

B: Well, yes, they're insecure. They are out of harmony with the great mother. And the main thing that guarantees that the church will wither up and dry away is, they insist upon a heavenly *father* being overall and everything. And it's not that way at all. It is the great mother.

D: *Well, they have to make him masculine, I suppose.*

B: Yes, and they gear everything towards the masculine way of doing things. Which is not right. That's leaving off half of humankind when they do that.

D: *That's true. For the masculine cannot do anything by itself really. Not in according to the laws of nature.*

B: And their great father has never had a wife. He once sent, they say, his spirit down to impregnate a virgin without her ever having known a man. That is unnatural. And they say that he has no need of a wife. That is unnatural, too. The great mother has had several consorts and lovers. And from her loins have sprung all life.

D: *Then you have probably heard the story about the virgin and the child she brought forth, that the religion is based on.*

B: Yes. Everyone has heard it. The church makes sure of that.

D: *This is the one they want everyone to believe then. (Yes) I don't know if you can tell me or not, but I am curious about the test. Can you tell me what the test was, now that it's over? How I was tested?*

B: I'm not sure it would be wise to tell you.

D: *Because you won't do it again now that it's over, I don't suppose.*

B: But if others of your kind come, we would need to test them, too.

D: *I don't think they will. I don't know of anyone else that will come. You never know, but I think I'm the only one that will come at this time.*

B: We went to the sacred grove. We are very fortunate here. We have the sacred grove of potent power. It's on top of a hill, which is good. And there's a focusing stone in the middle. And we used a focusing stone, and we brought along a pot and had it filled with water. And we called down the guiding forces. We presented you to them and asked them to tell us about you. And in the pot of water, there are some of us who can read what is shown in the water. And those that can do that gazed into the water and told us what they saw about you.

D: *Can you share that with me?*

B: It's hard to explain. There were many wondrous things that could not be expressed in the language of man.

D: *Could you try? I'm curious.*

B: They said that they felt sorry for you. For you have been raised up under the influence of the church, with the image of the church's father pounded into your head. But they could see that you basically were trying to walk the path of the great mother. But there was no one to help you and you were doing it by yourself. And that was the first point in your favor. That you were basically in harmony with the great mother, and with her realm of the power. And they said that you had wondrous things. You have a black object that takes the voices of men and holds them and can give them back again, without making anybody mute.

D: *Yes, I do. It's a wondrous object.*

B: And you have wondrous objects for writing. You are able to do this without having to have an inkpot and an inkstone on hand. We saw many things about you like this. But that was not the important part. They needed to find out about *you*. And they saw that you were a tool of the great mother. She is using you for her own end. We saw that you are not of our time. That you are from the time to come. And where you're from, the church is beginning to wither. Very soon it will dry up and blow away. But it has been waning for quite some time, and it is beginning to wither. And it's going into its death agonies, which can be very ... as you know, when anything goes into its death agonies the effort involved can be very strong and vigorous. And so the church in your time is going into its death agonies, which is making it appear strong, vigorous, powerful, but very unsure of itself, for it is being undermined all around. And shortly the church will wither up totally, dry up, blow away, and the great mother will still be there. It is seen that you live in a blessed time, in that followers of the great mother do not have to worry from the Inquisition. That is good. And that in your time there have been discovered many paths of following the great mother. And her followers have used various paths. Therefore, we have agreed that since you have contacted me, that I will help you all I can. Perhaps we might know something of the great mother that has been lost in your time, that might help you. There are things that are lost, and they are regained again across the ages. That is the natural cycle of things.

D: *Yes, this is true, because over time books are destroyed, parchments are destroyed, and people die and a lot of knowledge is lost. That's what I am always trying to do, get back lost knowledge that might help people. So that's why you are correct, I have no desire to hurt you at all. I'm just seeking and looking for knowledge. In our time we are not quite as persecuted as you are in those days. There are still some people who have incorrect ideas, but they are the ones that are totally into the church, and they don't understand. But there are no torturing or deaths now as there were in your time. There's the difference. That part is good anyway, isn't it?* (Yes) *We have persecution of a different type.*

B: Persecution that you have in your time is spiritual persecution rather than physical.

D: *Yes. Did they have any idea how far away from you in the future I was speaking from?*

B: Many ages. It's hard to say. For when finding information like that, things like numbers and such, the things of man are not important. It is the feelings and the impressions that you get that are important.

D: *Then they could tell by the objects they saw that it was a different time.*

B: And from the distance you were coming from. They said it seemed like they were gazing down a very long tunnel. And it's the length of the tunnel that gives them an idea of how far away in time you are. The Inquisition would kill me for saying such things, for they say that time is now. And what happened in the past is not important unless it was recorded in the Bible. And not to worry about the future. That there's no such thing as the future, except that which has been recorded in the Bible. But then they won't tell you about it because they say that laypeople would not understand, so they don't need to know.

D: *That's interesting. They base everything on what is in the Bible. Is that true?*

B: Supposedly they do. I think they adjust it to suit their own notions.

D: *Yes. I have been told that people in your time didn't read the Bible themselves. That the priest told them what was in there.*

B: We're not allowed to read the Bible, because the Bible is considered too sacred to be touched by ordinary hands, by profaned hands.

D: *Well, in our time we are allowed to read it and to study it and to try to understand it. But still people find many different meanings in it, even today.*

B: Yes. That's because they're not in harmony with the great mother. And if they were walking the path of the great mother, they could throw away the dross and keep that which is good.

D: *Because there are many interpretations and many meanings today. That anyone can get what they want out of it. This is one of the strange things about the Bible.* (Yes) *It is basically a good book, but people twist it to their own interpretations.*

B: It's a good book. But it's not the only good book around. Nor is it the king of books.

D: *Do you have anyone in your group of followers—I guess that would be a good word—that can read at all?*

B: Let me think. (Pause) I suspect there might be one. But *if* she can read, she keeps it a secret, because she's not supposed to be able to.

D: *Because I was wondering if you had anything written down. Any parchments or things that you would read whenever you were having your ceremonies.*

B: There are some parchments that have some ceremonies on them. For some of the ceremonies we don't use very often.

D: *The majority of it you just know?* (Yes) *Well, I would like to work with you over a length of time if you would allow me to.*

B: You have passed the test.

D: *I would like it, if they would let me, if you could tell me bits of magic or spells that could be used in our time, by the ordinary person.*

B: I will tell you if you be sure to let a follower of the mother know them. So as to make sure that other followers of the mother will have them.

D: *That's what I mean. To pass them on to the right kinds of people. Things that they could use to help themselves and help other people.* (Yes) *We don't want anything that will hurt anyone.*

B: Occasionally you have to have rituals of protection against those that would harm you.

D: *Yes, I'm interested in knowing those, because I want to be protected as I do my work. (Pause) Would you have anything like that you could share with me? For protection?*

B: Let me think. There are so many that I do just as a matter of part of my everyday life, that it's hard for me to separate them. (Pause) One thing that is good, at nighttime—I'll start out giving you the simple ones, so that you may make sure you understand.

D: *All right. I appreciate that.*

B: At nighttime when you're fixing to sleep, the room that you sleep in should have only one entrance and exit, only one door. And across this door on the floor—you get some salt and you think on this salt. And you think hard, and you imagine that the salt produces light of its own, much like a candle would produce light. That it would produce light of its own. And that this light can spread all about and repel all the evil forces. And you get this salt and you sprinkle it on the floor across your doorway. And it makes a protective wall so that you cannot be harmed in your sleep.

D: *That would be very good. Is there another? You said you would start at the simple ones.*

B: Whenever you're having contact with people, and you're not sure whether they mean you harm or good, have some salt on hand so that you can sprinkle some salt on them. On their back or shoulders or what-have-you, so they won't notice. And you think of a white wall between you and them to protect you. And this will confound their thoughts and their tongues, so that they won't be able to do the harm that they were planning.

D: *So far these are easy things to do. It would not require very many things to accomplish them. That's very good.*

B: The most important rituals are those which you do with your mind. And it's hard to describe them. That is why I am starting with simple ones. To get you ready to hear about the more difficult ones later on.

D: *I might be able to understand them, because I have studied the use of the mind in my time period. I hope I will be able to understand. Did you have another? Or do you want to wait?*

B: I was trying to see how I could tell you about it. In the spring and summer when the weather is warm and pleasant, and the moon is waxing, go and find a place where there are flowers that are blooming and smelling nice. It would be particularly good if they are night-blooming flowers, for you will go there at nighttime. And you pick a flower to represent you, and you pick a flower to represent the one you love. And you twine them together. You're in a clearing where you can still smell the flowers and the bushes, and where the moonlight shines upon these flowers. And you walk a circle around them thirteen times.

D: *Around the two flowers, or the other flowers?*

B: The two flowers, for you have placed them on the ground with the moon shining on them. And every time you walk around these flowers, you ask the great mother—in this particular situation, you're asking her as she is when she is embodied in the moon. You ask the great mother to intertwine the one you love, his heart and your heart, to intertwine them the way these flowers are intertwined. And to intertwine your lives, and so on. And every time you walk around the flowers you ask for a different intertwining. And you have to really stop and think of thirteen different intertwinings, so that you don't repeat the same ones. But so that you will be very fairly linked together and intertwined. And then when you are done walking around these flowers thirteen times, you will stop and face the moon, and stretch your hands up toward it. And you say, "I have asked the great mother for this, and I know it will be. As it has been asked, so make it be." And then you take the two flowers and you take them back to where you found them amongst the bushes of these flowers. And you bury them in the ground amongst these bushes where it's sweet smelling all around. And you walk away without looking back.

D: *That sounds like a love spell.*

B: It is.

D: *Have you done this on yourself and Roff?* (Yes) *That's very effective. Would there be any other ones you would want to share with me at this time? I don't want anything that will hurt anyone. But you said you're not allowed to use those type, are you?*

B: No, it is not needed. For if you're not in harmony with the Earth mother, if you go out and be harming people and everything, after a while the goddess will take things in her own hands and strike back. Simply because the person harming people has been going against the goddess. And after a while things have to be put back to the way they were.

D: *Then the goddess doesn't like violence either.* (No) *That's good, because I can believe that way. I don't like harming anyone or saying even bad words against anyone.*

B: That is true. That is why the church will end up destroying itself, for all the things it has done has caused nothing but violence. The Crusades, for example.

D: *Do you know something of the Crusades?*

B: I don't really know of them. I've heard stories about them.

D: *They were not in your time then, were they?* (No) *Have you ever heard of a group of women that were called the Druidesses? Do you know them by a different name? Druid or Druidess?*

B: If I understand you correctly, I'm not sure that I do, I think that's one of the names that they call us. Those who are not part of us who walk the path. And they are not sure what we do, and there's many different names that they call us.

D: *What do you mean by those that walk the path?*

B: Those of us that follow the great goddess.

D: *Well, what I have heard of the Druids and Druidesses, were they lived many years before your time. But it is possible they have some of the same beliefs.*

B: Those of us who have walked the path of the goddess have been around since the beginning of time. We have always been around. For many ages now we have had to be very secretive with what we do or be killed.

D: *Because I spoke to one who was practicing that. You know, like I speak to you?* (Yes) *And she was many hundreds of years before you. And she said they worshipped the Lady.* (Yes) *Do you think it might be the same type of thing?*

B: Yes, I think so. For we have always been around, and we do not go around making a big noise about our beliefs, the way the Christians do. We pass it on from parent to child.

D: *Some of these women though had never married, and they just followed these beliefs.*

B: Some have done that. Everyone has their own choice about

that. And we don't do anything to show our religion to anybody. Occasionally someone becomes interested on their own. They start walking the path as best they can without any help from anybody. And when we see someone doing this, we observe them for a long time. And if they continue to do this, then we approach them and start helping them. But this does not hardly ever happen.

D: *They usually don't try to do it on their own then.—I'm glad for anything you can tell me, because, like I said, the others have told me things. But sometimes they were so strongly bound by secrecy that there were things they couldn't reveal.*

B: It's difficult for one to find the path and walk it by themselves, when one has the Christian church in one's way warping your mind. Yes, being bound by secrecy is very necessary. Not all groups have the tests that we have for familiar spirits. For everybody has different gifts from the goddess. And we are very lucky in the gifts that we have in our group.

D: *But it's only natural. They have this fear because the church is very powerful. And they were always afraid that somehow there would be retaliation against them.* (Yes) *That's why I'm glad that you are able to tell me things. I've tried so many different time periods to find the answers.—Would you have any other spells, so to speak, that you might share with me at this time?*

B: Not at this time. Most of the spells, rituals that we have are for love, such as I have told you, and for protection. These are the basic everyday spells. There are also more difficult things, like knowing your enemy's thoughts and such as that. And also confounding somebody's thoughts if he means you harm. But these are very difficult to do. And it's almost impossible to describe them to somebody who is not a longtime follower of the great mother. I suspect that one reason why the Lady Joslyn gets mad at me, is because I always confound her thoughts. So that whenever she is around Roff she starts stammering and making a fool of herself. One time she made me particularly angry because she beat me for no reason. And I confounded her thoughts when she was going to a banquet with the lord of the manor. And she kept saying the oddest things, that made no sense for what was going on. She was very upset. And the more upset she got the worst it became.

D: *(Laugh) Did she have any idea you were doing it?*

B: No. She might have a feeling since she has not ever been able to get me upset. She can't prove anything.

D: *That's where you must be careful.* (Yes) *Didn't you say one time that you suspected that the lord was doing things up in that tower room?* (Yes) *Have you heard any more about that?*

B: From what we can tell, that which he does is not for the goddess at all, but a corruption of the vestal (?) (mystic?) aspects of his church.

D: *I thought the Christian religion didn't do things like that.*

B: The priest would have you say that. The priest would have you believe that. But the priests do many things in the course of a mass that, if they weren't so corrupted, would almost make the mass into a ritual.

D: *Oh? Can you share that with me?*

B: I'm sure you've seen how they have statues and burn candles in front of them. And many people spend time gazing upon the statues with the candles burning in front of them. That is one way of doing a ritual. And they have various parts of the mass that are supposed to be for symbology, that actually are things that they—I suspect what happened is that ages back when the church first encountered followers of the mother, some of the followers of the mother infiltrated the church and became priests. And started introducing some of our ways into the mass, so as to corrupt the mass. So that the power that they want to do with it would be ineffective. Because if the mass were not corrupted, they would be able to wield much power with it, spiritual power, invisible power that would do the world much harm. And so they corrupted the mass, so that it's valueless so far as power is concerned.

D: *What is some of the symbology that you think is part of the mass?*

B: Well, the mass is always emphasizing the numbers three, seven and twelve. And these numbers have meanings that are not connected with their Bible. They have meanings connected with the goddess instead.

D: *Oh? I don't know anything much about the numbers. How are they connected with the goddess?*

B: The number twelve is connected with the goddess through the cycles of the seasons. There are twelve months of the year. There used to be thirteen months in the year. But then a great change came over the Earth, and there was much crying from the goddess, because it was a horrible change. And when the change was wrought there was only twelve months in the year.

D: *Do you know what the change was?*

B: I don't know. It happened so many ages back before the Christian church ever existed.

D: *But the memory is carried?*

B: Yes, it's one of the legends we have.

D: *What about the number seven?*

B: The number seven is a spiritual number. But the numbers have different levels. The number of three represents multiplication. It represents growth and children. It takes two people to have a child, and then they are three.

D: *You mean it would represent creativity, the creation process?*

B: Yes. It's an active number. An active element. Something with three sides is active, it can move. Where something with four sides is stable and solid and will sit still. Thus, four is kind of a resting number. Five is a very physical number. It's the number of human, because of the five limbs of the body. The arms, the legs, the head. Six again is another active number but on a more spiritual plane. Six is going beyond human and reaching the upper planes. Six is spiritual creativity and spiritual multiplication. Seven caps it because seven is the perfection of six. It's hard to explain this and get across how I mean.

D: *I think I understand.*

B: Therefore, seven is an important number. All the numbers are important. They all have their meanings and their uses. But the church in the way that it has been corrupt in everything has corrupted this, too.

D: *What about one and two? You didn't cover those.*

B: One is the source. The origin of energy. There is a number before one. It's a nonexistent number. It represents nothing. This number is good to meditate on, for it represents the void, the universe. It represents the limits of consciousness and beyond. One is the source of energy from which all things were created. Two is a good number for love spells because it represents the great mother and her consort.

D: *You said that one represented the creator. Do you consider this creator the Earth mother?*

B: Yes, she is the source of the energy from which all things were created.

D: *Then that would represent the creator image in your mind.*

B: Yes. The central source of energy through which she is the primary channel. The energy behind the great mother.

D: *Then there is another behind her then. Is that what you mean?*

B: No, it's part of her, but the great mother is the part that we can see, and we can understand. But there's more than what we can understand. And the number one represents the energy behind that which we cannot understand. But the great mother is more than what we can understand. And the energy that drives this and the energy that is part of the universe is represented by one. That is just the energy. But the entire concept of the great mother, which is beyond what anyone can understand because she encompasses everything imaginable and beyond, is represented by the number that isn't.

D: *The number before the one.* (Yes) *All right. Let's see, we've gotten up to seven. What about eight? Does that have a meaning?*

B: Eight is a spiritual resting. After attaining the perfection of seven, eight is a spiritual resting and meditation. Nine is a spiritual link to three, for it is three threes. It is a very potent number for creativity and such. And ten represents the crowning achievement. Any numbers beyond ten are simply permutations of the numbers already covered.

D: *That would make sense because they would just become*

multiplication as they become higher. (Yes) *That's very interesting. But you think the numbers are part of the symbology that the church has taken?* (Yes) *Is there anything else symbolic in the church or the mass that you recognize?*

B: One thing they do that we do also, we often build fires and put herbs in the fires, to make the smoke turn certain colors sometimes and to produce certain smells to help evoke the goddess. And they use their scentsors** to help provoke the mood they want for mass. Because they have everyone—I guess you'd call it trained—to get into a certain state of mind whenever they smell the incense that they use.

** A thurible (or censer) is the incense pot used during mass. **

D: *Do they use the same type of herbs that you use?*
B: No. We use all kinds and they only use one particular combination all the time.
D: *Do you know what that combination is?*
B: Not exactly. It's a very harsh masculine combination.
D: *I thought maybe you could tell by the smell what it was?*
B: With some yes, and with some no. We suspect that they might sneak in a couple of drugs to help keep everybody in line. To make them more susceptible to what the priest has to say.
D: *And this is in the smell, too?*
B: Yes. There are certain plants that have powerful juices. And when the juices are burned it gets into the smoke and affects anybody who breathes the smoke.
D: *Wouldn't this also affect the priest?*
B: It could, except that the way they do the incense, I don't think the priests are exposed to it much. And if they are, they possibly have another plant whose juices affect that in a way that's favorable to the priest. Or perhaps makes it to where he's not affected as much.
D: *Hmmm. I wonder what type of plant they would use?*
B: There are several that they could use. I just don't know which ones they do use. But I suspect that they do use two or three of them.

D: *Do they have a name that you call them?*

B: No. We of the craft know what they look like. And whenever we need them for something we go to the woods and get them.

D: *Is this why you wouldn't have a name for the other types of herbs they might use, too?* (Yes) *You just know what the leaves and roots look like?* (Yes) *That's interesting. Can you think of anything else the church would use in the mass? Because I want to be aware of these things.*

B: Yes, it is good to be aware, to protect oneself from the incense of the priests.

D: *Any other symbology they would use?*

B: The most heinous of all. Even though they will not say it, they know that the great mother is the power of the universe. But hers is not a masculine direct power, it's more of an indirect power, like the effect of water on stone.

D: *A gradual.*

B: Yes. A flowing power. And they know that people will find this and follow it in spite of their teachings. So what they have done, they have taken the symbol to represent this power that people might find and explain it in terms of their church. And exploit it and profane it to make it seem like it has no power at all, or perhaps inferior power to their follower. And this is what they call the Virgin Mary.

D: *Hmmm. Yes, in our time she is almost worshipped. She is supposed to be equal to her Son. It is like they worship all three.*

B: Yes. That is the same here. They worship her but they make her subject to the Father. That she doesn't have any power of her own, but she can use feminine wiles to trick the Father, so to speak. Or to talk Him into considering being merciful.

D: *Oh, this is why they ask her for favors?*

B: Yes, and they make her very subservient to the Father. Making it seem that the goddess herself has no power.

D: *Do you think the story of the Virgin Mary was true or was it just introduced for this reason?*

B: I think it was partially introduced for this reason. I think there was a story behind it that got twisted to their own ends, so that they could consolidate their power. For I think what happened was that she who bore Jesus, Joseph was the father of. And that the first time that they made love she did not know what was going on. And so she did not realize that she had lost her virginity. She had been told to keep her virginity, and she didn't know what they were talking about. And so she didn't know she had lost it until after several times of making love with Joseph. Or sometime later she came to the realization that she was going to have a baby. And she knew that only women who were not virgins had babies. But she thought she still had her virginity. And it was due to her being young and not knowing things. And so the church took this and twisted it around so that she actually was a virgin. And it was just a spiritual influence that caused her to become pregnant.

D: *They couldn't have it be otherwise, I guess. What about the Son, Jesus? Do you have any thoughts on that with your beliefs?*

B: He was a servant of the goddess, and He was trying to turn people to the goddess. Trying to soften up the Jewish religion, so that people could be more acceptant toward the goddess. And He would have succeeded had it not been for the Inquisition. You see, it has been said that after He was killed His followers were in two different groups. One group was following the goddess in the way that she would be very pleased. And the other group was power hungry. And the group that was power hungry made up rules and changed things and consolidated their power and tried to stamp out the other group. I suspect they pretty much succeeded. Had they not stamped out the other group, the church would not exist. There would be followers of Christ, but they would not be grouped into an all-powerful church. They would be in groups worshipping the goddess the way we worship her.

D: *That makes sense. These are things I've never thought of but they do make sense. I really appreciate you telling me these things. I'm going to have to leave, but would I be allowed to come and continue our conversation?*

B: You have passed the test.

D: *And I'm trying to learn this information and pass it on to your own followers at this time.*

B: *I* have no followers.

D: *I mean the followers of your religion, your beliefs.*

B: The followers of the goddess.

D: *Yes, that's right. I said it wrong, didn't I? But you know what I mean. I will try to pass it on to those who are interested.*

B: Yes. Tell them their sister, Astelle, sends it with love.

D: *And if I come again, we can continue the conversation about the different spells and things like that.*

B: Rituals.

D: *Rituals? Is that what you call them?* (Yes) *I would also like to hear some of the legends. That would be interesting.*

B: You have heard some today.

D: *Yes. I would also like to hear some more. All right. I really appreciate it and I thank you. And I wish to come again at some other time. And we will continue our conversation. Thank you very much. I wish you well, have a good day.*

B: You, too.

(Subject brought forward.)

Chapter 6

Pentagrams and More
(Recorded May 13, 1986)

Used keyword and counted her back to the time when Astelle lived.

D: *We have gone back through time to when Astelle lived. What are you doing?*

B: I'm out in the field. I'm gathering some truffles.**

** A truffle is the fruiting body of a subterranean ascomycete fungus, predominantly one of the many species of the genus Tuber. Some of the truffle species are highly prized as food. French gastronome Jean Anthelme Brillat-Savarin called truffles "the diamond of the kitchen." Edible truffles are used in Italian, French and numerous other national haute cuisines. Truffles are cultivated and harvested from natural environments. **

D: *What is that?*

B: It's ... I am not sure ... it's a type of ... well, it's not really a plant ... it's like a ... (had difficulty describing) ah you've heard of mushrooms? *(Yes)* They're a plant but they're not a plant? Truffles are a plant but not a plant. And they grow underground a little bit, and you have to dig them up.

D: *Oh, it's something to eat then. (Yes) How do you find them if they are underneath the ground?*

B: Part of them is above the ground, but the majority of them is underneath the ground. Some people use hogs to root them up, because hogs can find them. And hogs like to eat them. But I don't have a hog with me. I'm just finding them myself, using, there's a way of sensing things that are not seen. The church teaches against this, but those of us with the old religion know better. And so, I'm using that ability to sense things that are not seen to find them. Mainly it's an excuse to get out of the kitchen for a while and be outside because it's a pretty day.

D: *Will these be cooked?*

B: Yes, they'll be fixed with ... there's a dish that the cook is making. Or that the cook *can* make. I don't think she's making it right now. And they can be fixed different ways.

D: *What else would be in the dish besides the truffles?*

B: Oh, it depends on how you fix it. One way of fixing it is as being a part of stuffing for either stuffing a roast or stuffing a goose or something like that. And another way is fixing it as a part of a sort of ... not exactly soup, but truffles and some other vegetables with a sauce, to be served with meat or something.

D: *I've never seen a truffle. That's why I was wondering what they looked like. Is it a certain color?*

B: Well, there are different colors of them, and some are considered more desirable than others. And they're usually kind of in shape. And the surface of them has different textures. It seems that the texture depends on what color it is.

D: *What colors can they be?*

B: Well, most of them are usually kind of a reddish-orange. And some of them are kind of a tannish-white color. And some of them are black. But that's just the surface of them. On the inside they're all white. Except for the reddish-orange one, it tends to be pink on the inside.

D: *Oh. I don't think I've seen one then. The white-gray one you were talking about reminds me of mushrooms.*

B: Yes. And they're solid all the way through the way mushrooms are. It's not a skin and fruit, it's just ... there.

D: *I probably wouldn't even know one if I saw one. (Laugh) I've never seen anything that color.*

B: They're difficult to find. They're not very common. The mushrooms and the spongy mushrooms are a lot more common.

D: *I think it's good if you can find these if they're underneath the ground.*

B: Well, part of them kind of stick up above the ground a tad bit. (Softly) Tad? Where did that word come from?

D: *(She had spoken so softly that I had not heard her remark.) Where what?*

B: I used a word and I realized it was an unfamiliar word.

D: *What was the word?*

B: Tad. I said, "a tad bit." I meant to say "a little bit."

D: *That's what it means. A little bit. Well, I know I've never ate them. Do they have a distinct taste?*

B: Umm, they have a mild flavor, but pervasive. You know that mushrooms have a mild flavor, but when you put mushrooms in something you can tell the mushrooms are there. Well, it's the same way with truffles. They have a mild flavor, but you can tell that they are in a dish when you put them in.

D: *You're pretty good at using your senses in this way then.*

B: Oh, it does good to use them, because the more you use them the better and more reliable they become.

D: *That's true, the more you use them. Well, do you remember talking to me before?*

B: Yes. You passed the test.

D: *That's right. You told me about the different things that the church did. I was wondering how you know these things. Have you ever been in a church?*

B: Everyone knows about the church whether they want to or not.

D: *Have you ever been to the mass?*

B: No. But those of us who follow the old religion, we have to know about what the church does, for protection. And many times, these things that we know about the church service ... see, some of us do go to mass to, I guess you could say, throw the priest off scent. And they can now tell us what goes on in the mass. And we say, "Well, ah-ha! That makes sense."

Because of such-and-such reasons.

D: *The similarities.*

B: Uh-huh. And they do things out of ignorance, just repeating it because the person before them did it. And so, we know that they don't know the true meaning of many of the things that they do.

D: *They don't really realize what they're doing.* (Yes) *Well, the ones that do go to mass, where would they go? Is there a church nearby or what?*

B: Yes. There's a priory* here on the grounds, plus the private chapel for the duke.

*From Wikipedia: Priory: a monastery of men or women under religious vows that is headed by a prior or prioress. *

D: *In the house?* (Yes) *But you have never been to either one of these.* (No) *Well, you once mentioned the Inquisition. Are these priests or what?*

B: Yes. There's a certain branch of the Catholic priesthood that all they do is go around torturing people. And it's usually ... you see, all types of men are attracted to the priesthood. And so that's why there are so many branches of the priesthood, to accommodate these different types of men. And there's a type of sick men who get their pleasure from hurting things. From hurting either animals or people. And the only time they feel like a complete person, like they are worth something, is when they are hurting something. And so these are the type that are drawn to the Inquisition.

D: *It doesn't sound very religious to want to hurt people.*

B: They convince themselves that they're doing it for the glory of God, and they pray themselves into hysteria.

D: *I've always thought religion was supposed to be doing good.*

B: It is.

D: *But to hurt other people doesn't seem right. Let me see if I understand exactly what the Inquisition is. Were they trying to find people who were not obeying the church or obeying the ways of the church?*

B: Yes. They feel that it is their duty to help keep the bride of Christ pure for Him, to use their terms.

D: *I wonder what they mean?*

B: It can mean whatever they want it to mean. Whatever is convenient at the time.

D: *What do they consider the bride of Christ?*

B: They're referring to the church when they say the bride of Christ. And they say they want to keep her pure for her bridegroom. And so they use that excuse for their own reasons. Frankly if such a notion were true and the bridegroom were to come to Earth for a church to take on as a wife, which makes no sense, the Catholic church would not be it. Whoever heard of such a notion.

D: *Yeah, I can't see how they're keeping it* pure *if they're hurting and killing.*

B: Exactly.

D: *That is like staining it.* (Uh-huh) *Well, what do they do? Just go throughout the land searching for people? Or how do they do this?*

B: They're all around raising trouble. There are agents of the Inquisition everywhere. And if there's not an agent of the Inquisition right there on hand, there's usually a paid informant or two or three around to inform agents of the Inquisition as to what's going on. I think they're paid according to how many people they turn in. The more people they turn in, the more they get paid. So, it depends on how greedy they are as to how many people get turned in for various made-up reasons.

D: *The informers get paid?*

B: Yes. So much a head, just like cattle.

D: *What do they look for? How do they know?*

B: They don't have to look for anything. They can make up what they need to find. They look for anybody who has the courage to look them directly in the eye. They look for anybody who asks questions about things. People who wonder about things. Like if someone says, "Why is it that the clouds that look so solid float above the Earth, when everything else that is solid sits on the Earth?"

D: *Yes, I wonder about things like that, too.*

B: Yes, anything like that. Or if someone has a deformity, they'll pick on them. Or if they have a marking on their skin. Sometimes if they are very short of people to pick on, they'll grab somebody and make a mark on their skin, and then say it's a witch mark. And many times, if there is somebody that they think is a burden of the community, someone who's worthless, they'll pick on them. Which usually means some of the old widows, and some of the old men.

D: *That's kind of scary, because to me that's not exactly religious. That means I would not fit in, would I? Because I love to ask questions. (Laugh)*

B: You would be in danger. You'd have to have protection from us. And you'd have to have several lessons before you could survive.

D: *I'm very inquisitive. I have a lot of curiosity. They wouldn't like that at all, would they?*

B: No, they wouldn't. You're just supposed to look down at your toes whenever one of them is around you and take your hat off and grovel. And when you're not at mass soaking in all they have to say without questioning any of it, then you're supposed to be on your land plowing and not asking anything about what's beyond the boundaries of your field.

D: *You're not supposed to* want *to know or have the curiosity?*

B: That is true. You're supposed to know your place and stay in it. That way the world will be nice and orderly.

D: *Yes, but the human mind always wants to know more, I think.*

B: That is true. They believe to *want* to know more is heresy.

D: *I always thought of heresy as being if you said something that was not in the Bible or not in their beliefs.*

B: That is correct, that is the meaning of heresy. *But* for the people in the Inquisition, heresy is anything they want it to be. Sneezing at the wrong time is heresy.

D: *(Laugh) You can't control a sneeze.*

B: If you sneeze at an awkward time, then it's obvious that you're an agent of the Devil trying to disrupt things. *(I laughed.)* So, if they can't get you for heresy, they'll get you for consorting with the Devil.

D: *Oh, boy! You'd be afraid of everything you did.*

B: That's what they're trying to do. They're trying to keep the people beaten down.

D: *But you wouldn't know if anything you did would be safe, would you?*

B: That is correct.

D: *I can understand then your hesitancy to talk to me.* (Yes) *But to me that would be very frightening. You would be afraid of every movement or every word you said.*

B: I think they do it to discourage people from traveling very much either, to keep people on their land because nobody trusts strangers.

D: *I've been told this before when I do these things that I'm doing now. They'll say, "You're a stranger and you must be careful."*

B: Yes. But you were lucky. You were wanting to find out about what we do, and you contacted someone of the old religion, and we have ways of finding out whether or not you can be trusted. And our ways are in harmony with the universe, so that nobody is harmed. And no pain is caused.

D: *Yes. And you could see that I am also in harmony this way.*

B: Hmm, pretty much so. You're out of harmony in some ways, but I think it's due to your surroundings. Because you are endeavoring to be in harmony, but some of the things that you must live with are things that cause you to be out of harmony. But it's not because you are basically out of harmony, because you're trying to be in harmony. It's just simply because of your circumstances.

D: *And the times that I live in. The times are different.* (Yes) *Well, that means anyone who is deformed in any way or has a mark ... some of these marks are caused from birth.* (Yes) *They view all of this as marks of witchcraft? Is that what you said?*

B: Yes. If someone has a mark from birth, that means that their mother made love with the Devil. Made love with Satan, and so the children are marked with the mark of Cain or some other such nonsensical label. And so the children should be killed because they're the spawn of Satan. And their mother should be killed for being in intimate contact with Satan.

D: *Then do the mothers try to hide any marks that are on their children?*

B: Yes, if they're lucky the mark is where it is covered up by clothing. And if they're unlucky, they keep the children where just neighbors and friends and family see them. And not let strangers see them until they get up older.

D: *Then they consider a deformity the same thing?*

B: Yes. A deformity is caused by the parents having indulged in some sort of horrible sin. And so, as punishment God, their God, supposedly deforms the child to punish the parents. And the child, since the child is merely being used as a form of punishment, is not fully human anyway. It's just being used as an object lesson. So, the child doesn't matter either.

D: *Then they would kill the child or the adult that had a deformity?*

B: Right. Or the child and their parents.

D: *Their parents too?*

B: It depends on which one it is most convenient for the Inquisition to kill. Like for example, if one member of the Inquisition desired the wife, they would kill the husband. Or if a member of the Inquisition desired the husband, they would kill the wife.

D: *Hmmm. You mean the informers? Or the actual priests?*

B: The actual priests.

D: *I thought that they were not supposed to have sex.*

B: (A loud laugh.) Ha-ha! It is true that they are supposed to be celibate according to their teachings. I personally say that it is unnatural to be celibate. It's not the way things are meant to be. It's out of harmony. Out of rhythm with the universe. Out of rhythm with the mother goddess to be celibate. And these priests maintain a front of being celibate, a mask. But it's false and hollow, because behind the mask they are not celibate at all. I don't know of any priest that has ever been celibate. They all are very debauched. And they make love as often as they wish with whoever they wish. And it doesn't matter of what sex it is.

D: *Then no one can say anything either, can they?*

B: No, because it happens behind closed doors. Priests have fantastic feasts because they get the best of the crops. And at these feasts it is said that all sorts of debaucheries take place. Usually the priests are taking advantage of the young boys who have just entered the priesthood.

D: *Do these things happen at the house where you live? Or do you know?*

B: No. Not to that degree. The priest that is here … I think he takes care of himself with his hand. Occasionally he might use a young page, you know, whenever he's in confessional. And someone wants to do penance for a sin, he sometimes thinks of an unusual penance for them.

D: *I see. Then you think most of this would go on in a place like the priory?*

B: No, the priory is here on the grounds. Like in the village. But the village is kind of small. But the larger places where there's more people and more priests on hand. You know, like in the cities.

D: *But these things are what your friends tell you?* (Yes) *Because you said you have no personal knowledge.*

B: Right. These are things they have seen. Plus, we have ways of observing things that go on, similar to how we observed you.

D: *Then you can see faraway events that way, of what is actually happening.* (Yes) *You would have more truth, wouldn't you?* (Yes) *More knowledge of the truth.—Is there a large city near where you live?*

B: I don't know. I think there may be one within a couple of days ride. But I don't know. I've never left this place.

D: *I was just wondering if you'd ever heard a name of a large city near there.* (No) *Well, then these priests, do they ever marry?*

B: Some of them do. It's supposed to be secret though and nobody knows about it. Most of them just have mistresses or young boys. Or both.

D: *To me this is not exactly what Jesus, the Christ, intended at all. I don't think he was teaching this.*

B: From my understanding, I agree.

D: *Especially they say they are trying to do what he wanted, and I don't think this is what he intended. The Inquisition or any of these things.*

B: That is true. That is why it is said that the church is declining. And it will follow the natural cycle of such things, and it will fade away and wither to death. And the mother goddess will still be there. That is the cycle of all patriarchal-based religions. They start out with good intentions, but with some selfish intentions thrown in. And as a result, they're not in harmony with their Earth mother, and they get out of balance. And after a while eventually they collapse upon themselves and wither to death. This has been the fate of religions that are not in harmony with their mother goddess.

D: *I am curious. You said a while ago that I might need to learn some protection if I was to be there?* (Yes) *Could you tell me how I could protect myself?*

B: Where you are you seem to have sufficient protection, although more protection never hurts. But the protection of the white light that you use is very effective. We have seen that you use this. Also what you can do to make many things come to pass is the casting of pentagrams for various reasons.

D: *Can you tell me about that? I'm unaware of those things.*

B: The tetragrammaton* or the pentagram is a design of a five-pointed star enclosed within a circle. You do that whenever you want to be protected against, say thieves and robbers and such. Some of the farmers do this, but the Inquisition doesn't know about it. For example, whenever they're bringing their crop here to turn it in to the storehouses, if they have to stop along the way overnight on the road, they cast a pentagram on their wagon. So as to protect their crop so that the thieves won't run off with it during the night. Some farmers not knowing the truth behind this will with some clay dust or something draw one on their wagon itself to protect the wagon. And this will do it. But it's best to do it with the mind. And what you do is—let's see if I can describe this— you know how sometimes when the sun is shining in between clouds, you'll see spears of light coming down to the ground?

*This word was difficult to spell phonetically. Tetragrammatons. According to the dictionary, this is the Hebrew name of God transliterated in four letters as YHWH or JHVH. *

D: *Oh, yes, it's very beautiful.*

B: Yes, it is. Well, take a spear of light like that and pretend that it's a quill to write with. And the spear of light can be whatever color you need it to be for whatever purpose you need the pentagram for. And in this case for protection, like the farmer needs for his wagon, it would be white. And you would draw the five-pointed star first. And you do it in one line without lifting your quill. And then when you get done drawing it and you're at the tip of the last point, from there without lifting your quill, or your spear of light in this case, go ahead and draw a circle around the star.

D: *Okay. Right from the pentagram to the circle without lifting? All one continuous line.*

B: Yes. And when you're drawing this, what you do in your mind, you picture whatever it is that you want to have protected. And you have this superimposed on it.

D: *I see. But some of the others don't realize you can do it with your mind, and they actually draw the pentagram.* (Yes) *It sounds like it would be very effective.*

B: You can use the pentagram in many different ways for many different things. For example, if somebody is ill and you want them to regain their health, you draw a pentagram of ... (pause) well, it depends upon what kind of illness it is. But just for illness in general, you'd draw a pentagram of golden-yellow color with a hint of rose in it. And picture this as enclosing their body. Where it's large enough with the circle going around it, to where it's large enough to enclose their body. And you picture it on their body.

D: *The circle surrounding their body?*

B: Right. And if you're wanting to arouse passion in somebody, you picture you and this person standing together. And then you project a red pentagram upon yourselves. A bright, intense crimson red.

D: *Surrounding the two people.* (Yes) *Hmmm, that sounds like that would be intense.*

B: You can use them for many different things.

D: *I was wondering if there were different meanings for the different colors.* (Yes) *Used for different purposes.*

B: Red is for passion. Yellow is for health. Blue is for mental clarity. Violet is for reaching the higher realms.

D: *Green?*

B: Green is for getting in touch with living things. Plants and animals. And the mother Earth in general. White can be used for any and all of these, plus just for general protection, since white is all the colors of the light together. At least that is what some of them say. The priests deny this. But some in the old religion say that since rainbows spring from the sun and the sun is white light, then all the colors must be in white light.

D: *That makes sense.*

B: But anyway, I digress. Let's see, white, red, blue, green, yellow, violet. Orange is for friendship. Blue can also be used for friendship, but orange would be for a loving type friendship, whereas blue would be for a friendship that stimulates you mentally.

D: *It would be different kinds of a friendship.* (Yes) *What about the rose by itself?*

B: The rose by itself is for true love and affection and caring.

D: *This is why you combined it with the yellow because it would be caring?* (Yes) *So you can use mixtures?* (Yes) *Let's see, what other colors are there? Do you ever use the dark colors like brown or black for anything?*

B: It's very dangerous to use those colors. Brown, if you cast a brown pentagram on any living thing it would cause it to become ill.

D: *Oh. Because it's dark?*

B: Because brown is a mixture of colors like mud. And since it's a mixture of colors they cancel each other out and have a negative influence. Now black pentagrams are very powerful, and we can use them for different things. Some people who have the weaker turn of character would use black pentagrams to cause bad luck for people. To cause negative things to happen to them, or to have them attract negative influences. You know that I mentioned that violet was for reaching the higher realms. *(Yes)* The next color beyond violet is black. And so once you go through violet you can use black to reach to the very core of the universe, and to find out secrets that sometimes the mind cannot handle.

D: *Do your people ever use black pentagrams to cause negative things?*

B: I don't know. Someone might privately occasionally when someone does them an ill turn. They might cast a black pentagram on them just long enough to teach them a lesson and then retract it, but that would be a private thing. Sometimes when the Lady Joslyn is being particularly obnoxious and negative, I'll cast a very small black pentagram in her path to make her trip over something.

D: *(Laugh) I just wondered how your religion felt about causing things like this.*

B: Well, if someone wants to occasionally tweak somebody's nose to teach them a lesson because they need a lesson taught, that is as it should be. But to be malicious and to cause bad luck for no reason, that is not allowed. And to cause bad luck in general, even if there are reasons, is not necessary. Because what they have coming to them will come to them anyway sooner or later, because of the way the universe is set up. But if someone is being consistently negative to you in your life and you want to kind of return a couple of the favors, you can as long as you don't cause them any harm. Sometimes I'll do it out of a little bit of spite when the Lady Joslyn's been particularly bad. And I'll do it in a sense of mischief, you know, of making her look graceful, shall we say, around Roff. *(I laughed.)* Sometimes whenever they're having a large banquet and she's wanting to show off and be the center of attention, I'll cast a small black pentagram onto her mouth, onto her lips, so that whenever she says things, they don't come out straight. She'll say something, meaning to say one thing, but she'll accidently say it in a way that's taken as a double-entendre, and people take her differently.

D: *(Laugh) You figure in these ways it's not really harming anyone though.* (No) *Because I've always heard that what you send out would come back to you.*

B: Right. Well, she's been sending out so much negativity that my occasionally doing something like this in self-defense would not rebound on me. Because it's just some of what will be rebounding on her.

D: *Then you can look at it that way.* (Yes) *You keep mentioning the universe, what do you know of the universe? Your world is really so limited. You said you cannot go from that house.*

B: It's true that my physical world is limited. But one of the advantages of my religion is that no matter how limited you are physically, there is no limit to you mentally. And you can go anywhere, anytime, with using just your mind. You can project your mind to anywhere. And so, what we tend to do is explore the universe in general, trying to figure out how things work, why they work, how they work. And try to figure out what the Earth mother had in mind when she created the universe. We don't ever talk about what we do, because it would be heresy of the highest order.

D: *That really would be inquiring and wanting to know. But do you do this as a group?*

B: Usually we do because it's more effective that way. As individuals we can do some of it as a personal meditation. But it's most effective to get together as a group and all join together and use our energy together, because it seems to magnify somehow.

D: *Where do you do this? In the grove of trees?* (Yes) *Do you have a certain kind of a ritual or ceremony?*

B: Well, before we start, we all go to the grove of trees, and all of us find that particular spot that we feel comfortable with.

The kind of a spot where we can tune in to the Earth mother. We all go to our favorite spot and get ourselves prepared for it, because it takes some preparation first. And we clear our minds, and relax the body, and don't think about things that have been going on during the day. But just start picturing, well, there's two things one can picture. One can either picture a white light, and you're diving into this white light like you would dive into a pool on a summer day.

D: *Okay. But the main thing, I don't want you to do it right now. I just want you to tell me the procedure. (I had noticed some changes in her physical reactions.)*

B: That's what I'm doing.

D: *Okay. Because it would be dangerous for you to do it out there anyway, while you're looking for your truffles. Just tell me the procedure.*

B: And another way of doing it would be to picture a night full of stars when the moon is not shining. And think that you are flying up to the stars in the depths of the blackness. Either way, you do it so as to push away the limitations of being one person.

D: *It sounds like it would be very enjoyable.*

B: It is. And then after you feel ready the group gets together. And we sit around in a circle on the ground and join hands. And usually when we do this there'll be something in the middle of the circle for us to concentrate on, for those of us who need something visual to look at.

D: *Anything in particular?*

B: Usually a design done on the ground with rocks or pebbles or something.

D: *Any particular design?*

B: It depends. Sometimes it's a pentagram, and sometimes it's a design that's not supposed to mean anything. Just to help you to push back the barriers.

D: *Then you look at this?*

B: Yes. And since we're holding hands our energy is all flowing together. And from there we can direct the energy for whatever purpose we're gathered for. If it's for the purpose of exploring the universe, then we all picture falling into either the white light or the depths of space. And we travel together with our minds and see many wondrous things.

D: *You don't have any drinks or any herbs that you use at this time to help with this?*

B: No. We do have some drinks on hand that we use for certain purposes. But for this it is good to have a clear mind.

D: *In our time people think your people sometimes used drugs in different ways.*

B: We do.

D: *That maybe the drugs would cause this feeling of being able to travel.*

B: No. This type of traveling you have to do with your mind. Now sometimes on certain days of the year for celebrations we'll get together with another group of the old religion that's not from this immediate area. And since we're not used to working with that other group, sometimes we'll take a drink that will help break down the barriers so that our energy can flow together, as if we were one group. Because with the group that you work with all your life, it's very easy to push the barriers away. But when you work with a new group it's difficult, and so the drink helps to break these barriers down. And see, it seems like we do it with the hidden part of the mind that most people are not in touch with. And pushing these barriers away like this also helps you to push away the internal barriers, so that you can get in touch with all sides of your mind and work them together into one person.

D: *What kind of a drink is that?*

B: I'm not sure. Only a few know how to make it. There are certain herbs and berries that go into it. The berries are considered to be poisonous. But they're not actually poisonous, they're just powerful. They have a drastic effect on the body. And if you were to take too many of them, yes, they could kill you. But not because it's poison, it is just because it's strong. But we use these berries plus some normal berries that taste good. And certain herbs and flowers that have certain effects. And they're mixed together in certain proportions to have whatever effect is needed. And then it's stored and allowed to ferment like wine, but it really doesn't become alcoholic. Somehow the way it ferments brings out the drugs and helps to combine them or concentrate them somehow. I don't know how it works. I'm not old enough yet to learn how to make that. But I watch them make it and I have gathered the herbs for it.

D: *It seems like you'd have to be very careful to get the right proportions.*

B: Yes, in order to get the desired effect because the different proportions cause different effects.

D: *What color are those berries that are considered poison?*

B: White.

D: *I was trying to think of what kind of plant it could be. But you mix them with other berries of different colors?* (Yes) *You would have to be careful. If you got it in the wrong proportions, I suppose it wouldn't be a very pleasant experience.*

B: No. It could be made into a mixture that would kill somebody, but we don't do that ... usually. But there are different proportions that cause unbalanced effects. Unbalanced meaning compared to what is supposed to happen.

D: *What kind of effects would it have on the body if it was mixed incorrectly?*

B: One effect that is particularly frightening, it would make the heart beat too hard and fast. Or you could break out in a sweat all over, and your skin would feel like it was on fire. Or one might feel a sort of paralysis coming over them. Or different things like that.

D: *No, it wouldn't be very pleasant if you got the wrong combination. It's better to leave that to the ones that know how to mix it.* (Uh-huh) *Well, are these the only times that you would use any kind of drugs when you got together?*

B: When one of our group is ill, sometimes we'll use a drug to help the pentagram casting to take effect. But usually it's just at these meetings.

D: *Do the ordinary people use any kind of drugs when someone is ill?*

B: Just meat and wine.

D: *Oh? When they're ill?*

B: No. Not unless someone comes who buys in herbs and such and uses some herbs to help them to feel better. There are certain tree barks that help to dull pain. From the willow. And there are certain herbs that when made into a drink are supposed to be a good tonic.

D: *I was just wondering how the church felt about using drugs and herbs for people that were sick.*

B: Oh, they're against it. But it doesn't prevent the common farmer from doing it anyway. What the church says people should do when they are ill, is to pay an arm and a leg to the church, and they'll send one of their educated doctors to take care of you. And that will also take care of a priest praying for your soul. So, depending on, I guess, your state of grace, how sick you are, how well you are, it depends on how much you have to pay the church.

D: *Oh, that's what you mean by paying an arm and a leg? You pay a lot of ... what? money or goods?*

B: Both. Either. Whatever you have.

D: *Then the only way you could be treated would be if you were wealthy. If you had these things, wouldn't it?* (Yes) *Then they wouldn't treat the common people, would they?*

B: Usually, no. Unless a particularly good servant to a rich person falls sick. The rich person would pay to have their servant treated.

D: *Then it would seem like the ordinary people would come to your people, the people of the old religion for help. Or do they do that?*

B: No. Sometimes some of the farmers will come and say, "I hear that you have a way with herbs. Could you help my daughter? She's sick." Or something like that. But that's all that is said, even though much more is understood than what is said.

D: *I have so many questions. I'm glad you're being patient with me.*

B: That is no problem.

D: *Whenever you explored the universe, what did you find out there? What's your version of it? What it's like?*

B: It's hard to say. The way the universe is it's hard to describe in things that you've seen on Earth that you can understand. On the one hand the universe is like a gigantic sphere. Yet on the other hand the universe is like a tunnel that goes on and on and on forever. And loops back on itself and tangles up on itself and such as that. That's kind of like the way time is, too.

D: *You've found this out?*

B: Well, it seems that time and universe are the same. We have found out many things. It's hard to explain what we have found out. And if we would try to put it in words, we wouldn't have to worry about the priests finding out, the regular people would kill us first.

D: *(Laugh) Why, because it was so strange?* (Yes) *When you're doing these things, do you go out there and explore for a while as a group and then eventually come back to the grove?*

B: First we'll go out and explore for a while as a group. And usually there'll be a purpose for us having met there anyway. And when we come back, we find out what's going on that could affect those of us in the old religion. And prepare against that event.

D: *You don't want to be surprised then.*

B: Right. And then we'll take care of other different things. Like if there's a woman in the group that wants to conceive, we'll make her body receptive to conceiving. And if there's another woman who's been having problems with her back, then we are able to make the pain go away. Just different other things like that.

D: *With this woman conceiving, you do this with your mind? With your thinking? Or do you use herbs?*

B: No, with our thinking.

D: *There have been tales told over long periods of time—it sounds funny to me—but there've been people that said that you people actually* flew. *You actually used your body to go do these different things and go different places.*

B: Well, sometimes some of the regular people would get an

inkling of what we were doing, or we'd mention something that had happened far away. And they couldn't picture anything but maybe one of us physically flying there and seeing it happen. It's hard to explain to them about projecting your mind and doing it with your mind instead. Because you can go anywhere you need by using the essence of your mind. Using your higher essence.

D: *Then this is where the stories have come from. Passed down.* (Yes) *I see. Well, we've heard the word "witch." Do they use that word in your time?*

B: Sometimes. There are several different words that they use. Sometimes they just say the phrase "an old lady" using it as a term of respect. They'll say, "Are you an old lady?" meaning someone who is knowledgeable with herbs and such, to be able to help one of their household with sickness or what-have-you. And they won't be meaning, "Are you old and gray?" but they're meaning, "Are you old as in wise?"

D: *In knowledge. What other terms would they use?*

B: Sometimes they say "people of the trees" because we always meet in a grove of trees.

D: *Does anyone use the word "witch"?*

B: The church does, but who pays any attention to the church?

D: *(Laugh) I was just wondering what they considered a witch.*

B: The church? *(Yes)* I'm a witch, you're a witch, everybody's a witch.

D: *(Laugh) Just anybody that's doing anything that the church doesn't like?*

B: That is correct.

D: *We've heard the words "witch" and "witchcraft." That's why I wondered what those words meant to you.*

B: Witchcraft is the word referring to the old religion.

D: *But is that a word that you use to describe yourself?*

B: What? Witchcraft? No, but then I don't really use any words to describe myself. Because I just think of myself as where I am. And since we don't really talk about it much, since we can't, a lot of words are not necessary.

D: *Then you don't think of your group as being witches?* (No)

Especially the way the church would use this.

B: The church would use "witch" for someone who is concentrating on the negative side of things. And worshipping the church's notion of the Devil. What the church doesn't realize is that Satan is a Christian invention. Because for any religion to take hold, for any figure of admiration to take hold, there has to be some sort of figure against them trying to kill this other figure, to make people feel sorry for the good one and follow the good one. So consequently, the Devil and Satan are an invention of the church.

D: *They have a war going on between the two powers, so to speak. Is that what you mean?*

B: Yes. They invent this to capture people's interest and to keep them involved with the religion.

D: *Then you don't really think there is a Devil?*

B: No, I don't think so because it's an invention of the church. Now I'm not saying there aren't any negative forces around. But what may appear to be negative isn't necessarily negative. Just balancing out what is apparently good, because everything has to be in balance. And it's all part of the mother goddess.

D: *I'm sorry to say that even in our day people still believe there is a Devil. Which I don't believe in, but other people still do. (Yes) The idea hasn't really gone away. Have you ever heard the word "coven"?*

B: (Pause) Yes. It's a group like what we are.

D: *Yes, that's what it means now, a group of people that get together to practice the things that you've talked about. But aren't you afraid that someone will discover you when you're all out there together?*

B: There's always that possibility, except that when we are projecting our minds, we can see many things. And we can see things that ordinary eyes can't see. We can see if anyone means us good or ill. And so, we can see danger well before it comes. So, we have time to come down from that plane and to scatter, and to disappear, so to speak. So that by the time whoever gets there, all they see is just a grove of trees and nothing else.

D: *That's what I was thinking. If you were meditating, they could surprise you.*

B: Yes. While you're using your mind for other things, you can also use it for protection.

D: *But you feel safest in that grove of trees.* (Yes) *You were talking about certain holidays when you meet with other groups like yourself. What holidays are those?*

B: There is the hallowed evening. And there is Beltane.*

D: *What is that? These are holidays that I don't know of.*

* Dictionary: Beltane: "The spring festival celebrated on May Day in the Celtic lands in pre-Christian times." This could also refer to what she said earlier about celebrating spring on May Day. *

** Beltane is a Celtic word which means "fires of Bel" (Bel was a Celtic deity). It is a fire festival that celebrates of the coming of summer and the fertility of the coming year. These rituals would often lead to matches and marriages, either immediately in the coming summer or autumn. Beltane is the Gaelic May Day festival. Most commonly it is held on May 1, or about halfway between the spring equinox and the summer solstice. **

B: We have four main holidays, and they fall usually as close as we can come to the solstices and the equinoxes.

D: *Can you tell me about these?*

B: Well, we get together. And due to the time of the year it is the Earth energies that are flowing a particular way that makes it good for doing things like that, so we take advantage of this.

D: *Do you have a name for that equinox in the spring?*

B: Yes. Sometimes it's difficult to keep the names straight because the names are not important. The Hallowed evening is in the fall.

D: *Around the fall equinox?*

B: Uh-huh. And winter is Lamas. And spring is Beltane. And summer is the high festival. The one in the summer is called the high festival because that's when the sun is at its strongest.

But the largest celebration is in the fall on the Hallowed evening. Plus, we like to meet and do certain things with certain phases of the moon.

D: *I was going to ask you about that. Why is that the largest one, the Hallowed evening? Is it more important than the others?*

B: Yes, because that's the ending of one year and the beginning of the next, in our cycle. It's like New Year's for the Christians.

D: *Do you do anything that's different at that time?*

B: Yes, we usually have more elaborate rituals then. And we're more likely to have the herbal drinks on hand. We tend to go all out for Hallowed evening, because sometimes the combination of meditation plus herbal drinks plus the energy of being with a group you're familiar with, can sometimes provoke some very profound experiences.

D: *What kind of experiences?*

B: Things like prophecy and such as that. Or sometimes just getting a very clear vision of what things are going to be like ages from now.

D: *And you think it has something to do with the time of the year and the moon?*

B: Yes, because all of this affects the way the energies are flowing through the Earth. And however, the energies are flowing through the Earth is how they are flowing through you.

D: *I see. I'm trying to understand all these different things. I have so many questions. Lamas, you said, is in the winter? (Yes) Is there anything different that's done at that time?*

B: Usually at that time we invoke the power of fire and use that power. Usually we'll have a fire built and we stare into the flames, and that seems to do something with the mind. And while the mind is changed like this, there are several things that the group can do.

D: *Like what, in particular?*

B: Nothing in particular. Just think whatever needs to be done.

D: *Like the traveling or if anybody in the group wants something, like you said before?*

B: Yes. Plus, we usually do something with the land. So that the energy will be flowing good in the land when the spring comes, so that the crops will grow well.

D: *What do you do with the land?*

B: We do it with our minds. Everything is done with our minds.

D: *It's like refreshing the land, or replenishing it, and getting it ready?* (Yes) *And you said Beltane is in the spring? What is special then?*

B: The equinox, and that is when everything is in balance. The balance is always tipping in one direction or the other, but at the equinox the balance is in balance. And so there are things that are done then.

D: *You mean part of your rituals have to do with the growing season?*

B: No. Because that's already been taken care of. The rituals have to do with things being in balance because of it being the equinox.

D: *I see.*

B: No, you don't see.

D: *(Laugh) I'm trying to. Usually I think of the equinox as the beginning of the growing season, when things begin to come back.*

B: Well, that's not true. Because the growing season has already started when the equinox comes. When the equinox comes, the proportion of day and night are in balance. And the celestial things are in balance. *(She sounded a little irritated or aggravated with me.)* You have to look to higher things. You're not looking high enough. I think you're not giving us enough credit, simply because we're from the ages past.

D: *Yes. I think people think you didn't really have this type of knowledge in those times.*

B: The church has been trying to suppress this knowledge, but we have continued to pass it down. Such knowledge used to be much more common, plus much *more* knowledge. But the church has been suppressing it all for several centuries now or trying to snuff it out like a candle.

D: *Do you think they have succeeded to a certain extent?*

B: Oh, yes. Just about all knowledge has been suppressed except for what little groups like us have been able to hang on to.

D: *Then there was much more in the past.*

B: Oh, yes. Even much more amazing than the things of your time.

D: *Do you know about that? Or is that from your legends?*

B: I don't know hardly anything about it.

D: *Do you think they were physical things or mental?*

B: Both.

D: *It's very good you have groups like yours that are trying to continue with these things. To try to preserve them.*

B: What makes it difficult though, is that since we know more than we're supposed to know, it's difficult to act as ignorant as everybody else.

D: *(Laugh) Yes, I think that would be the hardest part of all. I think it would be hard for me anyway, to not look them in the eye and say, "I don't believe in what you're doing." (Laugh)*

B: Yes, exactly. You do understand that.

D: *Yes, that would be dangerous. And then you said the high festival in the summer is when the sun is at its height. (Yes) Okay. I think I understand the holidays now and why they are important. And you said there are certain phases of the moon that are important?*

B: Yes, the various phases of the moon signify different things, because the phases of the moon correspond with the cycle of the year. Things that are done during certain festivals of the year, if you need them done in-between times, you do them according to the phases of the moon.

D: *Are any phases of the moon more important to you than the others? Or what is the significance?*

B: Well, I wouldn't necessarily say "more important." It's just that for certain things you need to know the phase of the moon to make sure that the phase is not in opposition to what you need to do.

D: *I know some things about the moon and the growing of plants.*

B: Yes, that is one thing. But also, certain mental things that we do quite often as part of our religion, for helping each other and helping ourselves. And depending on what kind of thing we're wanting to do; it has to be in agreement with the phase of the moon. For example, if I'm wanting to do a ritual that will help Roff feel close to me, I need to do it when the moon is growing. And if I'm wanting to do a ritual so that life will be particularly vexatious for the Lady Joslyn, I need to do it when the moon is shrinking. For certain things the full moon is in best agreement, and for other things the dark of the moon is in best agreement.

D: *What type of things would the full moon be best for?*

B: Having good fortune with material goods, having good relationships with those around you and things like that. The dark of the moon can be used for doing rituals for helping to push away the barriers between the various aspects of yourself. And the dark of the moon can also be used for getting in touch with those who have already passed to the next plane of existence.

D: *Then when you meet in your grove of trees, do you mostly do it during the dark of the moon?*

B: We meet during all phases of the moon, because there are always different things to be done. We meet fairly often.

D: *Then you wouldn't just wait till that time of the moon.*

B: No, because if the time of the moon isn't right for doing a particular thing, we can always project our minds to various places to see what they are like.

D: *Is this group composed of people that live and work there?* (Yes) *Is it a large group?*

B: I don't know. Large compared to what?

D: *I wondered how many. Well, thirty? That would be large.*

B: No, not that many. There are fifteen of us ... or seventeen? It depends on how you count it, because two of us are like peddlers and they travel.

D: *Oh, they're not there all the time?* (Right) *Then they meet with you when they are passing through?* (Right) *I just wondered how large a group it is. I've heard tales that you can contact the spirits of those who have passed over.*

B: Yes, that is correct. At first, we thought that *you* were a spirit that had passed over. Because your spirit takes on a body for a while, and then you pass over to contemplate the lessons you have learned. And then you come back and take a body again. And we thought you were one of those who had left a body and was doing some more learning and thinking before taking on another body. And we were surprised to discover that you were somebody, a spirit who is *in* a body right now.

D: *This is a little unusual, isn't it?*

B: Yes, but not unheard of. But that is okay, because you being able to contact us, and you having passed the test, means that you are a follower of the goddess, too. Even though in the portion of your mind that you are most conscious of, you call yourself a follower of the patriarchal God, you're really a follower of the goddess deep down.

D: *I think I'm a searcher for knowledge more than anything.*

B: That makes you a follower of the goddess. Seeking out the secrets of the universe and making them plain and laying them out where all can see.

D: *Yes, that's what I'm trying to do. I've often wondered when I do this, if you can see me or do you just hear me?*

B: We don't see you with eyes as eyes can see. But we see you with our minds. Or we can see your intentions in your mind.

D: *But when I come, you mostly hear me speaking? Is that what it is?*

B: It's hard to describe.

D: *Because I've often been curious as to how I appear to people.*

B: What it is is that I'm talking with you inside my head.

D: *Ah, that's what I thought. But many people aren't aware of this.*

B: That is true, because most people are not aware of the various aspects of their selves.

D: *For I travel like this through many time periods, and most people can talk to me but they're not aware that I am actually there. That's why I was surprised when you seemed to be aware of me.*

B: It's because we're both followers of the goddess.

D: *That must be the difference. The other people probably were not using that part of their mind.*

B: You are correct.

D: But I've never harmed anyone while doing this. I'm very careful. (Yes) *I'm very interested in these rituals because I would like to pass them on to the followers of the old religion that are living now. They are still secret. Some of these rituals may have been lost.*

B: That is true, or perhaps they use different aspects of these rituals now. But they are welcome to them. I can see that you are in contact with a few followers of the goddess. And so by giving these to all of them, it will get to the right places. I can see that some of the followers of the goddess that you know, are in contact with other followers. And there are some that are by themselves. I can see how you mean that they are needing to stay secret. There's one in particular that works by herself, but those that work by themselves do so because it's difficult to contact others. But they need this knowledge, too.

D: I was thinking they might be interested in how the rituals have changed. And they may want to go back to your way of doing it.

B: Yes or add our way to their way to develop a more complete way.

D: There might be many things that have been lost, or the reasons behind it. Some in our time wear *pentagrams, pentacles.*

B: Yes, I can see that. And it is good because that is a sign that the church is definitely withering away. When people can wear pentagrams openly without fearing the Inquisition, that is a good thing. And I'm very glad to see that. I wish I could wear a pentagram openly.

D: They wear them on necklaces, chains around their neck, and rings and different things like this.

B: Yes, and sometimes as a sword buckler. (She was probably referring to a belt buckle.)

D: Of course, most people don't know what it means when they see it. The people in your time don't wear pentagrams openly, do they?

B: No, we don't wear anything.

D: To recognize each other?

B: We don't *wear* anything, but we have subtle gestures that we use when we're talking. They look like just ordinary gestures, but someone who knows them and can recognize them can return them.

D: *Can you tell me?*

B: It's very hard to describe. It's of something you grow up with. You know how different people hold themselves a certain way and use certain hand gestures. It just seems to be the type of thing people around here do. And it's that type of thing but it's different in certain ways.

D: *You mean like placing your hand on a certain part of your body?*

B: Either that or sometimes holding your fingers a certain way when you're gesturing.

D: *Could you show me, so I could know if I see someone.*

B: I don't think that knowledge would help you any, because that's just something among our local group here.

D: *Your local group, okay. It would be a way of knowing each other.*

B: One gesture we do that is common amongst all of us is the Horns of the Goddess. (She held up her hand. She had all fingers folded under except the thumb and little finger. Very similar to the sign for the Texas Longhorns. I described for the tape recorder.)

D: *Oh, the thumb and the little finger?*

B: Yes. Some do it like this. (She gestured again.)

D: *The first finger and the little finger.*

B: Yes. And they get that from the phase of the moon. The first quarter.

D: *Oh. The crescent of the moon, as we call it?*

B: Yes, the crescent.

D: *That is called the "Horns of the Goddess?"* (Yes) *I've heard it called the "Horns of the Devil" in our time sometimes. (Laugh)*

B: That is the church working again.

D: *(Laugh) But this would be a gesture to know each other. I can see where you would get it from the horns of the moon, because they look like horns when they're in that last phase.*

B: Or the first phase.

D: *Yes, either way.—I was wondering if people wore crosses. Do you know what a cross is?*

B: (Indignant and disgusted tone of voice.) Yes, I know what a cross is.

D: *Do the average people wear them, or just the church?*

B: Priests do, of course. Some of the more superstitious of the farmers more often have a cross on their body somewhere. It's usually two sticks bound together. Sometimes a girl will have two sticks bound together and tied around her neck with a thong of some sort. It's supposed to give them protection from the Devil or vampires or what-have-you.

D: *Hmmm, do they believe in vampires?*

B: Not really. I have heard rumors that the belief is more strong east of here. But they do believe that there are fantastical creatures lurking about waiting to snatch their eternal souls.

D: *What do they consider a vampire? You may have a different meaning for the word than I have.*

B: No, there's only one meaning for the word.

D: *What does it mean?*

B: A vampire is another church invention. I'm not sure if vampires exist, but supposedly it is a spirit imprisoned in a body and the spirit refuses to let go and go on to the next stage of development. And in order to remain and retain its hold on the body it has to drink human blood.

D: *This would be a spirit?*

B: Well, it's a spirit in a body. You're a spirit, I'm a spirit.

D: *Oh, a spirit in a body. Okay. Because I was thinking if it were just a spirit, it wouldn't need to drink. You mean a spirit in a body.*

B: Listen to what I say. I said it was in a body.

D: *I see. And the church invented this idea?*

B: I think so. Either that or they miraculously grasped a notion about ... because, see, a spirit is in a body for only so long then it must go on to the next stage of development. And somehow the church managed to perceive that some spirits do not let go when they should. And so the church invented fantastical things about *why* they don't let go, and *how* they keep their hold on the body. And the affects they have on ordinary people.

D: *Do you think they've done this just to increase the fear?* (Yes) *I see. Well, I'm really enjoying this conversation, but it's time for me to leave again. (Laugh) I usually have to leave right when I have something I want to talk about. But I can always ask you for more information next time, can't I?* (Yes) *Maybe you can tell me some more about these things. Then it's all right if I come again and speak to you?* (Yes) *Every time you let me come, I learn so many things. And I thank you for allowing me to come.* (Yes) *All right, then I will meet you again and ask some more of my questions. Be patient with me when I don't quite understand.*

B: I will try.

D: *Then thank you, Astelle. (She strongly corrected my pronunciation with the accent on the first syllable.) I keep saying it wrong, don't I? But I know who you are anyway.*

(Subject brought forward.)

Chapter 7
Talk to the Animals
(Recorded May 20, 1986)

Used keyword and counted her back to the lifetime of Astelle.

D: *We have gone back to the time when Astelle lived. What are you doing?*

B: I'm in the stables.

D: *What are you doing there?*

B: (Her voice sounded sad.) Staying away from the Lady Joslyn.

D: *Oh, has she been giving you a hard time?* (Yes) *Do you want to tell me about it?*

B: What's to tell? It's what she usually does. (Sigh) They've been trying to get a suitor for her but they keep turning her down. And she gets upset and she hits me with her brush.

D: *Like it's your fault.*

B: Well, she feels that it is because I'm prettier than she is.

D: *I think one time you told me they had a large banquet when many people were coming. And they were going to try to arrange a wedding for her?* (Uh-huh) *It didn't work out or what?*

B: Well, they arranged the wedding, and then when the people got back to where they lived to let the man know about the wedding they had arranged, he had already gotten married while they were gone.

D: *I bet that didn't make the Lady Joslyn too happy.*

B: She *screamed.* And she kept screaming and rolling her eyes around and throwing things.

D: *Do they arrange weddings like that before someone has seen the other person?*

B: That's quite common.

D: *And she thought it was all set.*

B: Yes, she did. But the man had heard of her and had heard about how she is about things. And I guess he didn't want to marry her. It is said that he loved another lady and that's the one he married. He didn't want to marry somebody that he didn't love.

D: *I was just wondering if he really got married or if they just said that because he didn't want to marry her.*

B: As far as I have heard, he really did get married.

D: *So the Lady Joslyn really was unhappy.*

B: Yes. There have been other tries, too. But they have all fallen through. If only she would realize it, if the Lady Joslyn weren't so worried about getting married and quit screaming and worrying about things, she would not be so ugly. And perhaps then be more desirable to a suitor. But she doesn't seem to be able to look at it that way.

D: *You said she was upset with you, so I thought maybe something had just happened.*

B: Well, Roff turned her down again last night. And this morning she came down to the kitchen area early and found he and I together. And she was somewhat upset.

D: *And that's what did it.* (Yes) *Does Roff ever try to do anything when she hurts you?*

B: No. She saw us together and she just spun around and went off. But later in the day, I think it was close to a mealtime, she decided she wanted to eat up in her room. And she specifically wanted me to bring the food up. So when I brought the food up she was waiting with her hairbrush.

D: *She doesn't do anything in front of him then.* (No) *That would make her look even worse, wouldn't it?* (Yes) *So right now you're hiding in the stables?*

B: You might say that. She never comes down to the stables. She doesn't like to ride. And so I'm down here and I'm watching the men in the practice yard. And I'm not really needed in the kitchens just yet.

D: *Just trying to stay out of her sight?*

B: Yes. Besides it's peaceful here. I listen to the horses talking. And I hear the wind blowing.

D: *Can you hear the horses talking to each other?* (Yes) *I never knew anyone who could hear the animals talk before.*

B: Well, you can hear them talk, but sometimes you may or may not understand what they are saying. It depends on how well with the mother goddess you are. If you are of like mind with her then you can understand what they say.

D: *What does it sound like?*

B: With your ears you hear the sounds they normally make. But inside your head it's like listening to two people talking.

D: *It sounds like words, like mental communication?*

B: It sounds like words.

D: *Hmmm, I wonder what horses would find to talk about?*

B: Different things. They talk about the weather a lot. And whether or not they need to be shod again. The stallions that we use for breeding only have one thing on their mind.

D: *(Laugh) That's all they think about?* (Yes) *What do they think about people? About their masters?*

B: Oh, I hear some scandalous things about some of the people in the household here. Horses are very bad about gossiping, too. The different ones who come down here to the stables to make love. They think it's safe, but they don't understand what the horses say. They talk about everybody. *(I laughed.)* And they make fun of different identifying characteristics that the different humans have.

D: *Like what?*

B: Well, like there's one man that has a limp. And they imitate it by hobbling around in their stall. And there's another man with a large nose and a small mouth. And one horse is particularly good at imitating the way he talks. That's very funny. And it's just different things like that.

D: *You would normally think they would not even be interested or notice it. Many people think they're just dumb animals.*

B: That is true, and that is where they make their mistake. The animals are not dumb at all. There is just simply a wall between them and us so we can't talk. The people who go down there to make love don't know that the horses even notice. And if they do, they figure there is nothing they can do about it, because they only interact with other horses. And they don't realize that there are those of us who can understand what the horses say.

D: *(Laugh) Do the horses know that you can understand?*

B: I think so. There's one or two that I know for sure that do.

D: *I guess there's a lot that goes on in the animal world that people don't realize.* (Yes) *Have you ever tried to communicate with any other animals besides the horses?*

B: Oh, yes. I can't necessarily say anything in return, but I can hear what they have to say.

D: *Then if you tried talking to them, they wouldn't really understand you?*

B: I could speak with them with my mind, and they could understand me. But some of them are like people, they get suspicious whenever I do that.

D: *They're not used to it.* (Right) *But you are able to at least know what they're thinking.* (Yes) *I guess most people think that animals wouldn't have much on their mind to talk about anyway.*

B: Well, that depends on what animal it is and what it's been doing.

D: *Well, you remember me, don't you?*

B: Yes. You passed the test.

D: *Yes.*

Upon returning in another session, Dolores wanted to follow up on a subject she wasn't able to finish asking questions about. Here is what she found.

D: *And the last time I was talking to you, we were talking about something, and I had to leave, and we didn't get to finish it. You said some of the people wore crosses in the shape of pieces of wood that were tied together.* (Yes) *And they kept them around their necks for protection against things. One of the things you mentioned was they had a belief in vampires. And I never got all the information about that. You said it was a belief in something that the church had invented? Was that right?*

B: Yes. The church has used and will use anything and everything it can to keep the people scared and stupid. One of their best weapons is fear. And so they make up these wild stories to tell the people to make them scared, so they are easier to be controlled. I hear that it's a belief from some mountains that are east of here. But I don't know where it could be. No one has said. And I've never been there.

D: *Do you think the stories were based on any kind of fact? Anything that was real?*

B: That is hard to answer. Sometimes I think yes, sometimes I think no. There are many things that happen in the world that man does not know or know the why of. And these things are very puzzling. Sometimes a fantastic explanation will fit, and sometimes if you look a little bit deeper there's a reason there that the mind can accept.

D: *I was thinking maybe the church didn't make it all up. That there might have been something that they took and added to.*

B: I think they took stories of wolves carrying off children in the wintertime. Took that story and made up everything else from it, including the notion of the doll.

I must not have heard this mention of a doll, because I did not follow up on it. I wonder what she was referring to here?

D: *What is the belief that the people have? What do they think that a vampire does?*

B: Oh, what happens when the vampire takes blood?

D: *The story of what they're supposed to be.*

I wanted her story. I didn't want to influence her. But I was unsure how to word it.

B: Yes. Well, the church would have you think that they are the undead. That they should be dead but are not. But a wise woman in our circle has said that people who are like that are alive but are diseased in a subtle way. And that perhaps the only nourishment that will help keep them alive is that of blood.

D: *How do they get the blood?*

B: The story says that they bite you at the elbow or on the neck to get blood from you. I have heard they bite you anywhere where the blood may be close to the surface in heavy streams.

D: *Well, it seems like an odd notion. But then the church tells them that if they wear this cross it's for protection?*

B: Yes, they do. I have my serious doubts about that. The way the church has corrupted itself, none of its magic works anymore. And so it will try anything to try to hold on to the power.

D: *Do you think at one time it did have magic that worked?*

B: Yes, I do, even though the church would never admit to it.

D: *In the early days?* (Yes) *Well, do they have any other things like vampires that they want the people to believe are there?*

B: The church is always trying to scare the people with ideas about demons. And how demons are everywhere ready to do various things according to where the demon is. And it's a matter of setting aside all this that the church tells you and try to look at things clearly. Many people don't have the strength to do it.

D: *They just go along with it.* (Yes) *Do you think demons are real?* (No) *Do you think that there is any such thing as spirits like that?*

B: There are such things as spirits and people from the other side of the veil. I have seen them. But it's not the same as the church describes as demons, or angels either, for that matter. It's different from the way the church describes it. The church tries to put a mathematical significant onto everything, when it's not that way in nature.

D: *What do you mean, mathematical?*

B: For example, they try to tell you there are seven realms of heaven, because they consider seven to be a holy number. And they try to think there are thirteen divisions of hell, because they consider thirteen to be a number of witchcraft. And it's totally arbitrary. They just put the numbers down because it looks good to them. They don't know how to follow their feelings, and to let what is there be there naturally. They just try to make everything fit into their pattern for the world.

D: *What do they say angels are?*

B: That's one reason why they keep having councils. They can't agree on what an angel is.

D: *You mean church councils?*

B: Some of them say that they're very big and grand and tall, and others say that they're so small that several of them can dance on the surface of a spoon or something. But they can't agree. On the one hand they say they're spiritual, yet on the other hand they start giving them ridiculous physical descriptions. Spirits are not bound to the ground like you and I are. And so the church assumes that they have to have wings. But things from the other side don't need physical manifestations. It's confusing.

D: *I wonder if they have ever seen them or if they just make them up.*

B: They make them up.

D: *I thought they might have something in their holy books that might tell them that they exist or something.*

B: I don't know. I've not heard tell of anything about them existing.

D: *Well, what do they think an angel does? What is its purpose?*

B: An angel is to keep believers safe, especially from the Devil and his demons. But more generally, keep people safe from each other.

D: *Okay. And the demons are supposed to be ... what?*

B: Imps of Satan. This is a tiring subject to speak on.

D: *Well, I just wanted to get the information. (Laugh) Because some of these beliefs still exist in my day.*

B: I see.

D: *They still haven't gotten rid of those beliefs. That's why I was wondering where they came from. I'll talk of something else. They also believe in saints, don't they?* (Yes) *Who do they say the saints are?*

B: Well, the church would have it that a person who lives a particularly holy or blessed life for their church, of course, is particularly blessed when they die. And have advantages over other people who have died. And as a result, there are objects put up to represent these people, so that people can venerate them. And also so that I can use these different ... (Pause) I'm confused.

D: *What?*

B: My mind is all confused. It seems I'm having difficulty talking. It seems like there are two minds here at once.

D: *Oh? Is it bothering you?*

B: It's making it difficult to talk, because it feels like there are two minds here at once, which makes me feel very sleepy. And the other mind is thinking about things, too, and is concerned about things. And I'm thinking about the things I'm trying to tell you. And that other mind ... I'm having to work very hard to keep my concentration. And whenever my concentration lets up a little bit the other mind is there with the other thoughts. And I forget what I'm going to say. And it's making me tired trying to concentrate like this.

I think this meant that she was becoming aware of Brenda's mind, or Brenda's mind was trying to interfere or interject in some way.

D: *Maybe I can help. Maybe that's what it is, you're probably sleepy anyway.*

B: That could be. I didn't sleep well after the Lady Joslyn beat me.

I thought the best way to stop the confusion that was creating interference would be to move her to another scene. So I asked her to move forward to an important day in her life. When I stopped counting, she announced excitedly, "I'm at the banquet. People are eating and the musicians are playing."

D: *Do you have a job to do there?*

B: I'm done with it right now. I just brought some food out for the banquet. I'm listening to the musicians before I go back to the kitchen.

D: *What kind of musicians are there?*

B: Just the normal sort. They're a traveling company of musicians, and they stopped by here. They're going down the road. And they'll continue down the road after tonight.

D: *Are there many?*

B: Oh, six or seven of them.

D: *What kind of instruments are they playing?*

B: Mostly instruments that you blow into. And some with strings attached to it that you strum. I'm not sure. I'm fond of music but I don't know much about the instruments.

D: *Is the music nice?*

B: Yes. It's sprightly. It's good for a banquet. It sounds nice. And whenever they're not playing instruments, they're telling jokes.

D: *(Laugh) What kind of jokes?*

B: Usually risqué. Just different things. Poking fun at people here at the banquet.

D: *Can you give me an example?*

B: Well, for example, at one point they were saying, "When is a banquet-hall a stable?" And so someone asked, "When?" And they said, "When there are horses at the table." And they pointed at Lady Joslyn when they said it.

D: *Oh-oh! What did they mean? Because of the way she looks?* (Yes) *(Laugh) I wonder what she thought?*

B: She threw down the piece of meat she was eating and stomped out of the room. And she hasn't come back.

D: *(Laugh) Ummm. Are there any other jokes they are telling? Because I like to laugh, too.*

B: That's the main one I remembered because it was on the Lady Joslyn. They've been doing it all evening, poking fun at everybody. Not meaning it serious, but just doing it to give everyone else a laugh.

D: *Uh-huh. But it was the wrong kind of a joke to tell on her.*

B: Yes, except that everybody else laughed.

D: *Do they tell any jokes on the lord, the master?*

B: Oh, yes. Oh, yes. But they're the type of jokes that you know they're poking fun at the master, but at the same time they respect him. And so it's kind of as a compliment.

D: *Do they do any singing?*

B: A little bit. Usually whenever it's a song that has some words that someone has requested.

D: *Do you know any of the songs that they sing?*

B: No, I've not heard them before. This is a new troupe that has not come by here before. It's said they're from the south, and they have some songs that are not heard this far north very often.

D: *Is there any other kind of entertainment?*

B: Well, this is the main entertainment while the ladies are at the table. I suspect they have something else planned for when the ladies retire and leave. Normally the ladies would stay with the men till the end of the banquet, but with this other entertainment they have, they have decided that the ladies must cut their banqueting short and leave.

D: *Oh, I wonder what kind of entertainment that would be?*

B: There's no telling.

D: *Do you have any idea?*

B: I rather suspect it might involve doing unnatural things with a naked woman.

D: *Oh? They do this at these banquets?*

B: I don't know. It's just a rumor I heard.

D: *They think of this as a form of entertainment?* (Yes) *Would it be a woman that was brought in or somebody in the house or what?*

B: One who was brought in. One that is with the troupe.

D: *Hmmm. I can see why they wouldn't want the women to be there. I was just curious what kind of entertainment you have. Is there anything special to eat at the banquet?*

B: Various kinds of meat fixed different ways. And different kinds of bread. The meats have stuffings in them of various kinds.

D: *Do they ever have anything sweet?* (No) *I was wondering if your people ate things that were sweet.*

B: Sometimes yes, but not very often.

D: *Why is that?*

B: That which makes things sweet, be it liquid or solid, is very difficult to find. Particularly honey is very difficult to find in this part.

D: *Oh, I didn't know that. Then you wouldn't have sweet things very often.*

B: Right. It's just a treat for every once in a while.

D: *I've also heard something about salt, too. (Pause) Do you know what salt is?*

B: Yes. I know what salt is. There's a trade in salt. And we have some on hand, but not much.

D: *A trade in salt? What do you mean?*

B: There's a peddler that comes by who sells the salt occasionally. We don't use it too much at the banquet table. We use it mainly for preserving meat.

D: *You don't use it in your cooking?*

B: Well, the meat that has been preserved in salt puts plenty in the cooking. And so we use herbs and such to make the food tasty.

D: *I've heard from other people that salt is valuable. It's hard to find. Is that true?*

B: I'm not sure. We seem to have plenty of it, but it comes a long distance to get here.

D: *So you don't use it freely anyway.*

B: Correct.

D: *Well, you wouldn't have to, I suppose, if the meat was preserved that way. Is that how you keep the meat for the winter?*

B: That is one way of doing it. Another way is if you have a haunch or something. (Dictionary: Haunch: An animal's loin and leg together.) To coat it with wax, so that the wax seals it.

D: *This keeps it from going bad?* (Yes) *I wouldn't have thought that. Are these the only ways you can keep food during the winter months?*

B: This is the best way. The meat that is fresh killed in winter will keep for a while if the days are cold. On the other days you have to rely on salting the meat down. Usually when the meat is fresh killed, on the cold days they go ahead and cut it up and salt it down. So that it will be there for other days.

D: *Do you know what vegetables are?* (Yes) *Do you have those in the winter?*

B: Some of them. Mainly ones that grow in the ground, like beets and carrots. They keep well for a while after the growing season has ceased. And others don't keep as well.

D: *Do you know what fruits are?*

B: Oh, yes. We have many fruits. Apples, pears, berries of different kinds. There's a way of preserving them, too, for whenever you need them. And they'll keep for as long as you need them to keep.

D: *How do you do that?*

B: With brandy. A very strong alcohol drink. You get your fruit and you cut it up into the size of pieces you want it to be. And you pour brandy over it and just let it sit. Put a cover on it to keep out the dirt and bugs. And during the wintertime whenever you need any fruit, just dip some out of the brandy. And then afterwards, the brandy that's left, you filter it, you pour it through a cloth, because it will have the flavor of the fruit in with the brandy and that makes a very good drink.

D: *This gives the fruit a different taste, too, doesn't it?*

B: Yes. But then anything you do with food to help keep it for a while changes the taste to it.

D: *Oh, yes, it would. And these are things you eat during the winter?*

B: Yes. The lord of the household sometimes has other things brought in, but that's usually for the holiday season.

D: *What holiday season does the lord observe?*

B: He and his household usually observe those which the Catholic church says needs to be observed. Christmas. Easter. Saint Peter's Day. Saint Paul's Day. Different days of the saints are important, too, plus the days leading up to Christmas and Easter. Leading away from Christmas and Easter.

D: *Are there any special events that they do around Christmas?*

B: It's difficult to say. They do more singing then, about things that are religious. They have more masses then. And the people who are part of the church are expected to do certain things according to custom, to show that they are observing these holidays, whichever holiday it is.

D: *What do they do to observe these different customs.*

B: It's difficult to say. I try to stay away from it as much as I can, because we have our own holidays close to these times. And so in order to be able to be in the right frame of mind I try to stay away from the church's doings.

D: *Okay. I just thought maybe it was something very important that you had to help with.*

B: Just more cooking.

D: *More cooking. You said they have special things that they cook or special things they eat?*

B: Well, if they can get ahold of any fresh foods, they fix that surely. Plus whatever is there to fix in the storage rooms.

D: *Well, it sounds like a good time anyway. Why is it an important day?*

B: Why is what an important day?

D: *Is it just important because it's a banquet or what?*

B: Do you mean right now?

D: *Yeah, on that day.*

I realized on listening to the tape that this must have been confusing to her. I had been talking about the holidays and then switched and was asking again about the banquet without being more clear about it.

B: It's important for the household because this troupe stopped by, and it's a treat. And it's important for me because, although I don't know much about music, sometimes I make up a tune, and I like to hear what it sounds like. And I talked a couple of the musicians of the troupe into playing it for me. So I could hear how it sounded, to make sure it sounded the way I thought it should.

D: *Oh, the songs you've made up, you mean?* (Right) *That's why it was important then. You don't often have a musical group stop by.*

B: No, we don't.

D: *Then most of the time you don't have much entertainment at the house?*

B: We usually make our own entertainment. And it's the outside entertainment that's a treat. Usually the entertainment we have is like contests between the different knights and valets and pages and such, to see who's the most skillful or strong at something. And just different things that an ordinary household does.

D: *Are these contests ever dangerous?*

B: No, no, because the lord of the house couldn't be killing off all of his household for the contest. They're made to be challenging without endangering your life. If you're not careful you could get injured, but that would be only due to your own clumsiness.

D: *What kind of contests would they be?*

B: Archery, lances, knives, riding. Some of the valets and knights like to show off with their riding, by doing things that you wouldn't think could be done on a horse. And just different things like that. Sword-play.

D: *Then they're like games of skill. Do they ever have any challenges with other knights from somewhere else that might be dangerous?*

B: No. They're mainly kept in good form with the games of skill, to be ready in case we have to go to war. And so, usually there's much wagering that goes on during these contests. That's the main part of the entertainment aspect of it, seeing everybody go crazy betting on their favorite.

D: *Do you have money? Or what do they bet with?*

B: Usually you bet with things you have, or things that you can get.

D: *I have always heard that sometimes there would be contests between knights of different houses, and these could get quite serious.*

B: That is true if there is a feud between the two houses. And it keeps getting worse and worse until both of the whole households are involved. But if there's no feud, why have these contests to kill off the best of your knights? If it's just a contest like we have here for entertainment, it's just done to see who's the most skillful. Not to see who can be killed.

D: *That makes sense to me, because the knights do take years of training. Is Roff a knight yet, or is he still a valet?*

B: He's still a valet. I think he is to become a knight soon though, because he has mastered all the skills that he needs. And I think they're waiting for a big contest with a regular knight with more people to see, and so they make a bigger celebration. It takes a certain number of years to learn everything. And it takes different amounts of years for different people.

D: *About how long?*

B: I'm not really sure.

D: *Then when they're ready, do they have the ceremony for many at a time?*

B: No, usually only one or two.

D: *That's interesting. I know you're enjoying the banquet, but can I ask you some more questions about your religion?* (Yes) *Because no one else can hear us, can they? (Laugh)*

B: I wouldn't think so. I'm just standing next to the musicians. And most of the crowd is … over there.

D: *Well, they won't know what we're talking about anyway.* (Right) *You were talking about different rituals that you do?* (Yes) *Do you ever do anything involving candles?*

B: Oftentimes it's good to use a candle to get the mind calmed for doing the ritual. But usually the rituals we do don't really call for anything. Most of the time they just call for getting your mind in the right frame, so it can make it come to pass what you want to come to pass.

D: *Then you don't have to use different colored candles?*

B: It helps if you can, but if you don't have them then you have to make do without them.

D: *They're not* really *necessary then.*

B: They do help give more power to your rituals. But you can do the rituals without them.

D: *What about different kinds of stones? Not really jewels, but ...*

B: Gemstones?

D: *Yes. Do you have any beliefs in those?*

B: Ah, yes, they have magical powers for protection and such for the owner. All of the gems each have their own meaning. I don't know gem lore, but I'm young still. I'm still learning. There's an older woman in the group that does, and I'd like to learn it from her. But she's not had a chance to get hold of a large hoard of gemstones so that I could learn what she knows. To show me what they're good for, for the rituals.—The average person, all, each, everybody does at least something for protection or what-have-you. Usually they don't know if it comes from our religion, but they do it anyway, just out of habit. It's been passed down from parent to child.

D: *What kind of things would they do?*

B: Oh, whenever the tax collector rides by, they do the Horns of the Goddess for protection. And all they know is that it is a gesture for protection. They don't realize the meaning behind it.

D: *What else?*

B: Sometimes whenever someone who is diseased passes them, they spit over their own shoulder, because that's supposed to drive away negative influences. And sometimes the wives of the farmers in their kitchen will sprinkle salt around for good luck. And they are not aware that salt is very powerful for good luck and protection and cleansing.

D: *Well, what about these gemstones? Do people wear those?*

B: The lords and ladies wear the gemstones. They wear pearls and rubies and emeralds and opal.

D: *But they don't realize the powers behind these?*

B: No, they don't. They just wear them because they look pretty.

D: *Maybe whenever you learn these things, you'll be able to tell me. We have a stone that's called a crystal. Have you ever*

165

seen one like that? Maybe it's not in your part of the world?

B: A crystal? Is that like what I have seen my reflection in?

D: *It's clear, you can see through it. Do you know what glass is?* (No) *Well, it's a material you can see through.*

This was again another example of someone in those time periods not knowing what glass is. This has happened many times before.

B: Like water, but it's solid? Kind of like ice?

D: *Yes, kind of like ice, only it won't melt away. A crystal is a stone that is like that. It looks very much like ice only it's hard.*

B: I've never seen anything like this.

D: *There are some people in the world who believe these stones have great powers, even for healing.*

B: I can see where it would be good for that, but we don't have it here.

D: *But you said there was something you could see yourself in?*

B: Ummm. Well, sometimes the ladies of the household have a piece of metal polished to where you can see yourself.

D: *You told me one time you had not seen yourself.*

B: No. Sometimes you can see your outline in water.

D: *Yes, that's true.—Do you have any beliefs about the stars?*

B: It is said that the stars can help you determine the plan for your life. Perhaps that is true, because there are so many of them, they could be different for every life. It's just a matter of having the skill to interpret what they have to say. I know that skill exists, but we don't have it here. We just have a few dry things about the stars. Just small things.

D: *Like what?*

B: Like the love star. If you make a wish on the love star that it should come true.

D: *Which one is that?*

B: It's the early one of the evening. Or if you see a shooting star an event of some sort is going to happen in your life.

D: *Good, bad or what?*

B: Just an important event that you won't forget. It could be either way. And different things like that.

D: *One time you were telling me there were many legends that were passed down to your people. And there was one about the world a long, long time ago. You were telling me something about that.*

B: I'm sorry. About what?

D: *Am I distracting you?*

B: (Pause) It seems that our communication is not clear today.

D: *Oh, well, we won't be talking much longer anyway.*

B: And so I do apologize. I did promise to help you.

D: *I thought maybe the music was distracting you.*

B: It is. I keep listening to it and trying to listen to you, too. And sometimes it gets mixed up, and I can't remember everything you have said in your sentence.

D: *You could move away from the music, but I know you're interested in that, too.*

B: If you could ask your question again, I will answer it.

D: *All right. I won't be much longer, then you can enjoy your music. One time you were talking about legends of your people.* (Yes) *You mentioned something about what the world was like many, many years* before. *Do you remember talking about that?*

B: It seems to me that I must have mentioned that to you, but I don't remember what I said.

D: *I'm trying to remember. Something happened to the world.*

B: The only thing I can recall just now, is how the number of days in the seasons used to be different.

D: *It was something like that, yes. Something happened?*

B: We never have been clear as to what happened. We don't know. We just know that something happened. And somehow for some reason everything was different. The months were different, the years were different, the seasons were different. And according to the legends the crops wouldn't grow for several years. For some reason the air was poisoned or something.

D: *This went on for several years?*

B: Yes. And then the poisoning in the air went away, but the days never changed back to where they were.

D: *Do you think the days were longer, shorter, or do you know?*

B: I don't know. I only know about the number of days being different. Used to be, everything had good round numbers to it. And now the numbers are all kind of pointy and hard to remember. The number of days in the month, the number of months in a year.

D: *Were all different?*

B: Yes. And it is said that it took a while for people to figure out the months again. And so it was a difficult time for everybody.

D: *Hmmm. It must have been something really powerful that happened.*

B: That is true. But I cannot think of what it could be that would do something like that.

D: *No. Not if it would affect the crops and everything.*

B: And so, I think that is something we will probably never know, not even you in your wondrous time.

D: *No, we don't. We've never heard the story. Sometimes stories just die away and we don't know about them if they're not passed down.* (True) *How many days are in your time now?*

B: It's difficult to remember. It seems that the days are different for every other month. Sometimes thirty, sometimes thirty-one.

D: *How many days were there in a month before? Do you have that knowledge?*

B: I think it was twenty-eight. I'm not sure. It's hard to say.

D: *Of course, it would be easier to remember if each one was the same, wouldn't it?*

B: Yes. It might have been twenty-eight, or thirty, or even thirty-two. It was some number like that. It was the same number every month.

** In *The Legend of Starcrash* the story tells of something happening to the Earth that made the "moon walk a different path." It seemed that something catastrophic happened that changed the seasons and weather. **

D: *How many months in a year?*

B: Twelve. But legends say there used to be thirteen.

D: *Do you have different names for each month?*

B: The months are the months. There are names for the months. They're the same everywhere. Sometimes they differ slightly when they're in other tongues from other lands, but they're the same months.

D: *What do you call them? I want to see if they're the same as we call them now.*

B: I think that it is. There's no reason why they should change.

D: *You never know. That's why I ask so many questions, to see how things have changed.* (Yes) *Like do you know what month it is that you have your Hallowed evening?*

B: That's the harvest month. Also called October.

D: *And you said Lamas?*

B: February.

D: *And let me see. There was another one. I'm forgetting already what they were. You had the high festival and then you had another one that was in the spring, wasn't it?*

B: The one in the spring and fall for the equinoxes sometimes don't always correspond to the same month. Because sometimes the equinoxes doesn't always fall in the same month. The solstices usually fall in the same month, but the equinoxes don't always. Because the festivals are from before the change, and they're done according to the moon month, because the moon months are closest to what the old months used to be. And it's according to the lunar phases, and it's not always with the regular calendar.

D: *Then you mean that Hallowed evening would not always be in October?*

B: It usually is. I think they set that for the last of October just to make sure that everybody was celebrating at least that one festival at the same time to produce more power. The one in the spring, Beltane, is usually in April and sometimes in May. It varies. Sometimes I get confused what month the festival will be in, because you can't really tell until almost time for it. Because you have to keep track of the moon cycles to be able to tell when it's going to be.

D: *Usually by that time things have been growing for quite a while. It's not the beginning of the growing season.*

B: It depends upon how cold the winter was, but you are correct.

D: *Then the high festival, you said is in the summer?*

B: Yes. In June.

D: *That is on the solstice. (Yes) Well, it sounds like the months are the same. We have what we call a calendar that helps us. Do you have anything like that?*

B: I think the lord of the household has one. I'm not sure. I think he does, like you say, to keep track of the days.

D: *And the months.*

B: You don't need a calendar to keep track of the months. Just to keep track of the days so that you know when the month has changed. But it's not needed by ordinary folk like me.

D: *We would get confused if we didn't have our calendars today. (Ah!) That makes it a little easier for the ordinary folk. (Yes) Well, I'm interested in these legends of your people. Do you have any other legends about how your people began or the history of your religion?*

B: (Sigh) There's not been very much, because we've always had to be so secret about it. And just pass it on by word of mouth. You lose much through the years like that.

D: *Yes, you do. You don't have much on how your religion began or where it came from?*

B: It is said that our religion began when the Earth goddess wanted to give a gift to her children, so that they would grow up and be happy. And so she gave us this religion.

D: *In the long ago past. (Yes) And then people have passed it down all this time? (Yes) Have they always had problems being persecuted, if you know what that word means?*

B: Only since the Christian church came along. Before that, no.

D: *People were not afraid of the religion in those days then.*

B: No. Why should they be?

D: *Because you said the church has made people afraid of you.*

B: Yes, but before the church gained its power the people were not afraid. So I hear.

D: *I'm just curious where it all came from. Then you don't have any other legends that you can think of that have to do with your people? Stories?*

B: Only about how at one time men and animals could communicate, but I don't know the full story on that. That's kind of a half-forgotten story. And usually the storytellers will tell it for children, to entertain them. And they make things up to finish the story since we don't know all of it as to what happened.

D: *But you said* you *can communicate. You can hear them anyway.*

B: Yes, but that's not usual. It used to be everybody could without having to try.

D: *Can you think of any others? I'm trying to see if the people of my time may have forgotten the stories that you know.*

B: (Pause) I can't think of any today. I'll be thinking between now and the next time that you contact me. Most of the stories that we tell have to do with teaching a lesson to a child, to help them remember a ritual or something. And the stories are usually not true. It's just something made up to help teach the lesson.

D: *I'd even be interested in those, because there may be some that would help the people in my time.*

B: Perhaps so. I will tell you some sometime.

D: *Will you ask the others for some stories that you can tell me?* (Yes) *Because you said yourself stories get lost and forgotten over the many years. And they get changed.* (Yes) *There may be people in my day that would like to know these things.*

I tried to ask more about the rituals and spells that her group performed, but she again became unresponsive. It was as though she was immersed in her world and did not want to communicate with me. I apologized for taking her away from enjoying the music, which was a rare treat for her.

B: I apologize for not being able to communicate well this

evening.

D: *That's all right. Did the Lady Joslyn come back?*

B: I don't see her. Which is good. I'm enjoying the evening more with her gone.

D: *Then all the servants are allowed to come in and watch this?*

B: Yes, because the troupes don't come very often. It's a treat for everybody. After we have served the food to everybody, we're free to stay and listen.

D: *Then it sounds like the lord is pretty good to work for, isn't he?*

B: Yes, I've heard some are worse.

D: *One time you were talking about things that he did up in the tower room, that you thought were something he shouldn't be doing?*

B: Yes. Because every time he does it we feel like he is trying to corrupt the natural power that is inherent in things from the mother goddess. And use it for his own ends. Use it for selfish reasons rather than use it for the good of all.

D: *Did you find out what he does up there?*

B: No. But we're still trying to.

D: *Do you think he uses rituals similar to those you use?*

B: It may appear similar to an outsider, but they're basically different, because he has a different goal in mind.

D: *What kind of a goal do you think?*

B: Probably more money for himself.

D: *Can you get things like that through rituals?*

B: You can, but they may rebound on you some day if you do it selfishly. If you think only of yourself and don't think of where you are in relation to the mother goddess.

D: *The church doesn't like what you do, but they don't say anything about what he does?*

B: Yes, because we're a threat to their power, and he is not. Because whenever he gets more money, he gives some to the church.

D: *It sounds like he's doing the same thing you are, only he's doing it for different purposes.*

B: Very different purposes.

D: *Maybe someday you'll find out what he does up there and you'll be able to tell me.*

B: Yes, I will try. We need to know anyway. And you are probably curious, too.

D: *Yes. Does he go up there regularly or do you know?*

B: Almost every night.

D: *And he's always alone? (Yes) It would be difficult to find out what he was doing if he's always by himself.*

B: Yes. That's the main reason why we don't know anything so far.

D: *You told me about the strange fire he had up there.*

B: Yes. And we are trying to find out what he does up there. We have developed several ways of trying to find out. And we're trying to work out a way that will work the best. As soon as we find out anything, I will tell you. I might even tell you *how* we find out, too, because I'm sure we're going to have to do something unusual. He's being extremely secretive.

D: *If your people thought what he was doing wasn't right, would you try to stop it in any way? Or can you do things like that?*

B: We can, and we probably would. It depends on whether what he's doing is bad enough for us to risk being exposed.

D: *But do you think anyone else in the house is involved?*

B: No, he's the only one. The Lady Joslyn might be, but I really don't think so. She doesn't act like it.

D: *If she had enough power—if power is the right word—if she had enough knowledge to do anything like that, she would be getting what she wanted, wouldn't she? (Laugh)*

B: Yes. It's not working. It could be that she might be trying and is doing it wrong. And so that's one reason why she's ill tempered. She can't figure out what she's doing wrong.

D: *That's possible, too. Of course, her attitude is the big thing.*

B: Yes, but she'll never see that.

D: *(Laugh) That's true. Well, I think I'll just go ahead and let you enjoy the music. You're having a lot of fun there. And you don't get to do that very often.*

B: Not often. I've not been very informative for you this time.

D: *Oh, you've told me some things anyway. I can't expect it to be the same every time.*

B: No, I'm human.

D: *And I never know what I will find you doing. (Laugh) Maybe next time you can find out some more about the gemstones.*

B: I will try. I don't know if I will get all the information. I've heard some rumors about some of them. But I wanted to reconfirm what I'd heard before I told you, because the lore that I pass on must be correct.

D: *Yes, that's true. I want it to be correct. And then maybe you can find out some of these stories. They don't have to be the true stories, just the ones that you tell the children, you said so they won't forget the rituals. Those may be of help to people in my day.*

B: All right, if you think so. You would be able to judge better than I.

D: *Yes. Some may, some may not. I can't tell till I hear them. Maybe we could do that next time we meet then. (Yes) And I appreciate you talking to me and I want to come again some time. You go ahead and enjoy the music and have a good time.*

B: I will.

D: *All right. And thank you for speaking with me.*

B: Thank you for being patient.

D: *That's okay. I have lots and lots of patience.*

(Subject brought forward.)

One strange thing occurred this same day. I had another session with Elaine in Eureka Springs on this same evening. She also experienced the same disorientation and difficulty hearing me at times. She said it was as though I was speaking from another room. Brenda said I seemed to be fading out at times, or as though my voice was coming from the end of a long tunnel. I thought it was because of the circumstances Astelle was experiencing in her own life at that time that may have been causing confusion. But when it also happened the same day to Elaine, I wondered if it may have been that something else was involved. Atmospheric conditions, the phase of the moon or something involving time and other dimensions that was present on that day that we do not understand. Strange that it happened to two different subjects on the same day. It never happened again in any of my other subjects. Later occasionally Nostradamus would experience something like static, but I don't know if that was the same thing.

Chapter 8
The Little People
(Recorded June 3, 1986)

Used keyword and counted her back to the time that Astelle lived.

D: *We have gone back to the time that Astelle lived in Flanders. What are you doing?*

B: I'm with Grendell. She's an old lady who lives here. She's a wise woman. She's also one of us.

D: *Is she a very old woman?*

B: I don't know what you call "very old." She is bent and gray. But she never married to have children, so I can't tell you how many grandchildren she would have. But she's old enough to where her grandchildren should be having children, if she had grandchildren.

D: *Then that would be what I consider to be very old. This is how you tell the age of someone, by the children and grandchildren?*

B: Yes, if you don't know the age in years.

D: *Does she live there in the large house?*

B: Ahh ... not directly in the house. She lives in a cottage nearby.

D: *Why are you with her?*

B: I had a question and she's helping me find the answer. She has much knowledge.

D: *What kind of a question did you have for her? Or can you tell me?*

B: I can tell you. It's a matter of putting it into words. (Pause) As everybody knows there are magical properties in the various colors. And I was asking her if there were any particular rituals that had need of or took advantage of the presence of a rainbow, which has all the colors in it. And so she's helping me to explore some of the ways that rainbows can be used.

D: *Rainbows are very beautiful, but I never thought about that. That would be using all the colors at one time. Is this just an idea that came to you?*

B: Yes. I've been thinking about it for a while, because I've always liked rainbows. They're very pretty. As a child, when I was learning the meaning of the colors, whenever I'd see a rainbow I'd see if I could remember the meaning of the colors that I saw in the rainbow. And here lately I was thinking maybe there's a ritual that to be effective needs a rainbow. There are some rituals that need to be done at certain phases of the moon. Maybe there's a ritual that needs a rainbow. So, I thought I would ask Grendell, to find out. Mostly what she's telling me is how the rainbow can be used for meditation.

D: *Can you share that with me?*

B: I'm still learning it. After I learn it from her then I can tell you.

D: *I thought maybe you could repeat what she was telling you.*

B: Well, the way she explains things, she does it through a lot of examples, which sometimes makes it difficult to learn from it, and sometimes not. And after I figure out what it is that she's wanting me to learn, then I can tell you.

D: *Okay. But has she told you of anything else it can be used for besides meditation?*

B: Yes, there's a ritual that is done in the presence of a rainbow. It's supposed to help you be able to see the little people and unicorns. *(That was a surprise.)* Because they are both magical peoples and they have their own spells of protection, to where you can't see them. Unless you do this ritual with the help of the rainbow. So that you can see through their spells of protection and see them.

D: *I've heard of the little people, but I didn't know if they really existed or not.*

B: Yes, they really do. But they have very powerful spells, very powerful rituals of protection. They need it. They have been persecuted for so many centuries.

D: *Are they afraid of people?*

B: It depends. Most people, yes, they're afraid of. Because they know what they will try to do. But people who are in harmony with the Earth mother, they're not afraid of. Because they worship her also.

D: *Have you ever seen any of the little people?* (Yes) *Can you tell me what they look like?*

B: They look like ordinary people. They're proportioned the way they should be. Their heads may be slightly larger than what one would think it should be for the size of their body. And the only thing is that they're darker-skinned than what ordinary people are.

D: *Are they as tall as we are?*

B: (Emphatic) No! They're little people!

D: *How little are they?*

B: Oh? From the top of their hats down to the ground, they come up to just above the knees.

D: *Do they look like old people or young people or children?*

B: They come in all ages. The majority of them look like they are full-grown people. And a few of them look old. This ritual that you can do with the rainbow pierces the spells of protection to where you can see the adults, but you can't see their children, because they put even additional spells of protection on them.

D: *They're afraid something might happen to their children?* (Yes) *I've heard stories of these different things, but I didn't know if they were real.*

B: Yes, they're real.

D: *We have different names for the ones we have. I don't know if they're the same as you call them.*

B: There are many different names for them, because there are many different groups of them. And the various groups have different purposes in life. Sometimes the difference of purposes cause them to appear different because they have a different way of living. And so they're called differently.

D: *What are some of the different groups?*

B: Well, in general they are called elves. And there are different kinds of elves. There are field elves, and wood elves, and house elves, and ground elves. And there are the white ladies.

D: *White ladies?* (Uh-huh) *What are they?*

B: The white ladies are found mostly in the fields. The power they have has to do with the wind. If they get angry with you, they can call up a storm. If you trespass on their property, they will call up a rain of hailstones. But if they like you and you treat them with respect, they will cause it to rain on your crops at the right time.

D: *But how do you know where their property is?*

B: You don't. So, what one must do is be in harmony with the Earth mother and have respect for all of them. And they can tell whether or not you respect them.

D: *Then if you respect them, they don't consider you trespassing?* (Right) *Why are they called* white *ladies? Is that what they look like?*

B: I'm not sure why they're called white ladies. It is said one possible reason is that for one of their spells they appear to have the appearance of a large white lady who is kind of wispy and you can see through her, kind of like a cloud, sort of. And so they're called white ladies.

D: *Then they don't look as solid as the elves?*

B: Right. Whenever they cast this particular spell, when they get angry with an ordinary human being and they're going to call up the wind, they want the human being to be able to see what the source of the wind is, so they'll know they're trespassing. And the human being will see this large white lady, about, oh, tree-top tall. But they can see through her. She looks like mist. And they'll see her until the wind starts blowing and she's dissipated by the wind. They can't tell anybody about it because people will think they are crazy. And so that's why they're called white ladies.

D: *And she's large where the elves are small?*

B: Well, the elves themselves are small. It's just that when they cast this particular ritual, they have this appearance. But it's not their true appearance.

D: *Oh, this is just an appearance that they project. This would frighten people if they saw something large.* (Yes) *Well, are there other groups of little people?*

B: Yes, there are the field elves. They are related to the white ladies. All elves are related. It's like a large family. They are just different branches of the family who concentrate on certain things. The field elves are the ones that take care of the crops and the ground. To make sure that the dirt is good. And to make sure that the seeds sprout. The ground elves are the ones that some call gnomes. They're the ones that one hears tell of sometimes in the mines. The wood elves live in the woods. They help protect the wildlife from the lord's hunters.

D: *Tell the wildlife to hide and things like that?*

B: Often they're more mischievous than that. They cause the horses to trip and such as that, giving the wildlife time to run away. All of the elves have a mischievous streak in them. Particularly the house elves. The house elves have so much more opportunity to get into mischief than the other elves.

D: *(Laugh) What do they do?*

B: Sometimes they throw a plate across the room. Or they'll slam a door catching a lady's skirt where she's in an awkward position. Sometimes they'll cause something to rise up into the air, but with no visible means of being held.

D: *What are the house elves normally supposed to do?*

B: In a house that is in accord with the Earth mother and respects the elves, the house elves make sure everything works right. Makes sure that your bread rises the way it should. That your coals don't go out in your stove. That your beer or wine does the way it should, when you're making it. And that your cheese firms up well. And that your milk doesn't curdle. But if you get them angry with you, your milk will start curdling, your cheese will stay runny, your bread will not rise, it will turn out flat, and your beer and wine will turn to vinegar.

D: *Then they have good purposes if you are in harmony.*

B: Yes, all of them do.

D: *Then when they do the mischievous things, are they doing that because they're angry or do they just want to play tricks?*

B: Sometimes I think they get bored, and they just want to play tricks. If you're in harmony with them they're going to play tricks anyway. If you're not in harmony they just do everything opposite from the way they should. Like your fire keeps going out in your fireplace, and in the fireplace that you cook in. If they're really being mean, then every morning you'll have to go to somebody else's farm and get a bucket of coals to start your fire. And you know when you make bread you set some aside to put in your next batch of bread so that it will rise. Then the part that you set aside will not rise and it won't make the next loaf rise either. And you'll have to go to someone else who is making bread and ask to borrow part of their dough.

Unless someone has lived in rural areas, they would not know that the "old-timers" still do this. They often do not have yeast to make bread rise, so they use what is called a "starter" that they save from the previous batch to cause the new batch of bread to rise. This custom seems to be very old, yet it is still used in our Ozark hills.

D: *Well, it sounds like they are just like little children wanting to play tricks.*

B: Well, everybody plays tricks to have some fun. It's just that they have to resort to that more often than ordinary people because that's their main way of keeping big people in line, so to speak.

D: *Is there anything you do whenever they begin to make things go bad? Not bad—but when they cause these nuisances. When these things begin to happen, do you do anything to change them back?*

B: Yes. There are many things you do. First you put on some old clothes, and kind of tear them some, and throw ashes over your head, and make a big production of it, weeping and wailing about how sorry you are about having made them angry with you. And you do this long enough to let them know that you really mean it. And then you go and change into clothes for a solemn occasion. That is, if you have extra clothes to change into. If you're poor you just have one set of clothes anyway. Where if you're rich and you have more than one set of clothes, you change into something for a solemn occasion. And you get some baked bread and you break it up into a bowl, and pour some honey over it, and then add milk to it. And set it in a corner that you know they like, as a peace offering. Saying how sorry you were that you offended them, that you'll try not to offend them again. And would they please stay and live there and be friends again.

D: *Does it work?*

B: It's supposed to.

D: *Then they really don't mean any harm. They just do these little mischievous things.*

B: Yes. Unless they see that you're determined not to be in harmony with the Earth mother. Then they'll get angry with you and do things to try to make you straighten up.

D: *Do they ever do anything to try to hurt you?*

B: Well, yes, sometimes. Like when they throw a plate across the room, if you happen to be in the way it smashes against you instead of the wall.

D: *I wondered if they were ever* allowed *to do anything deliberately to hurt human beings.*

B: They will do whatever they like.

D: *They don't have any rules that govern them?*

B: They can't cause anybody to lose their life. For example, one thing that the elves do not like is hunters, if he's hunting for sport. If he's hunting to provide his family with food, they help him. But if it's a rich lord who's just gone out hunting simply because he has nothing better to do, and he just wants to show off his skill, they get angry with him. And they cause his horse to trip over tree roots. Or if the horse is shod, they will cause the horse to throw a shoe. Or the hunter's aim will be off. Or they'll cause his bowstring to be damp and not tight enough to shoot well. Various things they'll do.

D: *Would they cause him injury?*

B: It depends. If he gets violently angry and decides that he's going to hunt anyway, then they might cause him to twist his ankle or something like that, to where he can't pursue the game.

D: *Then they can't really hurt someone in a bad way.*

B: Not for bad reasons, no. But like in that case, if it's for a good reason, they can.

D: *But they're not allowed to hurt someone bad enough that they would be permanently disabled, or they would die.* (No) *Then they do have* some *rules. Do all of these elves look alike?*

B: They dress differently according to where they live, because they must dress to blend in. But if you took their clothes off, they'd look alike.

D: *Do you mean, like the ones in the fields wear green or what?*

B: Yeah. The ones in the woods wear brown mostly. And the field elves usually wear green and gold combinations. The white ladies usually wear gray and blues. And the house elves, they're the most mischievous of the lot, and the house elves like to wear bright red.

D: *(Laugh) Bright red. You can surely see them then.*

B: Only if you pierce their spells of protection.

D: *I was thinking that red would be very noticeable.*

B: Well, I think they think that since they're in the house it doesn't matter what colors they wear. And they like bright colors, all of them.

D: *The gnomes that live in the ground, would they wear dark colors?*

B: The ground elves, I'm not sure what colors they wear. I think they'd think it doesn't matter since they live in the dark anyway. But I think that they wear different colors but they're always dark. Dark red, dark blue, black, dark gray. The ground elves wear all these dark colors except for their hats. Their hats are always a bright color.

D: *All the elves have bright hats?* (Yes) *So no matter what clothes they wear their hats will always be different?*

B: Yes, and it must not be a color that goes with the other clothes. It always has to be a different color. For example, a wood elf that's wearing clothes of brown and russet and maroon may have a bright purple hat.

D: *Is that for a reason?*

B: Vanity, I think.

D: *(Chuckle)* They *have vanity, too, then.*

B: Oh, yes. But don't tell them I told you so. They might get angry with me.

D: *(I laughed.) Are there any other groups of little people besides the elves and the white ladies?*

B: It is said there are others who live in other parts of the world, because there are little people all over the world. I was just telling you the ones that live around here. They're the ones that I know of. Oh, there is one group that I forgot to mention. Not out of disrespect to the group, but simply because they are so well hidden. The water sprites. They are another type of elf, but they live in the water. They keep the water clean and pure for drinking. And they make sure that the fish and the plants and the water are taken care of. If you're going through the woods, and you've angered either them or the wood elves—they usually work together with the wood elves—and you stop at a stream to get a drink, suddenly the stream will be muddy and not fit to drink. Sometimes they help the house elves, too. If someone in the household is not doing like they should, then their drinking water is always brackish.

D: *Only their water?*

B: Yes. Unless they've done something to really anger them, and then they cause all water in the house to not be good. So that the people in the house, the big people, you and I, will start complaining and bring pressure on this other person to do right.

D: *To stop angering the elves.* (Yes) *What do the water sprites look like?*

B: It's hard to describe them. They're almost clear. They look like the other elves, except they're longer limbed. The water sprites have blond hair. And for clothing they wear water plants woven together into clothes.

D: *If they have blond hair, then the elves have dark?*

B: They usually have brown hair, sometimes black. Or gray if they're old. The water sprites are so blond it's almost white.

D: *And you said you can almost see through them because they're clear?* (Yes) *Well, in our stories there's one group called "fairies." And they're supposed to have wings. Do you have anything like that?*

B: I've not seen any. But I've heard tell from some of the elves of their cousins, the fays. That they're very small and they live amongst fields of flowers. And they do fly.

D: *These must be the ones I've heard of. They say they have wings. Do they look different or do you know?*

B: I don't know. I've never seen any. I just know that they're smaller than the elves.

D: *All right. You mentioned a while ago the unicorns.* (Yes) *I've heard of that animal. Many people think it might have been real.*

B: It is. The little people help protect it, because the men, the lords and such are always trying to get a unicorn's head for a trophy.

D: *I wouldn't like that idea.* (No) *Have you ever seen a real unicorn?*

B: Yes. Once. It's very beautiful.

D: *Then they are a real, physical animal?*

B: Yes. But as I mentioned earlier, you have to do a spell to pierce their veils of protection, so that you can see them.

D: *Then they're not visible to everybody.* (No) *I thought maybe they were a real animal and they were hidden and protected.*

B: They *are* a real animal. And they have veils of protection that the little people cast about them to hide them. The little people help protect them.

D: *Is there a special reason?*

B: The unicorn is a magical animal. And the Earth would not be the same without them. Probably a part of the Earth spirit would die if there were not unicorns here.

D: *What kind of magic do they do?*

B: It's hard to say. It's undisciplined magic. It's always for good but it's so undisciplined that you never can tell what form it's going to take. It can be done for a particular purpose, but you don't know how it's going to happen, or just how the final results are going to be.

D: *The other groups you were talking about had certain duties. The unicorn's magic isn't that way?* (No) *What did the unicorn look like that you saw?*

B: Well, on the tapestries they're always portrayed as being white. But it's not white. It's more like ... ahh, have you ever seen the inside of a clam shell?

D: *Kind of a gray?*

B: No, no, no, it's not gray. It's like a silvery color with all the rainbow colors in it. Or like opal or mother-of-pearl.

D: *Oh, yes, I know what you mean. That's beautiful.*

B: Well, that's the color the unicorn was. It was kind of a silver color with the colors of the rainbow in it. Kind of what you see in mother-of-pearl. And it had large dark blue eyes. And the horn was the way it's portrayed basically. It's a spiraled horn, also looking like mother-of-pearl. But what you don't see in the tapestries is that the spiral part has a line of silver in it.

D: *Along the spiral.*

B: Yes. And there's curly hair from the chin like a goat's goatee. There's a flowing mane. And the hooves are indeed cloven.

D: *They are?* (Yes) *Because I've heard they look like a horse.*

B: They look like a horse with cloven hooves.

D: *Are they as large as a horse?*

B: I've only seen one. I don't know if they're all the same size or not. It was the size of a pony. It wasn't as large as a warhorse. And as it had hair on its chin, it also had hair like that above the hooves on the back side of the leg. And the tail, it was like half-ass' tail and half-horse's tail. It went from the body being bare like an ass' tail. And then the bottom half was in the curly hair. You know, flowing like a horse's tail but curly.

D: *About half and half.* (Yes) *Was the mane curly or straight?*

B: I think it was probably curly. It looked wavy because it was so long.

D: Longer than a horse's? (Yes) *How long was the horn?*

B: (Pause as though thinking.) The horn was long enough to reach from my hips to the ground. The length of my leg. It was very sharp.

D: Oh, that would be much longer than I thought it would be. I've always thought they were like, oh, as long as from your hand to your elbow.

B: (Emphatic) No, no, they're very long.

D: Very long. It would be like the whole length of your arm then or the whole length of your leg?

B: It is the length of my leg. And it was very sharp and slender, but very strong. You can't break them.

D: Hmmm, it seems like the unicorn would have difficulty getting in and out of places, trees and things, with something that long.

B: That's why unicorns are friends with the wood elves.

D: If it was the size of a pony, that would be almost the length of the body, wouldn't it?

B: The length of the horn is very close to the length from the withers to the nose.

D: That would be long. The pictures I've seen show it much shorter.

B: Yes, the tapestries have the horn too short. But then usually things are distorted on the tapestries because they have to fit a lot in.

D: I wonder if the people who make the tapestries have actually seen one.

B: They're just going by old pictures drawn by monks who drew it from old pictures which were drawn from old pictures which were drawn from vague memories of someone who accidently saw one.

D: Well, when you saw one, was it in the woods?

B: No, it was in the field close to the edge of the woods.

D: And it didn't try to run?

B: Not immediately, because it knew that I try to be in harmony with the Earth mother. It stood and looked at me, long enough for me to look at it and admire its beauty. Then it turned and ran into the woods. And left a twinkling in the air afterwards.

D: *What do you mean?*

B: The way stars twinkle.

D: *Oh, that sounds lovely.*

B: And it faded almost immediately. But it was there for a moment.

D: *Oh, that must have been a very beautiful sight.*

B: It was.

D: *But you said they are magical animals.* (Yes) *Have you been taught how to use this magic?*

B: Humans cannot use this magic. It is possessed by the unicorn only, and the unicorn uses it as it wishes. It will accept advice from the little people, but then in the end it makes its own decision as to what it's going to do with its magic, in various situations.

D: *It's very highly intelligent then.*

B: Yes, but then all the animals are. More than what humans give them credit for.

D: *Then if you were in harmony with the Earth, could you talk to the unicorn and ask it to use its magic to help you?*

B: Yes. But then you would never know what form it would take. Because the unicorn's magic is always unpredictable.

D: *You mean it can't control its magic itself?*

B: *It* can. It's just that you don't know what direction it's going to go, because the unicorn is not a human. And so, it does not think like a human, it thinks like a unicorn.

D: *It thinks more like an animal?*

B: It thinks like a unicorn. (She was getting aggravated with my lack of understanding.)

D: *(Chuckle) I'm trying to put it into the category of an animal, I guess.*

B: It's a unicorn.

D: *(Laugh) Okay. Then the magic could turn out the wrong way?*

B: No, it's just that you never know what's going to happen in between initiating the magic and the results. And the results will be the results that you asked for. It may not necessarily be what you anticipated. Because if you word your question wrong, you get the wrong results.

D: *I think I know what you mean. You will get it but it may not be exactly what you want, because of the way that you say it.* (Yes) *But it wouldn't necessarily be something bad though.*

B: No, not deliberately bad.

D: *But it could turn out to be not what you want at all.* (Yes) *I think I understand. It still has a little mischievous streak, too, like the elves.*

B: Yes, but it's not as deliberate with it as the elves are. It's trying to help. If it likes you it will try to help. It's just that being a different creature, it thinks differently. And so, what happens often seems unpredictable from our point of view.

D: *Yes, I can see that. We think one way and we think everything else should think the same way.* (Yes) *Our kind of logic.*

B: It doesn't work that way.

D: *This was the main thing you went to Grendell for, to find out about the rainbow?* (Yes) *Is she the one who also knows about the gems?*

B: I think she does. I'll ask her.

D: *Because I asked you about the gems one time and you said you hadn't learned that yet.*

B: Yes, I've learned a little bit of it.

D: *Can you share with me what you have learned?*

B: Yes. The gems can be used in certain rituals to emphasize certain effects. For example, gems that are red like rubies can be used to emphasize the passionate feelings, love, hate, jealousy. Gems that are pink in color, and I was told the name of one, but I can't remember it. It was a long name, difficult to pronounce. They're pink in color, and can be used for loyalty, like if you want someone you love to be loyal to you. Gems that are green can be used for friendship and for growing. You know, for anything green and growing. And it can also be used for friendship. Gems that are blue, like sapphires, can be used for developing the mind part of the spirit. Because the gems that are purple, you use for developing the spirit part of the spirit. There are some gems that are bad luck, like diamonds.

D: *They're white or clear.*

B: Yes, they're clear. And they can be bad luck because they're not definitely oriented to a particular vibration of a particular color, giving them that color's influence.

D: *That's interesting because in my time when someone marries, they always give a diamond.*

B: How well do these marriages work out?

D: *Well, this is the custom for everyone to give a diamond to the woman.*

B: Yes. And I bet they have a bad marriage, too.

D: *Well, they must wear that diamond all of their life after that. Strange. They have not realized that this is the meaning for that stone.*

B: And stones that are black are for seeking the truth, or for initiating change.

D: *They're not bad luck then.* (No) *Only the diamond is bad luck?*

B: Or other gems that are clear. Because they can attract either bad or good forces. Now the diamond can be a powerful stone of good luck if you purify it and set it for good.

D: *In our time it's a very expensive stone. Maybe that's why they use it for marriages.*

B: I don't understand. How do you mean? Using stones for marriages?

D: *Well, when they have the ceremony to marry.* (Yes) *The diamond is in a ring. And it is given to the woman in the ceremony.*

B: Is it? I didn't know diamonds came big enough to be carved into a ring.

D: *Would you like to see mine?* (Yes) *All right. Here ... open your eyes and look at my hand. (She did so.)*

B: Oh! *Set* into a ring.

D: *Yes. You thought I meant the* whole *ring?*

B: Yes. Like gold is made into rings. Or silver, like yours.

D: *Yes. And this is what is given to a woman when they are married. It is* in *the ring.*

190

B: Perhaps the gemsmith that sets it in the ring purifies it and sets it for good for you, to bring power to your marriage.

D: *This tells everyone that a woman is married, by wearing a ring like that.*

B: I see. Like being betrothed.

D: *Yes. Would you like to see my other ring and tell me what you think of it. (I have a ring shaped like a pentacle which is made out of turquoise and surrounded by seven little silver balls. I had her open her eyes again and directed her attention to my right hand.) This hand.*

B: That is a ring of good luck. The silver is a good metal and it has a blue stone in it. That's good for developing the mental part of your spiritual development.

D: *Is that a pentagram?*

B: It's a pentagram without the circle. But it's enclosed by seven knobs of silver. Seven's a lucky number. So, it's as if it had a circle around it. That's a good ring to wear. It's a good amulet.

D: *That's what I wear it for. I never take it off.*

B: That's good.

D: *Is silver a good metal?*

B: (She had closed her eyes again.) Yes. Silver is also good for developing your ability to contact the higher planes. And the combination of silver plus the blue stone is a good combination.

D: *Then it should bring me good luck.*

B: Yes. Blue stones plus gold is good, too.

D: *But the other ring is just what women wear to show they are married. It is just like a symbol in our time.*

B: Yes, I see.

D: *Do they wear anything in your time to show that they are married?*

B: Yes. A bracelet.

D: *Of gold, silver, or what?*

B: Usually copper and set with stones. Gold and silver are very hard to get. And they usually put some kind of lacquer on it so that the copper will not tarnish.

D: *I see. And do even the poor people wear a bracelet?*

B: The very, very poor usually don't. But the various smiths, the iron smith and the blacksmith and such as that, and the tradesmen and such, on up do.

D: *It's the same in our time. If someone was very poor, they wouldn't be able to get the diamond either. They might just wear a plain gold ring. (Yes) It's just different customs. (Yes) What did you say the black stones were for?*

B: For truth-seeking and for initiating change. Black can also be used for protection. But a different sort of protection. Blue and purple can be used to surround your bodily essence with a protective essence that will repel evil and harm. But the type of protection that the black stone offers is being able to cut through the heart of things and see the truth of everything. And know whether or not something is going to cause you harm.

D: *Do you have any yellow stones, or anything that color?*

B: No. We have gold, that's yellow.

D: *Let's see, what other colors would there be?*

B: We have purple, blue, green, red, black and clear.

D: *With so many different stones, it's hard to know which one to wear.*

B: You wear different stones according to what situations you think you might be in.

D: *Or which stones to carry. A lot of times they're not in jewelry, are they?*

B: No, you'd wear them by putting them in a small pouch and wearing them about your neck.

D: *Because it's expensive to have them put into jewelry. (Yes) You told me before that sometimes the rich people, the lords and the ladies, wear jewelry and don't even know what it means.*

B: Yes. They just wear it to look pretty, and they often have several stones on all at once.

D: *That's the way it is in my time, too. People just wear it because it's pretty. They don't know what it means. But even if they don't know what it means, and wear these different things, will it still serve the same purpose?*

B: I don't think so. Because a stone has to know that you know that it's special for it to work good. And if you're just wearing all these different stones because they look pretty many times their essences can collide with each other, and they won't do you any good then.

D: *Then their magic won't work unless you know that the magic is there.*

B: Yes, you have to turn on the magic with your mind.

D: *Then the people just wearing it wouldn't be protected or draw passion or anything like that unless they knew that these stones would do those things.* (Yes) *Very interesting. Has Grendell told you anything else about the rainbow, and what it would do?*

B: You can use the rainbow for sealing amulets. There are several steps in making an amulet. First you must decide what the amulet is to be used for. And then if you have the materials you make the right parchment for it. But if not, that is all right. And then you go out and find a stone to go with your amulet, that will give the amulet the power it needs. And the parchment and the stone will be put in a pouch and sealed with a ritual so its power is concentrated and magnified so it will spread its influence all over, so it will do what it's supposed to do. And one very powerful way of sealing an amulet is with the use of a rainbow.

D: *Does it have to be an actual rainbow?* (Yes) *Sometimes you never know when a rainbow is going to appear.*

B: You do if you know where to look.

D: *What is the parchment for?*

B: You write symbols on the parchment that mean particular things to help draw and concentrate certain powers to your amulet for certain things. If you have an amulet to make money, you have a parchment that has symbols on it that work well with Jupiter.

D: *Why, because Jupiter is associated with money?*

B: Yes. He's also known by other names. And since you'll be using the parchment to bring the attention of certain deities to your amulet, you try to make the amulet on the day that deity is in power. And you try to do the majority of your work on that day. Until it comes time to seal it. And if it's in the spring or fall of the year, where it's raining a lot, and you have a chance of coming across a rainbow, then you seal it with a rainbow rather than sealing it on the day of the deity.

D: *You said Jupiter has many other different names. Do they all have different names?* (Yes) *What other names is Jupiter known by?*

B: Oh ... I'm drawing this from legends, you understand.

D: *Yes. I want to learn the legends if I can.*

B: Jupiter is also known as Zeus and Thor and there's another name that I can't pronounce since I'm always forgetting it. Oh, well. And so, the different deities have different names. I think it's because they're known all over. And so different people have different names for them.

D: *That makes sense.*

B: I think that's the reason why I can't pronounce that one. I never could remember it.

D: *(Laugh) Well, what would be Jupiter's day if you wanted to do the amulet for money?*

B: It depends on who you know Jupiter by. Some people associate Jupiter with Thor, and they would do it on Thursday. But here most of us say Jupiter is the same as Odin, and we do it on Wednesday.

D: *Then you take the parchment with the symbols on it, and the amulet and the stone and, what do you do?*

B: What you do is that on the appropriate day, and it's good if you can have the right phase of the moon, too, but, you know, you can only wait so long to have an amulet done. And you wait till nighttime. And preferably by midnight you go out to where you're in the direct light of the moon. And you take the parchment and the stone, and there's a certain way that you can fold the parchment around the stone, so that the stone is contained within the parchment and protected. And this is the part you can also do with the rainbow. But if there's not a rainbow around, you do it like this. And you seal it then, so to speak, and depending on what kind of amulet it is depends on how you're going to seal it. And then you put it in this pouch and draw this pouch closed. And then it is ready for the wearer to wear, after you have blessed the pouch.

D: *In my way of thinking, when you seal it it means it can't be opened again. Is that what you mean?*

B: Well, you seal it with magic.

D: *Okay. Not actually sealing it then.*

B: Sometimes you do. It depends upon what kind of amulet it is. You can seal it with wax, but not always. But always you do seal it with magic. So that it's tuned for a certain purpose and that purpose only. And it can't be reopened and retuned for another purpose. And the longer you use an amulet the more powerful it gets.

D: *The magic doesn't wear out, in other words.*

B: No, the more you use it the stronger it gets. And when you start passing the amulet down from parent to child, it just keeps gathering more and more power.

D: *But when you're doing all this, do you have any ritual or anything that you do or say?*

B: It depends upon what kind of amulet you're making. There're rituals for all of them.

D: *Would you be allowed to give me those rituals and those symbols sometime?*

B: I can't give you the symbols because I don't know them myself. I don't read or write, you see. But there are a couple that do. And they're the ones who draw the symbols for us.

D: *Oh, they draw them on the parchments?*

B: Yes. And I can tell you what you do afterwards, after you get that parchment with the symbols on it.

D: *I wondered if you saw them draw it, if you could copy it for me.*

B: No. But I'm thinking that if there are some of us still around in your world, that they would still have the symbols.

D: *There might be. There are people that believe the same things.*

B: Because we've been very careful to pass these symbols down, to make sure we don't lose them.

D: *I could show you some of the symbols we have now, and you could tell me if they are the same, because you would know what they look like.* (Yes) *That might be one way to do it. Then you could tell me if they were wrong, too.*

B: I don't know if I could tell you if they were wrong. I might tell you if they don't look right.

D: *Yes, if they're not the same as you know. That would be something we could talk about the next time we meet.* (Yes) *I'm very interested in these stories. And then you could tell me the rituals that you do whenever you do the sealing of the amulets.*

B: Yes, I can tell you that.

D: *And I can have the symbols drawn and show them to you and see if they are the same.* (Yes) *Maybe you can tell me on what day is the best for different things, too.*

B: I can try.

D: *I'm very interested in passing these along, because some of the knowledge might have been lost.*

B: Perhaps.

(Subject brought forward.)

Chapter 9
Signs and Symbols
(Recorded June 10, 1986)

Used keyword and counted her back to the lifetime of Astelle.

D: We've gone back to the time that Astelle lived. What are you doing?

B: I'm sitting under an oak tree. For discipline of the mind, there's a certain way of calming your thoughts. And I needed to get away from the house for a while and calm my thoughts.

D: Why, was something going on that you needed to get away from?

B: (Aggravated) Just what usually goes on. I was just tired of it. The Lady Joslyn was being her normal self, and the cook was being her normal self. Roff was in a bad mood. (Sigh) And everything was so noisy. I just wanted some quiet.

D: And you went out to the grove of oak trees? (Yes) What is the method you use to calm your mind? I'd like to try it sometime.

B: Different ways work better for different people. And the way that I use is, I get comfortable and I close my eyes. And I imagine that there is a unicorn standing beside me. I like unicorns. And I pretend there is a rainbow before me. And I get on the unicorn and we walk to the base of the rainbow. I'm riding the unicorn, and the unicorn keeps walking up the rainbow. And we follow it up, up, up and over. And when the rainbow comes back down, it comes down to whatever my heart's desires are. And I imagine all sorts of wonderful things.

D: *Oh, that's a beautiful mental picture. And whatever you want is there. Do you use this often for meditation?*

B: Yes. It's also a way of traveling, too.

D: *Traveling where?*

B: Anywhere you want to go.

D: *You mean when you come back down on the other side, you would be where you want to be?*

B: Yes. Not in your physical body, but in your mental body.

D: *Where would you normally like to travel to?*

B: It depends. I go different places. This time, though, I wanted some place that was peaceful and quiet and comfortable. And so when I came down at the end of the rainbow, there was a green pasture with some sheep. And there was a stream, and I was dangling my feet in the stream so they would cool off. And all I heard was the wind and the birds singing.

D: *A very peaceful scene. Is that what you're imagining now as you listen to me? (Yes) That's very nice. Well, you know I've spoken to you before. (Yes) And you were telling me some information when I had to leave. And there were some more questions I wanted to ask. Is it all right if I ask them? (Yes) Okay. One of the things I wanted to know was about the rainbow for meditations. And now you've told me that.*

B: That's one way of using the rainbow.

D: *Is there another way?*

B: Yes. There are different ways of using the rainbow. One way that some people use is ... well, first I'll tell you. In the house the grand staircase in the main hallway, the bottom two or three steps is in the shape of the outside edge of the moon. A partial circle. They are curved. What some people like to do is imagine that the rainbow is a curved staircase. And each color is a different stairstep. And they imagine they are taking each step up to the top of this curved staircase. And when they get to the top whatever they want or whatever they are imagining will be there. That does not work very well with me, but it is one way of doing it.

D: *Wouldn't there be more steps than there are colors?*

B: There are colors in all ways.

D: *I thought there are only about, oh, five or six colors in the rainbow.*

B: Well, it depends. If you use different shades of the colors, that would make more steps. As you float from one color to the other, there are many shades in between each color.

D: *Yes, I can see that now. But it would just go* up, *and it would be at the top of the stairs.* (Yes) *Are there other ways it could be used?*

B: Yes. I'm trying to think of ways that I've heard of but I've never used because they don't work well with me. I think some imagine that they are flying through the rainbow the way a bird would. But I'm not sure how they'd do it, so I really don't know. All I know is that's the way they described it. I don't really know how it works.

D: *Did Grendell teach you these methods?*

B: No. I'd heard about the stairstep method, and I asked her about it. And she said that's what worked for that person because that's what they could picture. And she told me it does well to imagine something that you liked real well. And imagine it in such a way to where you can accomplish something in your imagining. And somehow use a rainbow in your imagining. And I thought that, to myself, about how well I like unicorns. So that's how I came up with riding a unicorn over the rainbow. And when I get to the end, then whatever I want is there.

D: *That sounds like a very good method. I could picture that very easily. But everybody has different things that they can imagine.* (Yes) *And that's a very peaceful, happy thing to imagine to make you feel good.* (Yes) *The last time I was talking to you, you were talking about how you made amulets.* (Yes) *And you took different stones and you said they would take a piece of parchment.* (Yes) *And write a symbol on the parchment. I want to see if I got this right. And then they would wrap the parchment around the stone. And you put it in a little pouch or something?*

B: Yes. And sometimes they put more than one symbol on the parchment.

D: *And you carry this on your body somewhere?* (Yes) *We were talking about these symbols when I had to leave last time.* (Yes) *I think you were talking about the one for Jupiter that you use for money. That was the only one that you told me.* (Yes) *Why would you use more than one symbol?*

B: Sometimes, if I understand this right, there are symbols that stand for things like prosperity, happiness, love and such as that. But each one of these things have different aspects, so you use other symbols to emphasize the aspects you want to bring forth.

D: *I thought you had to concentrate on just one thing at a time.*

B: Well, you can combine things and use them like that.

D: *You said it was important that you use them on a certain day of the week?*

B: Yes. Jupiter would be on Thursday or Wednesday. Wednesday, if you were wanting riches, for example. You can get riches by coming across it miraculously. Or you can get riches by working for it, and money coming to you very, very easily. Or you can get riches by borrowing some money from a nobleman and not pay him back. The way some of the highwaymen do. *(I laughed.)* And so on the amulet you would put the symbol for Jupiter, for riches. And then you would temper it by putting another symbol down, to help guide the amulet toward the type of riches you want. And this you get at concentration. But the common person that you give amulets to, the peasants and such, are not always good at concentration.

D: *What other symbols would you use with Jupiter?*

B: With Jupiter, if you want riches by working for them and money coming at you from everywhere, for the work that you do, you would also use the symbol for the sun, also known as Apollo. Because that's a symbol for craftsmanship and skill as well as luck.

D: *And you would mark them both on the same parchment?*

B: Yes. And there's usually an outline drawn around to contain the power for a particular purpose.

D: *And then you would still do this on a Wednesday if you use both of those symbols?*

B: Since you're using both symbols you could do it on a Wednesday or a Sunday, depending on which symbol you are wanting to be slightly stronger.

D: *I'm trying to remember what you told me last time. You seal the amulet on those days to make it more powerful. Is that right?*

B: You seal it to help direct the power through the amulet. Because if you don't seal it, the powers may dissipate trying to affect everything, rather than just what they're supposed to affect.

D: *It directs it then.*

B: Right. It also helps protect it from outside influences.

D: *I think you said you had some kind of a ritual. Is it the same ritual on every amulet?*

B: I don't think so. It doesn't seem like it. The ones that I've seen made, it depends on what the amulet is for as to how the ritual goes. The purification part of the ritual is always the same. But then there's differences in the rest of the ritual depending on what kind of amulet it is.

D: *What is the purification part?*

B: For purification, you get the amulet and you surround it with a circle of ashes from the yew tree. And then within the circle you sprinkle salt in the shape of a five-pointed star. And then you sprinkle water over it in the four directions. And meanwhile you are saying the appropriate words. And after you've got everything together, then you let it sit like that for a particular period of time. There are different lengths of time for different amulets.

D: *You mean the amulet is in the middle of this circle.*

B: And star, yes. And it usually has to sit until a certain day, so that when the amulet is first exposed to the world, so to speak, or when you give it to the owner, it's on a day that's lucky for the amulet.

D: *Would it be for a week or longer?*

B: Usually a week or less. Three days is good. But if it happens to be slightly longer, that's all right. For example, an amulet for money, the purification would last six days. You do it a number that is lucky for the amulet. An amulet for learning things, for knowledge, you would do it either five or seven days, depending on whether you're meaning mental or spiritual knowledge. An amulet for love you would do either three or nine days, depending on how strong you want to make the amulet. And it goes on like that.

D: *But they have certain words that they use when they're doing this?*

B: Yes. I think they go by feel mostly when it comes to the words, as to which words would be appropriate. But usually they chant over the amulet during the end part of the purification. That helps direct the amulet.

D: *Do they do the sealing at the end or at the beginning?*

B: The sealing is done partially at the beginning when you draw the amulet and then it's completed by the purification. And then when you chant the words over it, it activates the amulet and completes the sealing.

D: *Which would be the symbol for love?*

B: The symbol for love. I do know that symbol. Usually the Horns of the Goddess is used for love. Another face of the goddess is also the morning star or the evening star. In amulets done for love it is very good to start out on a Friday, which is the day ruled by love. And you can either complete the sealing of the amulet the following Sunday or the Sunday after that. That's the right number of days, and you also have the luck of the sun behind it, too.

D: *Then it can get very complicated, can't it?*

B: Yes, it can.

D: *Because I know you said the moon was also the Horns of the Goddess.* (Yes) *Let's see, maybe it would make it easier if I went down the week and asked you which day represents which sign.*

B: I'll try.

D: *Okay. I'm trying to understand this. Let's see, you said Sunday would be Apollo?* (Yes) *What would Monday be?*

B: The moon.

D: *Tuesday?*

B: Mars. Tuesday is for contests and fights and anything like that.

D: *And Wednesday you said is Jupiter?*

B: Jupiter.

D: *And what about Thursday?*

B: You hear different things about Thursday. Some say Jupiter's brother, and some say his nephew for Thursday.

D: *Who is his nephew?*

B: I don't know the name.

D: *Well, what kind of powers would his nephew have on that day?*

B: Hmmm, communication. It has been said that the Romans have called him Mercury.

D: *What about Friday?*

B: The Horns of the Goddess.

D: *Then she has two days. You said the moon is on Monday?* (Yes) *And also Friday?* (Yes) *She has two days of the week, but like you said, she has many faces. This is why?*

B: Yes. It's possible to link all the days of the week to her if one really wanted to, because she is everywhere.

D: *They're just different phases of her, I suppose. Different ways of looking at her.*

B: You understand.

D: *Then Saturday?*

B: Saturday is for Kronos.* Jupiter's father. He has to do with ancient knowledge, history and time.

Dictionary: Cronus: In Greek mythology, a Titan who overthrew his father, Uranus, and was himself overthrown by his son Zeus; identified by the Romans with Saturn. Also spelt Cronos.

D: *So that's what you would use these different days for, according to who they are named after, or who they represent?* (Yes) *You said you have seen many of these symbols, haven't you?*

B: A few of them, yes.

D: *You know, I told you I would bring some symbols and have you look at them and see if you could recognize any of them. (Yes) Would you do that for me? (Yes) Because I don't know if they are the same. We may have changed them.*

I had brought an astrological calendar that had all the symbols of the planets and the zodiac in large print on the cover. I handed her the calendar.

D: Let me see if you can move your hand out. I want to give you a piece of parchment here.

B: That's a very thick piece.

D: Yes. But I want you to open your eyes and look at the top. Up here.

I directed her to look at the signs and not at the picture on the cover.

D: There are some symbols at the top and they go down the side.

B: (She seemed fascinated with it.) Yes.

D: See if any of those look familiar to you.

B: Some of them do. (She was studying them, and she began at the end of the first row, by pointing at the symbol.) This is for the sun. This is the Horns of the Goddess. (The moon.) This is for Monday. This is for Friday. (Mercury)

D: That third one is for Friday? (Yes) All right.

B: This is for Sunday. (Venus) This is a variation on the one for Friday, but we usually put the horns on it to honor the goddess.

D: Then the one next to it is a variation? (Yes) Would that be used for any certain day?

B: It's also used for Friday. Some other groups use it for Friday. But in our group, we do it like this to honor the goddess.

D: With the horns. (Yes) What about the next one to it? Does that look familiar? (No) (I don't know what that one stands for either.) That is just two lines crossing, isn't it?

B: Yes. It could be used to represent a crossroads. Also, it could represent the four directions. When you honor the four directions, when you need the power of nature behind your work.

D: *All right. But it's not a symbol that you would use with the others.*

B: Not that I know of. I'm just saying what it looks like it could be used for.

D: *Now there's the next one. Does that look familiar?*

B: That looks like a symbol that could be used for Tuesday.

D: *It's like an arrow, isn't it?* (Yes) *All right. Then the one below it.*

B: All right. This symbol and this symbol. (Jupiter and Saturn) These two symbols I recognize. I sometimes get them confused because they look similar to me. Let me see if I can make sure I tell you correctly. I don't want to tell you incorrectly. (Pause)

D: *Because I feel our meanings could have changed over the years.*

B: Yes. These two symbols, one is for Kronos, and the other is for Jupiter. And I'm trying to remember which is which. I feel that this one is for Kronos and this one is for Jupiter. (She might have had them backwards. I don't remember and the tape does not indicate.) This one is for Saturn. (She was pointing to the symbol for Neptune.)

D: *Saturn? (She had not mentioned that before.)*

B: Yes. Saturday.

D: *Let me see. Didn't you say that Kronos was on Saturday?*

B: Yes, Kronos is also on Saturday.

D: *There's two that can be used for Saturday?*

B: Yes. Kronos can also be used on Wednesday along with Jupiter.

D: *Because of the relationship there?* (Yes) *But this one is called "Saturn"? What is that used for?*

B: This one is called Saturn. Some also say that it's for Neptune because of the trine. And it is used for … let me think. (Pause) Neptune and Saturn are used for things having to do with hidden wisdom.

D: *All right. Some of these you may not recognize. You're doing real well. Then there's one below that. (Uranus)*

B: I've seen that on some amulets every once and a while, but I don't know the meaning of it. It's not used very often. I do not know this one. (She indicated Pluto.)

D: *All right. Now the ones below. (The signs of the zodiac.) Do they look familiar? They are not the symbols for the days. They are different symbols.*

B: Yes, they are symbols for the seasons of the year, for the months.

D: *Let's see if you know them as the same as I know them.*

B: Well, I can tell you how it appears to me. These symbols here is for the growing of spring. These first three. (Aries, Taurus and Gemini.)

D: *Do you have any names for those, or do you just use the symbol?*

B: I think there are names for them, but I can't remember them. And this one is the beginning of summer. (Cancer) And these are also for summer.

D: *Those next three? (Cancer, Leo, Virgo)*

B: Yes. They look to be in order to me. Because here's the ones for winter. And there's the ones for fall. (She indicated the correct ones.)

D: *Then there's three for each one. Do you use those symbols for anything?*

B: Sometimes when we're in the grove of trees doing rituals, we will draw them upon the ground. Sometimes we orient them to the directions: north, south, east and west. It depends. If we're celebrating one of the equinoxes or solstices, we use these symbols.

D: *You would use all three?*

B: It depends on what's going on.

D: *Well, it looks like the symbols have not really changed that much, have they?*

B: What you have here is incomplete. There are more symbols.

D: *Are there? Could you draw them for me?*

B: I don't know them well enough to draw, but I have seen them. They are more ornate than this. They are more complicated than this. These are some of the simplest symbols. And there are others that have more lines and loops in them. They're used for calling upon particular spirits. Spirits of protection, spirits of prosperity or what-have-you.

D: *These are the ones that are used in my time. I guess they're the most common.*

B: I suppose.

D: *They haven't really changed very much if you can recognize them.*

B: There are variations on them. Like the variations of these two for the goddess up here. The one with the horns and the one without the horns. (Mercury and Venus) There are variations on these down here as well. (I don't remember which ones she indicated.) But some of them are similar. And so I recognized the ones that were similar.

D: *Which ones have changed the most?*

B: This one is not as ornate as it should be. (Aries) This one is still very similar. (Taurus) This one is not as ornate as it should be. (Gemini) It has changed quite a bit. There are several variations on this one, but they all have similar themes. (Cancer) This one is still very similar.

D: *Let me see. We have names for these. I was trying to see which one that was. That would be the third one in the summer then? (Virgo) (Yes) That is very similar?*

B: Yes. And this one, the first one of autumn (Libra) is still very similar. The second one of autumn is very similar. (Scorpio) The third one in autumn (Sagittarius) we have a couple of variations for.

D: *It looks like an arrow. What is the variation you would have?*

B: Sometimes there is a figure shown holding it rather than just the arrow.

D: *Oh, yes, I've seen that.*

B: And … (She was pointing to Pisces.)

D: *The last one of winter?*

B: Of winter. Sometimes it is shown with fishes.

D: *This one over here that you said had changed quite a bit. That's the third one of spring. (Gemini)*

B: The third one of spring. We use an animal for that one.

D: *An animal? Do you know what animal?*

B: (Pause) I don't remember. And we use an animal for this one as well. (Aries) Sometimes we use an animal for this one, but it's simpler to draw this, for everyone knows that it looks like a bull. (Taurus)

D: *We have animals for those first two, but that third one we usually show two people. (Gemini) But you have an animal?*

B: Yes. I think it's a mythological one. I don't know the name of it.

D: *There are animals representing some of these. This one is an animal in ours. (Leo)*

B: I don't recall seeing an animal for this one.

D: *What do you have for that?*

B: A symbol very similar to this. Those are the basic simple symbols. The more complex ones, I imagine, have been lost or changed.

D: *Yes, those are the ones I would like to have back. Because we probably have lost quite a bit.*

B: No doubt, because of the Christians.

D: *You don't think you could draw those symbols for me?*

B: Nay, I don't think I could. I would feel uncomfortable drawing them without doing the proper rituals with them.

D: *I wouldn't want to do anything to make you uncomfortable.*

B: And we usually do these more ornate, too. But just for teaching the basic symbols, we use symbols similar to these. And when we're using them, we make them more ornate.

D: *They're easier to draw this way. (Yes) See, the picture has the Horns of the Goddess in there, too, doesn't it? (The picture on the calendar showed a crescent moon.)*

B: Yes, I see that.

D: *And it has a woman with all the food. (A woman pouring out food from a cornucopia.)*

B: Yes, the harvest time.

D: *Yes, that's what it's supposed to represent. Well, we still have these symbols as to those times of the year. So that has not been lost.*

B: That pleases me to hear that. That the Inquisition has not been successful.

D: *These other ones that have to do with Jupiter and Saturn. We have those representing stars in the sky. Do you also have that?*

B: (Emphatic) No! The stars are the stars.

D: *Like they gave a name to a certain star up there and they say that is Jupiter.*

B: That is true. But I think the alchemists deal with that.

D: *Then you are more or less dealing with the name of the deity or the god?*

B: Yes. With the power behind it.

I had her close her eyes again, and I took the calendar away.

D: *I want to thank you. That was a lot of information there. And I'm very pleased to see that it has not really changed a lot. You know the stars are up there and sometimes they say they form patterns in the sky. (Yes) And they have given them some of these same names. (Yes) You mentioned the alchemists. What do the alchemists do?*

B: I'm not sure. There are rumors. From what I can understand alchemists are men trying to find what we have. But they don't want to get in trouble with the church and they don't know where to look. And so they keep looking under every rock and stone trying to find the powers that we use.

D: *In material things.*

B: Yes. And some of them realize there must be some spiritual development, but they don't know how to go about it.

D: *It would be so much easier if they could just ask one of you, wouldn't it?*

B: Yes, but the Inquisition prevents that.

D: *We have heard the tale that alchemists tried to turn ordinary things into gold. Would this be a tale you have heard?*

B: Some have done it.

D: *(Surprised) Have they been able to? (Yes) Oh, we have always heard that it was just a tale. That they never really were able to do it.*

B: Some have done it.

D: *It would be very difficult, wouldn't it?*

B: At first when you don't know what you're looking for, yes. But after you know what to do, it shouldn't be too difficult, I would think. As long as you have a good bellows on hand to make the fire hot.

D: *Have you heard how they were able to do this?*

B: They take different things and mix it together into a powder. And they take something made out of lead and rub the powder on it. And when they heat it in the fire, where the powder has been rubbed it turns to gold. But it must be a very hot fire. The gold is only temporary gold though. After a certain period of time it reverts back.

D: *It doesn't stay that way?* (No) *I've heard the tale that sometimes the alchemist would get very frustrated trying to turn things into gold. And I thought they didn't succeed.*

B: The ones that succeeded are still frustrated.

D: *Because it doesn't stay?* (Yes) *Do you think this is because when it cools it changes?*

B: Perhaps so. It takes quite a while for it to cool. And it starts changing back. And it's very gradual of a change. And you finally know about a day or two afterwards that it has changed back.

D: *Then if they tried to use this gold, like to buy something, it wouldn't work, would it?* (No) *Well, there have been tales that rulers wanted their alchemists to make gold for them so they would have more riches.* (Yes) *But if they are more interested in the material things than the spiritual, maybe this was why it didn't work.*

B: Perhaps. They are always boiling and cooking things and mixing things together, rather than doing any meditating and trying to find their inner spiritual path.

D: *Would your people be interested in doing anything like that?*

B: Like alchemy? No.

D: *That would be a way to get rich though.*

B: But riches are not needed. We have a place to live. We have food to eat. As long as we please the lord of the manor, there's nothing to worry about.

D: There's nothing that you would want then. That's a good way to look at it. But you know there are selfish people out there. Some people want more and more and more. They can never get enough.

B: They are not happy. The Lady Joslyn is like that.

D: Nothing will ever please those kinds of people. (No) You said the lord goes into the tower and you were curious what he did. Do you think he's involved in alchemy? (Yes) You told me once that if your people ever found out what he did that you would share it with me.

B: We fear that it is a combination of alchemy and the dark side of our work. Because whenever he's up in the tower working on his work, sometimes things happen. Like a tree will fall down with no warning and for no reason. And different things like that.

D: Then you think he is doing something he shouldn't be. (Yes) I was curious how he could call on the dark side. I thought your beliefs were all positive.

B: They are. But the universe must balance.

D: And do you think he would do this intentionally or just because he doesn't know.

B: We're not exactly sure, but we think he does it intentionally.

D: You said one time you were going to try to find out. I didn't know how you were going to do this without being discovered.

B: Well, we work on it.

D: Is this a bad thing to try to do the dark side?

B: It depends on the circumstances. If you call upon the dark side for selfish reasons, then, yes, it's a bad thing, because it will rebound on you. But if you call on the dark side to help someone else who is truly in distress, then it works out all right.

Apparently, I wasn't watching it and the tape ran out. I don't know how much was lost before I noticed it and turned it over. When I resumed on the other side, apparently, I was referring to the sound of shutting off the recorder and turning the tape over.

D: ... the atmosphere. I didn't mean to disturb you.

B: Atmosphere? What is atmosphere?

D: Air. Like you have the birds and the trees and the leaves rustling. (Yes) It was just a noise. It had no meaning at all. (Oh) Like dropping something? (Oh) Okay. But I'm curious because I would like to know the warnings, you know, that I won't do things that I shouldn't do. You said that if you use the dark side for the wrong reason, selfish reasons, that it will rebound on you?

B: If you use the dark side to curse somebody, simply because you don't like the way they dress or something like that. And since they haven't done anything against you, whatever curse you put on them will not take hold but will come back and be upon you. Some say two-fold, some say ten-fold.

D: Yes, I've heard that in different words. That whatever you send out comes back. Good or bad.

B: Well, when it's good it takes effect and you don't have to worry about it rebounding on you. And you don't get *that* back. But you get the results back that you were needing.

D: And you said that the dark side could be used for good?

B: It can be used to help somebody. For example, if someone you know has been cheated by somebody else. You can use it on these cheaters to help set things aright.

D: You mean it causes harm on the cheaters?

B: It wouldn't have to.

D: What would you call the opposite? Using things for good? The light side?

B: There's the dark side and the other side is the way or the path. Because that's the path of which we guide our lives.

D: Then you don't use the dark side that often? (No) That's very good. Because the church has given us different ideas.

B: That doesn't surprise me.

D: They have tried to give the wrong ideas of your people for a long time. (Yes) This is why I wanted to learn the truth about what you really *are like.*

B: This is good.

D: *One time you said that you had stories that you told the children that helped you remember the rituals? Do you remember telling me that?* (Yes) *And you said you might tell me some of these stories. It made it easier to remember. Can you tell me some of those?*

B: (Pause) I'm trying to think of some. Sometimes usually the stories are about how the rituals got started.

D: *Can you tell me, share with me?*

B: There's a ritual that we do—I'm trying to think of one that would be good to tell without being too hard of a story, too complicated.

D: *That's all right. I'll try to understand and try to follow you.*

B: All right. There's a ritual we do for love that involves a lot of hand gestures. And the hand gestures really explain and help to remember the basic feeling of the gestures, by telling the story of these two swans. Swans used to be able to talk. And there was this one swan that was real bad to spread gossip about everybody. And since all swans look alike to humans, this one swan was giving the other swans a bad face to the human beings. And the human beings didn't like the swan going around telling everybody else's secrets. Because a swan could walk around and find out things and people really wouldn't notice. Who's going to pay attention to a swan? Swans are very beautiful when they're flying or swimming, but when they're walking, they're somewhat clumsy. And so it got to the point to where life was very difficult for all the swans. They called the council, and the goddess was there also. And they told her the situation and asked the goddess what they should do. And she said she could straighten out the situation to where this one particular swan could not gossip anymore. And at the same time, she would alter people's memories to where they would remember swans as the beautiful creatures they are. And they said, "Well, what will we have to give in return in this? Because something must be given in return so everything will stay balanced." And she says, "I will take your power of speech from you to where you all will be mute." And they said, "We can understand why you're doing this, but then how will we communicate? How can we tell our wives, our husbands, that we love them?" And she says, "I will give you a beautiful way of telling it." And so the goddess did all that she promised. And now in the spring when you watch two swans courting, they're doing it by twining their necks and heads around. It's very beautiful to watch. And we imitate these gestures with our hands in some of our love rituals.

During this story she intertwined her two hands and arms in a gesture imitating the actions of the birds.

D: I can see. Yes, that would be very fitting. That's a very beautiful story, I like that. And this way you would remember the hand motions you had to do with it. (Yes) *Do you have any other stories like that that you could share with me?*

B: Let me think. That's the one I remember the best because it's my favorite.

D: I can see why it would be.

B: There are other stories, but I don't remember all the details. I can't call them to mind good now. But I will be thinking of them, trying to get them in order and ready to tell the next time you come.

D: All right. You said you had some that explained how your religion began? If you call it religion. Your way?

B: Yes. There are several legends about how our religion began. I'd have to think on them too to make sure I don't mix up the details of one into the story of the other.

D: I'm grateful for anything you can tell me.

B: Just be patient with my slow memory.

D: I know when anyone tries to tell a story they can always get things mixed up. (Yes) *That's a very normal thing to do. But I would like to have them then I could pass them on to other people that may have forgotten these stories.*

B: Yes. Make sure it is only those who walk our way.

D: Yes. That's what I'm trying to do, pass all this information down. And they can see how it has changed. (Yes) That's why I wanted to have the information to pass on to them. They may have forgotten these stories.

B: Could be.

D: *Do you want to think on them, or do you want to ask other people?*

B: Both. I'll talk to Grendell about it, too.

D: *Oh, she must have a* long *memory.*

B: Yes, she does.

D: *I would also like to know what plants you use, but you said they have no names.*

B: Yes. I know they have no names. But it seems like this tongue that I'm speaking in seems to have names for some of the plants. I'll see if I can think on that too and connect the right name with the right plant.

D: *Because you know what they look like. (Yes) We may have different names now, too. You said some plants are poison, and you must be very careful. (Yes) Then the next time I see you maybe you could have the stories together and things that I could pass on. (Yes) Well, how are things going with you and Roff? (She corrected my pronunciation.)*

B: In one way good, in one way bad. We get together for loving and it goes very good. But it is said that he is to be sent away and he won't be coming back.

D: *Oh. I'm sorry to hear that. Is he still a valet?*

B: He's soon to become a knight and that's when he'll be sent away.

D: *Why can't he stay there?*

B: He's not needed here. There's enough knights here.

D: *I know you would like him to stay there, wouldn't you?*

B: Yes. He doesn't know but ... last night I could have married us by our ways. But he doesn't know our ways, so I didn't do it. It's secret, and he wouldn't realize until I had the rope around his arms ... at one point. And then he would start to wonder what was happening.

D: *Can you tell me how you would have done it?*

B: I couldn't figure it out. That's why I didn't do it.

D: *Oh, you didn't know all the little parts?*

B: I knew the parts. I was just trying to figure out a way of doing it without getting Roff upset.

D: *How would you do it if you were going to marry yourself?*

B: First you walk around the grove of trees, and you go to the center. There's a stone in the center. And you place something on the stone for the Earth mother, depending on the time of year. Last night we went walking around the grove of trees, and I put a bouquet of flowers on the stone. And after you place something on the stone for the Earth mother, then you turn, and you look into each other's eyes. And there are different ways you can pledge faithfulness to each other. And you're doing it before the goddess. And after you pledge faithfulness to each other, you seal it by putting a rope of flowers around both of the people. A rope of flowers that the girl has made beforehand, in preparation. And this seals it in the sight of the mother Earth, and anyone who may be watching. It's best to do it in the waxing of the moon. It should not be done in the dark of the moon. There should be moonlight for it.

D: *Why weren't you able to do it?*

B: Because he has not proposed to me, and he would have wondered about my pledging my love to him. And he would have wondered the reason why my draping a flower chain around us and doing the ritual gestures.

D: *You couldn't have told him it was just a meaning of love or something?*

B: No, I could not, because he does not suspect about us.

D: *Oh. I thought maybe he knew some of the things you did.* (No) *You couldn't just say this is a way I have of showing my love? But then that would have been tricking him, really, wouldn't it?*

B: Yes, and you can't do that.

D: *So this is why you're sad because you weren't able to do it?*

B: Partially. It looks like I'm not willed to do it. And it looks like if I am to be married, I need to find someone else. Roff … he's good at tumbling in the hay, but he has no desire to marry.

D: *You mean you feel the need to be married?* (Yes) *Is there a reason? (I was thinking she might be pregnant.)*

B: (Sadly) So that I won't be alone all my life. I need someone to be part of my life. I've always been alone. I need someone to care. Someone to be there until we're old.

D: *But you're not that old, are you? Why are you worrying about being alone?*

B: I'm old enough. I'm of marriageable age. But one must think about it soon and early. Because one never knows when disease of some sort may come and take you. Or take your companion. Or take all your friends and family.

D: *That's true. These things are unexpected. But he is going away. If you married him, could you go with him?*

B: No, I couldn't. That's what helped me to realize I had to find someone else.

D: *You would not be allowed to follow him?*

B: No. Not under these circumstances.

D: *Then he really wouldn't be a good choice, except that you love him, you said.* (Yes) *Is he going to leave soon?*

B: (Uncertain.) I think so.

D: *Then he would not have been a good choice for the Lady Joslyn either, would he?*

B: But the Lady Joslyn could follow him, because she is not bound here like I am. She's a lady. She has a horse she can ride anywhere she likes. And if she and Roff were to marry, wherever he would go to and live, she could go, too.

D: *I see. I thought it would be the same, and you could go with him.*

B: No, I'd have to have the lord of the manor's permission.

D: *Wouldn't he give it to you?*

B: One never knows. He acts very different. He acts strange. Some people would say he's been hexed, but we know better.

D: *What do you think it is?*

B: I don't know. I think perhaps some strange and wondrous disease is affecting him.

D: *How does he act that's different?*

B: Just from spending so much time in the tower. He doesn't

like to be bothered in the daytime. And he talks in circles and throws sudden fits of rage, all out of proportion for the situation.

D: *These were things he didn't do before?*

B: (Sigh) Well, he did them some, but he's been getting worse and worse. (Suddenly) It's hot! How did it become hot?

It was hot in the small room and we had the fan blowing on Brenda. She is very affected by the heat. It bothers her. The only way we could have a session in the summer was to have the fan on, although the tape recorder picks up motor noise. I always had to work around this when I transcribe, because it is essential that the subject be comfortable.

D: *Oh, I don't know. Is there a breeze blowing?* (No) *Maybe it's because the trees are blocking the breeze.*

B: No, it's pleasant here. But I feel where you are is hot.

Strangely she was being affected in her time by what was occurring in our time.

D: *It is a little bit. But it won't bother you. A cool breeze will blow through.*

B: I don't feel a cool breeze. I'm just sensitive to where you are. It's too hot where you are. It's not comfortable.

D: *All right then. But you can always move somewhere else where it would be comfortable.*

B: *I'm* comfortable. I'm talking about, where *you* are it's not comfortable. In my mind.

D: *Ummm, that's strange that you can sense that, isn't it? (I was trying to get her mind off the heat in the room.) Well, I'm sorry you and Roff are having problems. I keep pronouncing his name wrong. I'm sorry.*

B: That is all right. You have difficulty with mine, too. You seem to have difficulty with everybody's name, except Joslyn's.

D: *You're right. It's because the names are not names I am familiar with.* (Oh) *They're different names than we use.*

218

B: You know Joslyn, too, then. I pity you.

D: *Yes, that's a name I have heard, but the other names are not common.*

B: I pity you knowing her, the Lady Joslyn.

D: *I don't know her. But I know the name. (Laugh) I don't think I'd want to know her. (Oh) No, I just know the name. It is a name I have heard. The other names I have not heard. That's why I have problems pronouncing them. (Yes) All right. But in a few moments, we're going to make it cool here, too, so it won't bother you. We can open windows and let the breeze come in.*

The curtain was drawn across the nearest window to darken the room, and it could have been blocking the breeze.

B: Windows? What is a window?

D: *It's an opening in the wall.*

B: Oh! We have openings with shutters.

D: *Yes, I will have to open the shutter and that will let in the cool breeze. The shutters are closed, maybe that's why it's hot.*

B: Perhaps.

D: *But it won't bother you at all as long as you are comfortable where you are.*

B: It's hard to breathe.

I continued to give reassuring suggestions to alleviate any discomfort, but it didn't seem to help. Astelle seemed to sense that the body in our time was uncomfortable. I got up while I was talking to her and pulled the drape away from the window nearest her. I hoped this would allow some air to come in. I also decided to move her to another scene in the hopes of further distracting her. Either it worked or the air was finally circulating, because as she entered the next scene she appeared to return to normal.

D: *What are you doing?*

B: I'm getting married.

This was a surprise. I asked her to tell me about it.

B: Yes. Roff did leave.
D: *He did?*
B: Yes, he went away.
D: *As a knight or what?*
B: Yes. And I've never seen him again. I suppose I shall always have fond memories of him. After he went away there was a man who worked with the horses. He was new. And he understood the pain. Something very similar had happened to him, and we would talk a lot. And we got along real good. And we feel very comfortable together. And he started doing special things for me. And we found out that he was one of us. He didn't realize there was some of us around. And he was hoping ... he was wishing that there were. And one evening I caught him gesturing towards the moon similar to the way we do in honor of the goddess. I didn't tell him that I noticed it, but I told the elders of the group, so that they could make their decision as to what to do about it. And one of them approached him very cleverly. And while they were talking, they would make obscure references to the goddess, in ways that only a follower of the goddess would pick up on and notice. And he made the proper responses. And so they were able to finally come out openly about whether or not he followed the goddess.
D: *This way there was no danger of anyone from the Inquisition, if you were sure he was one of you.*
B: Yes. And so we decided since he was planning on staying here and spending his life here—he came here to get away from the pain. He came from afar off. I'm not sure where. The Inquisition got hold of his wife. He's a widower. He's young. His wife was about my age. And so there were too many memories there for him. He wanted to get away. And since he had some skills, he's good with horses, he can communicate with them and he's good with shoeing them. He knew that he would be able to go to another manor and they would allow him to live there and work.

D: *Normally strangers don't come to your part, do they?*

B: No. And so he understood the pain that I had gone through.

D: *What happened with his wife? Did he tell you the story?*

B: It's very painful for him to talk about. The Inquisition tortured her, because she was one of us, too. They suspected, but she never did admit to anything. And they tortured her until she died.

D: *Do you think they just saw something, or suspected something? Normally your people are so careful.*

B: Yes. I suspect one of the Inquisition members wanted to bed her, and she wouldn't do it. Because he said she was very beautiful. And since she wouldn't bed with this member of the Inquisition, they decided to get their pleasure another way. Because it is said many times that they will come while they are torturing people.

D: *Oh. This gives* them *pleasure in* strange *ways, doesn't it?*

B: Yes. And so he was able to help me and I was able to help him.

D: *Were there any children?*

B: She was with child at the time.

D: *This would make it more painful to remember, wouldn't it?* (Yes) *I could see why he would want to leave and go somewhere else. He would have been in danger too, wouldn't he?*

B: Yes. They were going to come after him next. And so he gathered together all of the tools he could get hold of and take with him, even though they weren't properly his. He took the tools with him so that he could go anywhere and be able to work.

D: *Did he come a long way?*

B: I think so. He looked very dusty and foot weary when he got here. He has been here several months now. We were needing someone like him. And also when he's not busy with the horses, he helps repair the armory. But his chief responsibility is with the horses.

D: *I'm very happy for you. Are you being married in your own way?*

B: Yes. All of us are here. Those of us who follow the goddess. It's not often that we're able to hold a marriage in honor of the goddess. And it's a reason for celebrating.

D: *Are you in the grove of trees?*

B: Yes. At the rock.

D: *Are you going to live there at the house with this man?*

B: No, he has a hut of his own. We'll be living there.

D: *What is his name? I didn't ask you.*

B: That is true, you didn't. I'm debating whether to tell you his inside name or his outside name.

D: *What do you mean?*

B: Those of us who follow the goddess have names that we're known to each other only by, and we have the regular names that we tell other people we are called.

D: *Can you tell me both?*

B: I don't think I'll tell you his inside name, but I'll tell you his outside name.

D: *So I will know who you're speaking of.*

B: My husband, yes. Yes, I was thinking about Roff for a moment. I wonder what he's doing now?

D: *Well, it's natural for you to think of him, too.*

B: Yes, I think so.

D: *What is your husband's outside name?*

B: Let me think of it. I never use it. *(I laughed.)* One moment. My memory has gone faulty again.

D: *(Laugh) Well, you have other things to think about at this time.*

B: This is true.

D: *What do the other people call him?*

B: His outside name is Gundevar. (Phonetic. I had her repeat it.)

D: *Oh, that's going to be hard for me to pronounce. Can you say it again?*

B: (Slowly) Gun-devar. (Phonetic. I repeated it after her.)

D: *Okay. And this is what others call him?* (Yes) *That is a rather strange name.*

B: Yes. I don't know what kind of people his family was that use such strange names.

D: *Well, the only name I've ever known you by is Astelle.*

B: Yes, that's my outside name.

D: *Could you tell me your inside name?*

B: No. I think not.

D: *I thought you trusted me enough that you could tell me.*

B: I *do* trust you. But they say even the trees have ears. The Inquisition is everywhere. They've been very bad lately. Perhaps when the Inquisition is not so fierce, I can tell you then. (She paused, and then said quickly:) I'll tell you real quick. Sharra. (Phonetic. It had a strange roll to the rs. I had her repeat it and I tried to say it.) Close but not quite. It's difficult to pronounce if you're not used to it.

D: *Does that have a meaning?*

B: I think it means follower of the star goddess.

D: *Why do you have two names?*

B: Our inside names contain power in them. Outside names don't really mean anything. They're just sounds. Astelle, Gundevar, Roff, Joslyn. They're just sounds that you call somebody. But the inside names have meanings to them that give them power that you can use in the rituals.

D: *Then everyone of your people has two names.*

B: Yes, except for the very young children. When children are born, they're given their outside names. We have to observe their personality and characteristics and what rituals they do best before you can give them an inside name that will work well with their lives.

D: *Then they're not given their inside name for quite a while.*

B: Not until their primary initiation. It is usually when they are seven, after they've been well taught at home by the parents of the things they have to know.

D: *Are they questioned during the initiation?*

B: Yes. And they are also tested on similar rituals to see if they know how to do them and know the proper responses for the group rituals that we do. Plus, they're tested on how well they're being secretive about it.

D: *Yes, you couldn't tell a child anything that might be a danger to the group, could you?*

B: Unless the child has been taught to be secretive.

D: *Would you be allowed to tell me those initiation rituals at some time?* (Yes) *And then I can see how they have changed.* (Yes) *What do you do tonight after the ceremony? Do you go to the hut?*

B: Tonight, after the ceremony the others will leave and we will sleep in the grove of trees, underneath the stone arch. There are two pillars of stone, and there was a stone that was a crossbeam, but it had fallen, so we have put a beam of oak across to take its place.

D: *Was that something that was there, or did you build it?*

B: I don't know. It's very old.

D: *Is that what you meant when you talked of the stone?*

B: There's an altar … well, not really an altar stone. There's another stone in line with the stone arch that we use for rituals. It's somewhat flat on top.

D: *But the stone arch is not used for anything?*

B: Yes, it's for rituals. And tonight, Gundevar and I will sleep within the arch and the stone. Then in the wee hours when it's still dark when no one will see us, we will go to his house so that the people of the manor will not suspect.

D: *Would they have any objection to you being married?*

B: No. They don't mind if we get married or if we just live together. They know that we don't have the money to pay the priest for getting married.

D: *Are you very old when this happens?*

B: I'm twenty-three, which is considered somewhat old for getting married. Most get married when they're sixteen or seventeen.

D: *Well, I want you to enjoy yourself and then may I speak to you again when I come again?* (Yes) *And I will have many questions to ask you at that time then. I'm very happy for you.*

B: Thank you.

D: *I hope you will be happy with him.*

B: I will.

(Subject brought forward.)

After I pulled the curtain back from the window, she did not seem to be affected any longer by the heat in the room. I think it was an interesting way that the other personality found to let me know that the body she was speaking through was uncomfortable. She sensed it in some way across time.

Chapter 10
Legends and Stories
(Recorded June 19, 1986)

Used keyword and counted her back to the lifetime of Astelle.

D: *Let's go back to the time that Astelle lived in Flanders. She was going to tell me some of the legends and stories of the time and she wanted to be sure that she had them accurate. I would like for us to go back to that time, at a time in that life when she would have access to this information that she was going to give me. I will count to three and we will be back at that time. 1, 2, 3, we've gone back to the time when Astelle lived. What are you doing?*

B: I'm sitting in front of the fireplace in my home.

D: *Do you have your own home now?*

B: Since I've been married.

D: *What is it like?*

B: You go in the door, and to the left of the room is the fireplace that heats up my home. And that's where I do my cooking. And there's a few things about to cook with. And a little bit from the fireplace is the table with two chairs and a stool. I'm sitting on the stool beside the fireplace. And then to the right of the door at the other end is where my husband and I sleep. We have a bed frame with ropes tied across and the covers and such put on top of that.

D: *Are there many rooms?*

B: No, just the one.

D: *Have you been married very long now?*

B: Yes, we've been married about five years now.

D: *Do you still work at the large house?*

B: No, I don't now. I have my family to take care of. I have three children and a fourth is on its way.

D: *Oh, you've done a lot in five years. What are they, boys or girls?*

B: The oldest one is a girl. And the one in the middle is a boy, and the youngest one is a girl. And the one on the way is a girl.

D: *How do you know?*

B: I have ways.

D: *That's always been one of the best kept secrets.*

B: Those of us who follow the old way know of ways to find out. If you work in harmony with the goddess, the goddess will tell you many things. And the goddess is particularly attuned to life and the giving of life. So there are ways of finding out the quality of that life, whether it be boy or girl.

D: *Can you tell me how?*

B: There are different ways of doing it. One way that you can do it, you take a small pebble, one with a hole in it is easiest. But you take either a pebble or you get a coin, and you tie a thread around it, to where it will swing. And you hold the thread with the pebble hanging on the thread. The length of the thread should be the distance from your wrist to the inside of your elbow. And you pick it up with whatever hand is comfortable to pick it up with. For some people it's the right hand and for some people it's the left hand. You pick it up and you hold the pebble hanging on the string over the top of the wrist of the other hand, with about a four-finger span distance between the two.

D: *The outside or the inside of the wrist?*

B: The outside. You have your hand resting on your knee or something like that. And you hold it there and relax and think about your baby. You have to be pregnant when you do this. You think about your baby. And if it's a girl it'll swing in a circle to the right. And if it's a boy it'll either swing in a circle to the left or just swing back and forth.

D: *Did you do this when you were pregnant with the other children?* (Yes) *Was it accurate?* (Yes) *And you said there are other ways to tell?*

B: Yes, more involved ways. But they're not any more accurate than this way. And this is the way that I use because it's not as difficult to do, and it's accurate. But it is said that there are some that cannot use my way of doing that, because just like there are some who cannot witch for water, the ability is just not there. It's some trick of being in tune with the Earth mother.

D: *Do you know how to witch for water?*

B: I know about it, I know how, but I've never done it myself. I feel that I could. It's just that there's one in our group who is very good at it, so I leave it to him to do. The way it is usually done, he takes a green branch that is split at one end and grasps it and walks over the area where underground water needs to be found. And the branch will twitch at the right place. And depending on how it twitches and how it feels he'll be able to tell you how deep you'll have to dig for your well.

D: *This is a method that is used in my time also.*

B: It's a very old method.

D: *Then that is one method that has not been forgotten.*

Two examples of dowsing that shows it has been around for a long time, and the methods have not changed much.

D: *I thought that you had to keep working in the large house. There was no way you could leave when you were a servant.*

B: I haven't left. I still live here on the grounds. My husband still works for the lord. It is true that usually I would have to stay in the kitchen. But the group of us decided it would be better if I worked in the kitchen part of the time. And so we did a ritual to change the situation.

D: *So they would let you stay home?* (Yes) *It would have been difficult with the children, wouldn't it?* (Yes) *Unless you would have brought the children to the kitchen, too.*

B: If I had one that was suckling, then I could have brought it. The other two would have to … there's a place for the servant's children to stay to play. And I'd have to take the others there.

D: *Well, you probably don't mind not working in the kitchen anyway, do you?*

B: No. (Chuckle) It has made life interesting for the Lady Joslyn.

D: *In what way?*

B: She doesn't ever get to see me anymore. She can't call for me in the middle of the night to beat me up.

D: *I wondered about the Lady Joslyn. Did she ever find a husband?*

B: No, I suspect she won't. She's an old maid now. She's thirty-two.

D: *I bet she's more frustrated than ever.*

B: Very sour, yes.

D: *I imagine she probably is jealous of you anyway because you're married now. She always was jealous, it seemed like.*

B: Yes, but she would never admit to it. It would be beneath her dignity, I think, beneath her station.

D: *I feel sorry for her in a way.*

B: She brought it on herself, because every person has their path to walk. The fates spin out the yarn of the life, and your actions determine the weave of that yarn. And the way it turns out in the end is determined by your actions in your life. So whatever happens you have brought upon yourself, either in this life or the last.

D: *That makes sense to me. Then in your beliefs do you believe that you have more than one life?*

B: Yes, which the church has declared to be heretical. But they used to teach it also. But not many people remember that.

D: *I know today they have taken it out of the teachings. And I wondered if it were taught in the olden times.*

B: It was, but it began to be suppressed. And after it was suppressed long enough then they were able to take the writings out of the Bible. They had to suppress it long enough for it to pass from living memory, so no one would miss it having been taken out.

D: *Have you ever heard about the writings that have been suppressed and taken out?*

B: One hears some stories, but there are so many rumors about the church that one doesn't know what's true and what's not.

D: *Do you know what it was?*

B: Well, it was teaching about the more than one lives. I never have known what it said.

D: *I was just curious. Because I'm always looking for the things that have been taken away and lost.*

B: Yes. And it is said that in the Bible it says that one should not take any away. But the priests indulge in it regularly.

D: *Why do you think they wanted it out of there?*

B: If one knows that one will have another chance, the priests' threats are not as effective. But if you think this life is your one and only chance, then that helps the priests to wield more power, and helps you to be more suppressed. It's not right that they took it out.

D: *They're doing all these things for power and control?*

B: Yes, that is true. For they don't realize that they may not have as much power the other way, but they'd have a lot more respect, which is a power in itself.

D: *Is the Inquisition still going on?*

B: They have concentrated their efforts elsewhere. They're in another part of the country now, concentrating their efforts there. They haven't been here in, oh, a couple of years.

D: *Then you feel safer? Your group doesn't have to worry so much?*

B: Yes, but we're not going to grow careless.

D: *You're still going to be secretive just in case.* (Right) *I am curious about something. If I'm out of turn ... if I ask a question you don't like, just tell me. You said you have three children now and you're going to have another one. I was just curious as to why you didn't get pregnant when you were with Roff.*

B: There are ways of preventing pregnancy or encouraging pregnancy. If you're in harmony with the Earth mother you can determine whether or not, and when you want to have a child.

D: *Because I was thinking you could have gotten pregnant then.*

B: Under ordinary circumstances, yes, but I didn't want to, so I didn't.

D: *Can you share these methods with me? Because in our times some people don't know how to control it.*

B: It's a mental thing. Something you have to practice since you're young. (Pause) It's hard to explain. I'm not sure I can put it into words. There comes a point about midways between one period and the next. There's a certain number of days involved, but that varies from person to person. And at this point one must go through a certain ritual in mental discipline, or a month later one will be pregnant.

D: *Can you tell me what the ritual is?*

B: You go to the grove at night and you have certain objects with you. You have some hair from your lover's head, and you have some of your hair, and you have an egg. And in the ritual you tell the powers that be that even though you and your lover are united together in love—and with this you do something with the hairs in the ritual. I'm not going to go into great detail here. You tell them that you desire no fruit from the union. And at this point you break the egg and smash it on the ground, symbolizing nothing coming of the union. And then you focus your thoughts inward, focus in on yourself down at the female parts, focusing the thought of not getting pregnant. So somehow this is what I do. It does the job.

D: *Then you mentally know when that time of the month is?*

B: Yes. If you are in tune with your body you can tell when that time of the month is.

D: *This is one of the problems women in our day have. There are many times they get pregnant when they don't want to because they don't know when is the safe time.*

B: If they take the time to listen to the Earth mother, they will find out what the time is.

D: *Then do you have a fertility ritual if you want to get pregnant? Or do you just don't do anything to prevent it?*

B: There are several rituals to encourage getting pregnant. They are popular with women who have difficulty getting pregnant.

D: *Can you share those with me?*

B: I'm not very familiar with them. I've never had that problem.

D: *It doesn't sound like it. But there are many women in our time who would like to get pregnant also. We have the same problems. It seems like the times don't change that much.*

B: No. One thing that is said that has helped is to bathe one's female parts with baby's urine.

D: *I've never heard that one. You never know. Different things might work.—I was curious because I knew you were with Roff for quite a while. Now you have all these children. Are you happy there?* (Yes) *He's a good husband?*

B: Yes. He works hard. We have a place to live. He doesn't beat me. And we really care for each other.

D: *And Roff has never come back?*

B: No. I don't expect that he will. If he comes back the Lady Joslyn will think he's coming back for her, and then where would he be?

D: *(Laugh) Oh, poor Lady Joslyn. What about the lord? Does he still have his things that he does in the tower?*

B: The lord, I think he tried to handle more than he could handle, because he's a broken man now. His mind, it's almost gone. They've locked up the tower, and no one goes up there anymore. And the lord is confined to his chambers.

D: *What happened?*

B: One night he called down a storm. There are ways and there are ways of calling down rain. And if you do it wrong it can overtake you and do something strange to you. He called down a storm because he was angry. He was wanting to hurl lightning bolts at a neighboring large house. He was angry with the lord of that house. And so he was wanting to throw some lightning bolts down on the house. And so he called up this big storm and he overspent himself. Not realizing after calling up the storm it would still take more strength to hurl the bolts down. And so he lost control of the forces that he had called up. And he's not been the same in his mind ever since. He is said to see strange things now. Because … well, this world is not the only one. There are other worlds, invisible worlds, all around us. Some of them more wondrous than others. And it is said that ever since that day he has been able to look into whichever world he was tied into, for the power to call down the storm. He can't get out of it completely now. And he's caught in between two worlds. And it's tearing up his mind.

D: *That must have really been some night when that happened.*

B: Yes, it was very stormy, and it damaged a lot of the fields.

D: *I didn't know it was possible to have control over the forces of nature like that.*

B: You don't really have control over it. You simply have them to work with you within their natural confines. Because you can't have the forces of nature do something totally unnatural. For example, you cannot call up rain and cause it to fall upward instead of down.

D: *Oh, no, that would really be against nature, wouldn't it?* (Yes) *But through these rituals he learned he could control weather to make a storm.*

B: Yes. But the rituals he learned were *man* centered instead of goddess centered. And so they didn't work. Or rather I should say they backfired on him. They messed up on him. It turned out differently than he had anticipated.

D: *There was more power than he could handle.* (Yes) *Then you said he is kept confined. Is he dangerous?*

B: Hmmm. Some days he is. Most days he isn't. It's just a matter of waiting for him to die. Because he just eats and sleeps and mumbles to himself, for the most part.

D: *I wondered if he was ... crazy, that he might do things that would hurt other people.*

B: You never know. I think they keep an eye on him all the time to make sure that he doesn't turn that way.

D: *Do you know if the church has said anything about what happened?*

B: I don't think they would. He's been most generous with offerings in the past.

D: *They have no explanation for what happened?* (No) *That's an example though of what happens when somebody uses the forces in the wrong way, or for their own gain.* (Yes) *Your people would never do anything like that, would they?*

B: No, I don't think so.

D: *Unless they would know how to control it better.*

B: Right. Usually to control a storm just right it takes two or three people. If you just want to call up a little bit of wind and a little bit of rain, one person can do it. But for a full-sized storm it generally takes about three people working together.

D: *Yes, sometimes you might want rain for your crops or something.* (Right) *I can see why several people would be able to control the power more than one person could.* (Yes) *You said before you weren't sure what he was doing up there.*

B: I think it had been building up across the years and this last thing was what it took.

D: *How long ago did this happen, and he was confined to the room?*

B: It's been about a year now.

D: *Okay. But you are happy with your life there now, and you don't have to work in the kitchen. And your husband works with the horses?*

B: Yes. And he's a chief armory now, too.

D: *What does he have to do with the armory?*

B: He has to keep the various things in good condition. Any repairing or forging that must be done on them, he's supposed to do. It takes skill and strength.

D: *Would it be the same as working with horseshoes?*

B: Yes, but it would take more skill, because there's the chain mail and such as that that he has to keep in good condition.

D: *Well, it shows that he is very skillful.* (Yes) *Okay. The last time I spoke with you you were telling me some things that you said you had to get more information on. And you wanted to make sure you were accurate. I was asking you some questions. Is it all right if I ask you now? Will you give me the answers?* (Yes) *All right. You were talking about the legends. And one legend was about the beginning of your religion. And you said you wanted to make sure you had it accurate before you told me. Can you tell me about that now? The legend about how the religion began?*

B: Yes. It happened so long ago. At the beginning of time everybody was in tune with the mother Earth, for the souls had just begun their journey. And they were but newly separated from her, and so they remembered how to be in harmony with her. And they knew how to be in harmony with nature. And so they observed the things they knew needed to be observed in order to stay that way. Time passed, they had children, their children had children, and such as that and they continued doing this. And it continued like this and developed into what we have today. Things had to change greatly after Christianity became powerful. But their time is limited due to how they are set up. So many times, we'll tell our children that our religion is like ... let me think. We use different examples depending on the circumstances. Our religion is like the horse and Christianity is like the saddle. The horse is in harmony with the Earth mother. The horse has the strength. And the saddle thinks it is in control. But it's not the saddle that's in control, it's the horse that's in control. The horse's thoughts and such. And the horse chooses to allow the saddle to think it's in control. And such as it is between our religion and Christianity. Christianity thinks it's in control simply because for the time being, since our members are scattered, it's convenient for us to allow them to think they're in control.

D: *That would be a good way of putting it. You said you had another example also of how you explain it to children?*

B: That's the main one I like to use. Sometimes the comparison is made between the grass and the grasshopper. Our religion is like the grass growing under the strong summer sun, growing strong and tall and beautiful, in harmony with everything. And Christianity is like the grasshopper hopping from one thing to another looking for things to occupy itself with.

D: *I can also see that. That's very good. Sometimes these make it easier to understand.*

B: Yes, that's why we have them for the children.

D: *That's very good. You also told me you had stories that you told the children so they would remember certain rituals.* (Yes) *Can you tell me some of those?*

B: Yes. Some of the rituals are easy to remember simply because they make sense. But sometimes a ritual may not make sense at first because you don't know the story behind it. I have told you about the swans ritual.

D: *Yes, that's a very beautiful one.*

B: Because many times the hand gestures are very complex and hard to remember. And it's hard to remember just how to do them unless you remember the swan. And then it becomes easier to do. Another thing that's often difficult for children to learn is the various phases of the moon. What rituals are good for what phases of the moon. And so to help them remember it we compare the phases of the moon with the seasons of the year. And that way it makes it easier for them to remember what kind of rituals go well with the various phases of the moon. With the new moon being winter and the full moon being summer, and the waxing and the waning being spring and fall. Rituals for increase and growing you do in the spring or the waxing moon. Rituals of fulfillment and completion you do in summer or the full moon. Rituals for finishing up the last details of things you do in fall or the waning moon. And rituals for cleansing and preparing for another cycle of things you do in winter or the new moon.

D: *We do believe there are things you can do in certain phases of the moon, but it's very difficult to remember. That makes it much easier to understand.*

B: Good.

D: *Thank you for telling me that. Are there any other ones that you tell the children?*

B: There are many. I'm just telling some that I can think of right off hand. There are many rituals to be done that involve using a crossroads. And usually these rituals involve a choice of some sort, and you're not sure which choice to make. And so that's the type of rituals that are done with crossroads, so that the choice may become clear. So that you know what path to take, so to speak.

D: *Do you have a ritual that you do with that?*

B: There are different ones. I was just speaking of the general circumstances. For when one is constructing a ritual and one needs certain elements in the ritual, one must remember what the various elements are good for. So that you may put the right elements in your ritual, so you'll have the right results.

D: *Then if you were trying to make a decision, how would you do that with the crossroads?*

B: Depending on what kind of decision you're trying to make, you'd get something that is compatible with it. For example, if you're trying to decide whether or not to trade some wool for some corn, or something like that. Or perhaps you have a chance to trade some of your wheat for some dye. And you're trying to decide which way to go. You go to a crossroads at night with a coin. And in the center of the crossroads there are certain symbols that you can draw indicating which crossroad is for which choice. And you bury the coin there. And you wait a specified amount of time, depending on what is compatible with the ritual, and you return. And whoever is the first to come down the road and cross the crossroads, whichever way that he goes, that indicates the choice that you would be best to make.

D: *What kind of symbols do you make on the ground?*

B: Usually there's a pentagram and then depending on what kind of a ritual it is would depend on what kind of symbols you put down. If it's a ritual for love you'd put down the symbol for Venus.

D: *Oh, the symbols we talked about earlier.*

B: Yes. And if you have something like a coin to bury, it is good to draw these symbols in the dust of the crossroads with this coin and then bury the coin right there with the symbol.

D: *Hmmm. What kind of coins do you have? Have you seen very many?*

B: No. Or hardly any.

D: *I was thinking they would be hard to come by.*

B: But sometimes ... it's really funny, one of our old women is known to be a wise woman. And often the rich nobles will come to her for advice on what to do in matters of love and such as that. They get desperate and they want to try anything. And so they don't mind going against the church to try our way.

D: *(Chuckle) As long as nobody else knows about it.*

B: Right. And so that is how I knew about the coins being used in some of the rituals, because these nobles would have some coins.

D: *Did you ever see what the coins look like?*

B: Not really up close. There's usually a picture of some sort of royalty on one side, and then a crest on the other side. And it was the equivalent in another metal of what this coin is worth. Like, for example, a piece of copper may be worth a piece of silver of thus and such size.

D: *And this is written on the coin?*

B: Usually there are some symbols to symbolize this. They're on the coin. And the coins are different sizes so it's easy to tell them apart. So you don't really have to look at the symbols if you don't want to.

D: *Do you mean that the larger the coin, it is worth more?*

B: It depends on the metal of it, but usually, yes, because a large copper coin would not be worth as much as a small gold coin. The coins are mostly copper and silver, but occasionally gold. But the gold is somewhat rare and difficult to get hold of.

D: *Okay. Once when I was talking to you, you were talking about the primary initiation of the children.* (Yes) *And you were going to tell me more about how that was done. You said there was a ritual to be sure they could keep secrets.*

B: Yes. Usually the way we test whether or not they can be secret, we'll get a grown person that they know, but they don't know whether or not they're in our group. But they are. The children don't know this. And the grown person will sit down and talk to them and use all manner of ways to try to get information from them. And depending on how free they are about giving the information or holding it in, determines whether or not they pass that test. Their age is taken into consideration when we do this. But even when they are young you can tell whether or not they're going to be able to stay secretive about it.

D: *Would a young child know very much that he could tell?*

B: He could tell some names, that's enough.

D: *Because they wouldn't really know many of the rituals yet, would they?*

B: Not really. But then the Inquisition is not interested in rituals. The Inquisition is interested in people to torture.

D: *This is why they would be looking for names.—I've been curious as to why they have to torture people. Why don't they just kill them if they're looking for witches or whatever they call them? Why do they have to go through the business of torturing them?*

B: Because they get twisted pleasure out of someone else's pain.

D: *I always thought they were trying to get them to confess.*

B: Yes, but if you have enough pain applied, you'll confess to anything even if you've never done it. Anything to stop the pain. They say they're doing it in the name of their god. And if someone is weak enough to confess under pain, if they haven't already committed whatever they've confessed to, then they will be committing it in the future because they were weak enough to confess of it.

D: *Hmmm. But still they don't release them after they've confessed, do they?*

B: I don't think they do. Occasionally they'll let one go, to teach the rest of us a lesson. And it's usually someone who is horribly scarred and disfigured, but that doesn't happen very often.

D: *Torture doesn't prove whether they are a witch or not. That doesn't sound normal, does it?*

B: No, it isn't.

D: *Well, getting back to the initiation. After you have seen that they are able to keep secrets, then you said they go through their first initiation?*

B: Yes. It's a very simple ceremony. They light a white candle, and they take up a handful of Earth and put it before it. And promise to keep in mind that they are part of that Earth. And that they must stay in harmony with the goddess, who is the moving force of that Earth. And they take a ritual symbolic drink of wine. And usually afterwards there is a celebration of some sort.

D: *Are there many of the children that do this at one time?*

B: No, it's all done individually, one person at a time. We just do it whenever a child is ready for it, because it's a very individual experience. Because to get ready for the ritual a child has to exercise the meditation that he has learned, to get their mind opened and in tune.

D: *Then you have been teaching them meditation from the time they're very young?*

B: From the time they're born. From before they're born.

D: *Hmmm. Because everybody thinks a baby can't know anything.*

B: That is not true.

D: *Are you doing this mentally or do you talk to the baby?*

B: Both.

D: *Because it is hard for me to understand how you could teach a baby to meditate.*

B: There are ways of doing it. You have to be very patient and be able to say it in words that they understand.

D: *Can you share that with me? I think it would be very nice if we could quiet babies down sometimes. (Laugh)*

B: What you do is use the various ways to help alter their breathing, either slower or faster. So that when they are excited and upset, you can calm them down by slowing down their breathing.

D: *How can you do that?*

B: It's hard to explain. You do it with your mind somehow. And when they're a little bit older and can talk a little bit and can understand, you tell them about breathing in and out slow. And you draw some parallels between them and how still and peaceful things are when the wind is still. You tell them the same thing happens in your mind when your breathing is still. And help them to explore themselves like this. After a while they get to where they want to do it themselves, just to find out what they can find out. And they'll start doing it just out of curiosity. And they'll get better and better at it.

D: *Yes, I can see it's easier whenever they learn to talk. When they're a baby I thought it would be difficult.*

B: Babies are usually good at doing it anyway. They just don't realize what they're doing. And it is just a matter of pointing out to them when they're doing it so they'll be aware of it.

D: *Then they learn at a very young age and it's not hard for them to remember this. They just grow up in it, and they can learn how to do this much easier. I don't think there's ever any danger in a child learning how to meditate, is there?* (No) *Because I think sometimes a child isn't as disciplined.*

B: A child doesn't seem as disciplined because it's not bound by manmade rules yet. It is still acting spontaneously and usually in tune with the Earth mother.

D: *So there's no danger to a child in doing any of these things.*

B: No. We would not endanger our children.

D: *I didn't think you would. But then are there any initiations that occur later?*

B: Yes, when they reach thirteen, they become full members of the group.

D: *What is the ritual that is performed at that time?*

B: It's very elaborate with much symbolism in it. And they are at that time confirmed in their secret inside name. Up to this time they have been preforming individual rituals that just takes one person to do it. Or perhaps two, they and their teacher. And this time for the first time they get to partake in a ritual that involves several of the group for a specific purpose. Up to now they've been involved in rituals with their teacher and is in tune with the teacher. And now they learn to expand themselves and be able to tune in with the other members of the group for various rituals.

D: *And you said at this time you give them their inside name?*

B: That's given to them earlier, but they're confirmed in it if it seems to fit their character. Unless they have a familiar** of some sort. And that being the case, their familiar is given an

241

inside name.

** In European folklore of the medieval and early modern periods, familiars (sometimes referred to as familiar spirits) were believed to be supernatural entities that would assist witches and cunning folk in their practice of magic. The main purpose of familiars was to serve the witch or young witch, providing protection for them as they came into their new powers. **

D: *What is the ritual that they do at this time?*
B: It's very long and elaborate.
D: *Do you have any other rituals that are performed as the child grows older?*
B: There's a ritual that's preformed when a child, a young adult, feels they have met their soul mate. There's a ritual that is preformed to see if this is true. And then they are helped, kind of guided along the way, as to what to do and which rituals to preform to cause what they want to come to pass in that relationship.
D: *How can you tell if it's really your soul mate?*
B: On the night of the full moon you get either a crystal ball or a black kettle with some water in it. And you go outside in the light of the moon. And you stare into the reflective surface of this, thinking about the person. And if the person is the one, you will see an affirmative sign. It's different for everybody, so you can't really describe it. But there's no mistaking it when you have received it.
D: *Something that happens or something in nature or what?*
B: Both. Or something that you feel, or some thought that pops into your mind, or something that you see in the reflective surface. Anything. A shooting star. It could be anything. But you'll know it when it happens that it is the sign to you for whatever.
D: *But if it's not, will you also have a sign?* (Yes) *It would be a way of knowing if it was not your real soul mate?* (Yes) *Then those are the most important rituals, initiations, and things that you do?*

B: Yes, there are others for smaller, everyday things, but those are the big things in life. There's one other celebration that we have, that the church particularly does not approve of. And that's at the death of somebody. We celebrate that they have completed one cycle of their life and they're ready for the next cycle.

D: *Why doesn't the church approve of that?*

B: Because the church says that when someone dies their soul goes to purgatory, and they're held either in limbo or in some sort of torture until they're ready to enter paradise.

D: *Odd belief, isn't it?* (Yes) *A very negative belief. Then they don't like it because you are happy when this happens.* (Yes) *Then there is no grieving when anyone in your group dies?*

B: Oh, you miss them, certainly, and you grieve in that way. But you don't grieve for their soul. You just grieve because they're not with you anymore, and you're going to miss them.

D: *What do you do with the body when someone dies?*

B: We can't do anything about it. They have to be buried.

D: *I thought you had a special way that you got rid of the body.*

B: We would if we could. But the church is too powerful.

D: *They take the body then?* (Yes) *Could you have a ritual whenever the person dies, or just celebrations?*

B: You place them within a sacred circle of salt, and you project a pentagram upon them. And depending on what they were best at, you arrange around them the things that they used for the rituals they did best. And it goes on from there. It's hard to say. We've never been able to do it. We just hear tell of it. And pass it down from generation to generation.

D: *Yes, something like that would be difficult to hide with the church watching. I'm going to have to leave now. And I wish to come again and speak with you.* (Yes) *And I'm very glad that you're happy with your children. I will come again at some other time and speak with you. Thank you.* (Yes)

(Subject brought forward.)

Chapter 11
The Inquisition Returns
(Recorded June 24, 1986)

Used keyword and counted her back to the lifetime of Astelle.

D: Let's go back to the time when Astelle lived and worked in Flanders. The last time we were there she was married and had several children. I would like to go to around that time in Astelle's life. To an important day in her life at around that time in her life, after she was married. I will count to three and we will be there. 1, 2, 3, we've gone back to an important day in Astelle's life after she was married. What are you doing?

B: I'm sitting in front of my home. I have a mixing bowl in my lap and I'm mixing up some bread.

D: Do you have many children now?

B: Do you mean children alive or children that have been born?

D: Oh! The last time I talked to you, you had three children and were expecting another one. (Yes) What did you mean?

B: That one died in childbirth. And a plague came and killed two others. Then I had another child, and so now I have two children.

D: I'm very sorry to hear about that.

B: (Sadly) It happens. It happens to everybody.

D: Did you have any warning that the one would be born dead?

B: It wasn't born dead, it died while being born. The cord that connects the baby to the mother was wrapped around its neck and it choked while it was being born.

D: *You had the feeling it would be a girl.*

B: (Sadly) It was a girl.

D: *I'm very sorry to hear about that. What kind of plague took the others?*

B: It was some sort of disease. It wasn't the Black Plague, thank goodness. But they became sick with fever and were coughing. The moisture would collect in their throat and thicken up. And they tried to cough it out. And they'd be sick and weak and not be able to cough as strong as they could otherwise, and this liquid would build up and choke them. It hit many of the children. For some reason it doesn't affect grownups. It's just a plague that affects children.

In my work of studying history through past-life regressions I have discovered that in the past the word "plague" referred to anything that was contagious. They did not have names for specific diseases unless it had a particular quality. This was why I did not question her use of the term. I had heard it from others in various time periods.

D: *Wasn't there anything you could do with the ways of your people?*

B: I tried. I tried to have them inhale steam that would loosen it up some, but it only worked for a little while. Because every time I would have them inhale steam, but when the thick fluid came back it would be even thicker than before.

D: *Wasn't there any herbs or anything you could use?*

B: Oh, I had some herbs in the steam, I mean, in the water that was producing the steam. And I was giving them medicines. But it was beyond my abilities. Our group's children lived longer than the others that had this plague, but ... This plague has come before, it wasn't that strong. Sometimes plagues are stronger and sometimes they are weaker. This time it was particularly strong.

D: *The one child you had left, was that one of the older ones?*

B: It was my second child.

D: *It didn't get the plague?*

B: No, it didn't. I don't understand why, but it didn't.

D: *That would be strange that some would get it and some would not.*

B: Yes, that's true.

D: *But you said you have another baby now?* (Yes) *Does this happen a lot in your land? That children have a hard time growing up?*

B: Yes. That's why we have many children. To make sure some live to carry on. And if you have many sons, if they make it through childhood, when they reach becoming young men, then they go off to war and get killed. So.

D: *You don't know how it's going to turn out. You just take your chances. Does your husband still work at the large house?* (Yes) *But you never had to go back to work in the kitchen, did you?*

B: No, not in the kitchen. What I do now is, I do some weaving and such as that for the ladies in the house. Weaving fine veils and lacy things. Making things of beauty.

D: *How do you do that?*

B: It depends on what I'm making. I just told them in the house that I weave it. For the veils I *do* just weave it. But for the other things of beauty I don't exactly weave it, I loop the thread around on itself. There's a stick that I have to help me with this. A small slender stick with a crook at one end. And I use it to help loop the thread around on itself. (It sounded like crocheting.)

D: *When you're weaving, do you use a loom? If you know what a loom is?*

B: I know what a loom is. I don't use a full loom because that is for making bolts of cloth and blankets and such. I have a smaller loom that is the type you hook one end to the wall. And the other end you tighten or loosen by tying it to a chair and setting the chair either further or closer to the wall. And the parts of the loom are held in place by stringing it up with thread. You have to string it up with thread before you can hang it up on the wall. And you weave with that.

D: *It sounds complicated.*

B: Well, most things are.

D: *Of course, this way you can stay home, can't you?*

B: Yes and watch after my two sons. Sometimes the weaving's difficult to do in the wintertime, when my hands get cold. But at least I'm not in the big house. I can pretty well do what I want here.

D: *Are you very old at this time?*

B: I'm thirty-seven.

D: *What ever happened to Joslyn? Did she ever marry?*

B: No. What happened was that Joslyn followed in the footsteps of the old lord. The old lord ... they had locked him up in his chambers. And he finally got so bad to where they had to tie him down on his bed and keep him tied up all the time. And finally, someone slipped him a poisoned drink and put him out of his misery.

D: *Was he still hallucinating or what?*

B: It had gotten worst. And he was believing what he was seeing was real instead of what was around him. That's why they had to tie him down.

D: *Did he try to hurt himself or hurt others?*

B: Yes. And the Lady Joslyn, not having the excuse that the lord had, she was just getting more and more extreme with her temper. She went insane also, but it was a different type of insanity. They locked her up in her chambers. And finally, they had to end up walling her up in a small cell with just an opening large enough to pass her food and water, because she was too violent.

D: *Hmmm, that sounds pretty extreme to do that.*

B: It was for the safety of everybody else. Because she'd be sitting there acting perfectly normal. And you never knew when she would suddenly *scream*. And she had this particular scream that was very blood-curdling. And she would attack whoever was the closest person and try to kill them.

D: *Did she have any reason?*

B: No! She might be sitting there in front of the fireplace doing some embroidery with the other ladies. And suddenly she would scream and throw her embroidery down and turn to the nearest lady and try to kill her.

D: *Hmmm. Well, you know she was always angry and violent in a way, because the way she used to beat you.*

B: Yes. Apparently, she had started going insane then, but people just put it down as bad temper. But she just got worst and worst about it, till finally they had to wall her up. I suspect she's still alive and they're still feeding her. She's probably a poor pathetic creature by now. But it is said that at nighttime you can hear her screaming. And with the way her chamber is situated, it tends to echo through a good part of the big house. And I rather imagine that when she dies there's going to be a restless spirit there in the big house.

D: *What about the lord? Do you think there will be a restless spirit from him?*

B: Well, he's already dead. And he was ready to go. I don't really think there'll be a restless spirit from him. Because I suspect the minute they released his spirit it went ahead and crossed over into that other dimension that he had been looking into for so many years, after he went insane.

D: *But did he also try to attack people like she did?*

B: No, he didn't try to attack people. He just tried to work twisted magic on them. Most of the time it would not work. But sometimes it would work in a very bizarre way. And so in our group we've been very busy trying to keep all of this under control.

D: *Can you tell me of any incidents that were bizarre?*

B: Well, he was talking to a friend of his, and the friend mentioned that his prize cow was with calf. And would be giving birth to a calf in a few months. You see, the old lord sometimes he would be feeling good and sometimes he would be feeling bad. And that day he was feeling good, and he thought he would help out his friend. And so he worked a ritual on the cow. When the calf was born it had two heads and didn't live.

D: *Oh. He was hoping to make it have twins or something?* (Yes) *That is bizarre. I wonder what the lord thought when that happened?*

B: He wasn't aware of it when it happened because he had swung back over to the bad side and he didn't really know what was going on.

D: *So he was not as violent as Joslyn was.* (No) *I don't imagine he liked being tied down to his bed though.*

B: No. But sometimes he would get violent and start trying to work some rituals in his violent stage, which could be very dangerous. He was very cunning. And he liked to conceal a knife and wait for one of his servants to get close to him. And then he'd slit their throat. He'd just do it real quick and he wouldn't be violent about it. He'd just ... he was sneaky.

D: *Then he was dangerous in that way.* (Yes) *It shows that it's not always good to try to work with these powers, is it?*

B: If you don't know what you're doing and try to go up to the negative side. And so all could see that he was weak and wouldn't live much longer. So they just tied him up and left him on his bed to die. They still fed him, but they knew he'd be dying soon. But the Lady Joslyn is very healthy and strong still. And so they walled her up.

D: *I didn't think if these were the lords of the house that the servants could do this.*

B: No, no, it was the other people in the house. Because the new lord, the lord's oldest son, was the one that ordered us to tie him to his bed. And when the old lord died, that made the son the new lord. And one of the first things he did was to order us to take stronger measures to keep the Lady Joslyn under control. And finally he knew that he couldn't order a servant to wall up the Lady Joslyn, so he did it himself.

D: *That's what I was thinking. The servants wouldn't have had enough power, or authority, to do this.* (Yes) *I imagine the Lady Joslyn didn't like that too much.* (No) *But the only way anyone has contact with her is just by passing her things through the opening?*

B: Yes, the opening is a handspan tall and about a cubit wide.

D: *Then nobody ever goes in to take care of her in any way?*

B: There's only that one opening to the chamber. The only thing that can be passed in is a platter of food.

D: *I guess I'm thinking of her bodily functions and things like that. And clothes. How could she live in there like that?*

B: There's a hole in the corner of the chamber for her to take care of her bodily functions. And there's another opening into the chamber, it's in the roof of the chamber. It's high up to where she can't reach it. And with a rope and a hook they lower a pitcher of water to her. And they pass food through that opening where they walled her up. The opening is wide enough to pass through folded clothes, but we don't know if she wears them or not.

D: *That's what I was thinking. It would be very hard for someone to live in a room without having contact. It sounds pretty drastic.*

B: The situation had gotten very bad. Words cannot describe how bad she had gotten. You never knew when her temper was going to strike. Her eyes always looked funny. She would be sitting there very calm and acting almost normal. And all of a sudden she'd just … turn around real quick and try to stab you.

D: *Do you think things would have been different if she had married?* (No) *I thought maybe it was frustration.*

B: I think it was just an extension of her bad temper that she always showed. The Lady Joslyn was just basically not right upstairs. And she never would control her temper. And had passions and temper she directed in a negative direction. And it overwhelmed her.

D: *What about the new lord? Does he show any signs of anything like this?*

B: No. The new lord had that tower walled off, and no one can go in or out. And the new lord has his interest in other things.

D: *What about the Inquisition? Is that still active in your country?*

B: Yes. As a matter of fact I suspect the Inquisition is here now. Some strange lords came up just a few days past to visit here at the big house. And instead of doing the normal things that lords do when they're here visiting, hunting and such as that, they keep asking questions and talking to everybody and snooping around the servants' quarters. So I suspect they are the Inquisition.

D: *Then they are not really priests?*

B: They're priests in disguise, because the priests have much money. It's easy for them to disguise themselves with rich clothes.

D: *But of course, you must be suspicious of any strangers anyway, shouldn't you?*

B: Yes. I'm just afraid that someone is going to let something slip.

D: *Yes, you must be extra careful at this time. I just wondered if they were still active. It hasn't passed away then.—But are you reasonably happy in your life?*

B: Yes. My husband's good to me. And I'm good to him. And we work rituals well together.

D: *That's very good that it turned out well for you.*

I decided to move her to something important that occurred later. I had an uneasy feeling the Inquisition was going to get her. I gave her instructions to view anything that might be bothersome with objectivity. I had had this feeling throughout this story that she would not be able to escape a final confrontation with them. I could not see her living this secretive lifestyle in that time period and growing old. With her mention of the renewed activity of the Inquisition and her apprehension about it, I felt the time was drawing near. I counted to three and moved her ahead in time.

B: I have baked my bread and I have just taken it out of my oven. And there is a knocking at my door. I go and I answer the door. And it's one of the visitors standing there. He comes in and wants to talk to me. And I ask him why he would want to talk to someone as lowly as I. I don't really think this, you understand, but I must say it so as he won't be suspicious. And he starts making remarks about things that he says he suspects, but he's really fishing for information.

D: *To see what you'll say?*

B: Yes. So I pretend that I'm very dumb. And act like I might be slightly touched. There are those who are slightly touched, and they do not *know* things as well. They do not talk very good.

D: *That's always a safe way.*

I turned the tape over before it was really to the end, because I did not want it to run out at what might be a crucial moment.

D: *Then what happened?*

B: The lord, the man there, he's not getting any answers from me. And I can tell that he's getting angry. And he's going to get dangerous. But if I tell him what I know it would be even worse.

D: *But he could just think that you are dumb or stupid.*

B: He could, except that he's heard of my reputation of being able to heal people.

D: *Do you think somebody said something they shouldn't?*

B: Yes. I think one of the children might have. One of the children here at this place, not one of mine, but someone else's, has accidently let something slip.

D: *Yes, children are innocent in that way. It's difficult. Then he doesn't believe you?*

B: No. And so he gets violent and he starts to bruise me and hit me. And he rips my clothes off. And he gets very violent.

This was all said in a very calm, detached manner with no emotion involved. Apparently, she was obeying instructions to remain objective so that it wouldn't bother her. I was grateful that she chose this way to report it.

B: And so he ... at one point he grabs ... I have this iron rod that I use for taking care of the fire in the fireplace. He grabs that and sticks it in the fire to make it hot and threatens to burn me with it if I don't tell him what he wants to know.

D: *But it's all right for you to observe it this way, isn't it?* (Yes) *It's not as painful.*

B: No, I'm floating above watching what's happening.

This could also explain the detachment. She had the ability to leave her body through years of practice with her religion. She may have chosen to do that when the pain began.

D: I don't want you to be uncomfortable. That's why I asked you to be objective. (Yes) *I try to be kind with you.*

B: Yes. This man is bewildered. He gets pleasure from pain. And he starts making welts on my arms and legs with this hot poker. And finally he rapes me. But the way he rapes me is not the normal way. What he does is that he gets the hot poker and ... and sticks me with that instead. And while he's doing that ... because he has tied me down ... while he's doing that with one hand, then he's doing himself with the other hand. And he gets pleasure seeing me being in pain like that. Because he is sticking my privates with this hot rod.

D: Yes, that is perverted.

I found this whole mental picture horribly revolting.

B: And he comes all over me, and meanwhile I'm rising in pain. And afterwards he's angry because he still hasn't gotten anything from me. And so he loses his temper. He gets the rod hot again and he strikes me across the throat with it. And the way he does this, it crushes my windpipe. And I choke to death.

She reported the entire horrible episode with total detachment, no emotion involved.

D: So he got no further pleasure anyway. That's a very perverted type of person.

His anger may have been further provoked if she was actually out of her body and not exhibiting the proper agony responses needed to fuel his perverted desires. This may also have caused him to strike out at her in anger because she had not provided him with the full pleasure he had been seeking. He probably felt unfulfilled.

D: *Were you alone in the house when this happened?* (Yes) *And you are now floating above it watching?* (Yes)

I was grateful for that. I'm glad she didn't reexperience such a horrible death.

D: *What happens? What does the man do then?*

B: Well, he covers his privates back up. And he puts the poker back over beside the fireplace. And he just leaves me where I'm laying. He leaves, and he shuts the door behind him like he found it to start with. And he goes back to the big house as if nothing has happened. And so my husband comes home and he discovers my body. The children have been out in the fields with the other children. And so they haven't made it home yet.

D: *That at least was good that they were not there.*

B: Yes. And my husband discovers my body and he knows immediately what has happened, due to the condition my body is in. And he is trying to figure out something that he can do about it. Because, unless he is wanting to get killed in the process, he can't take direct physical action against that man by himself. And so what he does, he calls a meeting of the whole group of us. And two of the stronger men trick the man away from the big house. They tell him that they have some information for him. That there's a young girl who is wanting to give him information. And so they tell him to meet them at a certain place. And they meet and they take him out in the woods where the rest of the group is waiting for him. But it's far enough away from the big house to where nobody can hear what's going on. And they tie him up on a large stone spread-eagled, to where he can't move. And they're going to find out from him what happened to me. And so they ... they have to resort to pain to get it from him.

D: *They were pretty sure he was the one?*

B: Yes, they could tell. One of his hands was bandaged from a burn, because his hand had slipped at one point and he burned himself on the poker that he was ramming me with.

D: *And you said they had to resort to pain. That's usually not the way of your people, is it?*

B: No, it's not. They tried other ways first. And he refused to tell them anything. And so they decided that he was going to have to die anyway, because people who are sick like he is should not live. The pain they used mostly was mental pain rather than physical pain. But they had to turn to some physical pain. At first they weren't going to use very much. And they saw that the amounts they were using, which were enough for an ordinary person to not like and to hurt, this man was getting pleasure from.

D: *But he was perverted anyway.*

B: Yes. And so they had to change what they were doing. And they found out from him what he had done to me. And they discovered that he was part of the Inquisition. So they knew that if they let him go, he would kill all of them. And so ... they went ahead and killed him. After finding out from him what they were trying to find out.

D: *No, this is not the normal way of your people. But sometimes it is something that cannot be avoided.*

B: True. They went ahead and buried him. And they put some spells over his grave so it would never be found.

D: *How do you feel about all that happened?*

B: I'm sorry that my people had to dirty themselves by resorting to the Inquisition's tactics.

D: *In a way that made them just the same, didn't it?*

B: Somewhat. However, I must admit the ones who resorted to using the pain were the younger ones that were more impatient. The older ones knew that they could do it just by using mental torture, rather than physical torture.

D: *But do you think it was justified?*

B: That's hard to say. Because when he didn't return to the big house the others became suspicious. And they stayed longer than they would have otherwise.

D: *Trying to find out what happened to him.*

B: Yes. And they finally decided it was some highway robbers that got him.

D: *That would have been a safe assumption anyway. It would be safer for your people.* (Yes) *Well, how do you feel about what happened to* you? *I mean, do you have anger? Or how do you feel emotionally about what happened?*

B: I feel sad, because I didn't feel like my time was finished yet. I had other things to do. And I feel confused. Why *me?* Why me? I had never done anything to the man.

D: *Yes, you were a very gentle person. But do you feel anger?*

B: Anger, no. I could very easily. But it wouldn't help anything. It would just start the cycle all over again.

D: *Yes. You would be creating bad karma, so to speak, that would have to be repaid later. If you know that word.*

B: I understand the concept. And what happened has not adversely affected my karma but has done bad things to his karma.

D: *I'm very sorry about what happened. But I've been in such close contact with you that I wanted to know what happened to you. I appreciate you telling me about it. And I'm glad you did it in* that *way so that you wouldn't have to* feel *it.*

B: Yes, it was very painful, plus it was too much.

D: *But it was not painful just to observe it. I'm glad you chose that way to do it.* (Yes) *All right. Let's move away from that very painful and sad scene. Let's move away from it and drift up from it. I want you to drift up through time to now when you're living this life as Brenda. And be able to look at that life objectively from this point. This is June 24, 1986. And you can look at the patterns easier now. Is there anyone in that life that you know in this life now as Brenda? That you can see a relationship with?*

B: Let me look to see. The pattern is very complicated.

D: *It sure is. And there were many people involved.*

B: The lord of the manor is involved in this life. I'm trying to trace the thread through my father.

D: *What about the Lady Joslyn? Do you have a relationship with her this time? Have you known her?*

B: (Pause) Not yet.

D: *Because it seems like a lot of karma there, the way she was treating you.*

B: Yes, there is a lot of karma there. But some has been worked out in some intervening lives. And there will be some more worked out in future lives. She hasn't been involved with this life yet. It's hard to see whether or not she will be.

D: *I would hope she wouldn't be.* (Yes) *Well, what about the two men in her life? Do you see any relationship in this life with them?*

B: Let me look.

One thing that makes it complicated is that in the present life she's at a nexus point. Where all the lines come together and then come out in new patterns.

B: (Pause) Let me look. Roff was in her life briefly. He followed a similar pattern again. He was the one known as Rick. And in this present life the one known as Rick is not doing well with working out karma. He's just adding a little bit more to it. Positive as well as negative. Gundevar is in this life. He is having difficulty working out this karma. Because in that life he was committed to Astelle. And when Astelle was brutally murdered, it tore him up inside, and he could hardly face it. And he didn't want to go through it again. And so in the lives since then whenever these two souls have met, Gundevar has always drawn back in pain and horror and tried to avoid the karmic connection. Because Gundevar does not want to go through that kind of pain again.

D: *I can understand why.*

B: He's afraid it will happen again.

D: *Well, we were told that if we looked at this life, Brenda would understand the problems she was having in her love life.*

B: Yes. Gundevar is the one known as John. And Gundevar is afraid to be involved in this karmic connection and to work out the karma there. Gundevar needs to work out this karma. The sooner he works it out the better it will be for him. And so it looks promising that he will work it out in this life. But he might decide to go ahead and wait until the next life again. But he's had several chances in past lives to work it out. And each time it gets a little less painful for him. And he gets a little bit closer to working out the karma before he runs away from it.

D: *Well, I think you've done very good at looking at this and trying to understand what was going on. And as you think on it, you will probably be able to understand more. We'll have to leave it at this time now. But I do appreciate you giving me the story. And I hope as you think on it, you will be able to figure out a great deal in your life that will begin to fall into place and make sense from this. (Yes) Even though it was a violent life, it had its points that you can learn from.*

(Subject brought forward.) She had some strange physical reactions upon awakening in spite of instructions for mental and physical well-being. I suppose the death was so violent it still left some emotional residue.

As she was coming out of trance I noticed a curious physical phenomena that I have observed a few times in the past. For some reason in the other cases this also involved the area of the neck. I noticed a red area appearing on her neck over the larynx. A red mark about an inch square. The other cases had involved hangings and had left a wider mark on the throat. I wasn't too concerned because in the other cases after the first initial shock and surprise the marks vanished after about five minutes leaving no lasting effects. This time when she awoke, she did not know about the mark, but her breathing was bothering her. She sat up and cleared her throat and coughed. I turned the tape recorder back on and recorded her reactions. She said she was having difficulty breathing. "I just can't breathe. I'm not getting any air in me."

I turned the tape recorder off to look at her neck. I gave suggestions that the mark and the discomfort would be gone quickly. As I watched the redness faded gradually until her neck appeared normal. She seemed to be breathing easier and when she was comfortable, she talked about some scenes she remembered from the session. I wanted to hear any memories before I told her about her death. All she consciously remembered about the session was seeing a fireplace and a mixing bowl with some dough in it. And the whole picture had an aura of brown, which she thought is a depressing color. This is common for subjects who have experienced the somnambulist state. The only memories are usually at the beginning or the very end of the session, and they often seem like dream images. They also fade quickly as dreams do upon awakening.

I then told her what the session and the death was all about. I thought it was interesting that the red mark had appeared in the same place where Astelle had been struck with the hot poker. Her initial reaction of not being able to breathe had faded within a few seconds. The mark took a little longer, a few minutes to fade away. She found my account of her gruesome death revolting, but it did not evoke any personal reactions. It was as though I were telling her about a movie I had been watching. Although she did say she had a birthmark in an unusual place. A dark birthmark on the fleshy part of her genitals.

The Astelle I will remember is not the tragic figure who died so horribly at the hands of the ruthless inquisitor. The one who will remain forever in my memory is the gentle, golden-haired girl who rides her unicorn across the top of the rainbow into a land of peace and beauty on the other side.

Section 3
More Lives with Karen

Chapter 12
The Minstrel, Part 1
(Recorded May 13, 1983)

We had just left the life of the Druidess. She had just died.

D: Let's go back in time about another hundred years. Let's go into the 600s, way back there. Going back in time about another hundred years from this life you've just been talking about. I will count to three and it will be about another hundred years before this time. 1, 2, 3, what are you doing?

K: I am stringing my harp.

D: Do you play the harp?

K: Aye. I make an attempt. (An accent was emerging.)

D: That's a beautiful instrument. Is it difficult?

K: It has its intricacies.

D: Have you been playing it long?

K: All me life.

D: Is it a big harp or a small harp?

K: It is a lap harp.

D: A lap harp? I've seen some that are very large. It's not like that?

K: No. It is not quite a carryin' harp, but it is one that you would use for a grand hall performance so that everyone in the hall could hear. (Definite strong [Irish?] accent.)

D: Are you a man or a woman?

K: I be a man.

D: You be a man. What is your name?

K: It 'tis O'Keefe.

D: *O'Keefe? What country are we in?*

K: 'Tis Erin. (She said it so fast it ran together. I had her repeat. I thought it was Er or maybe Ireland.) It is called Erin. (Very deliberately.)

D: *Okay. It was just a little hard for me to understand you. About how old are you?*

K: Um, I'm maybe twenty-four, maybe twenty-five.

D: *You're a young man then.*

K: I be in my middle years.

D: *Is this what you do for a living, play the harp?* (Aye) *Where do you go to play the harp?*

K: (Smile) Where *don't* I go? 'Tis a bard** I be by trade.

**Bard: a tribal poet-singer skilled in composing and reciting verses on heroes and their deeds. **

D: *Oh, you mean you travel everywhere and make music wherever you go?*

K: Aye. I tell the songs of what is happenin', and tales of past glories and whatever they want to hear.

D: *Do you go to the towns or to the castles—am I using the right words—or what?*

K: I go to the keeps and to the inns. And sometimes there are gatherin's.

D: *Anywhere there are people?* (Aye) *Do they pay you to do this?*

K: Oh, aye, otherwise I would not play. Sometimes it is just my meal and a place to sleep for the night. Other times they pay me in gold coins. But it makes a living.

D: *But you don't have a regular home that you live in?*

K: No. My home is where I lay my head.

D: *How do you travel?*

K: Mostly on foot.

D: *Oh, I thought you might have a horse or something.*

K: Occasionally I manage to make enough money to afford a horse, but ah, then something usually happens. And sometimes you get on bad times, so I trust my feet.

D: *Isn't that hard though? Do you have to walk a long way?*

K: Sometimes there are long ways to walk, yes. And sometimes you manage to get a ride with someone that feels sorry for you and different things. But it's not bad.

D: *And then you would ride on a horse with someone else?*

K: Aye, on a horse or perhaps a cart with a farmer maybe.

D: *How many harps do you carry with you?*

K: I have my own travelin' harp that I carry. This one is—it belongs in the hall, and I be using it for this performance. But it not be mine.

D: *You only carry one with you then?* (Aye) *And other places, you can use other people's harps?*

K: Mostly I use my own, unless it's like for a performance like this. If there's a grand hall to be performin' in, then a small travelin' harp would not be big enough to be heard. But it does me fine.

D: *It wouldn't be loud enough.* (No) *You said you're getting ready for a performance? Are you going to do one today?*

K: Tonight, aye.

D: *Where's that going to be?*

K: At the hall here!

D: *Where are we? (Pause) This place where you're going to do the performance.*

K: It be the Keep** O'Connor.

D: *The Keep O'Connor? It's in someone's house? (I didn't know if house was the right word to use.)* (Aye)

** English term corresponding to the French donjon for the strongest portion of the fortification of a castle, the place of last resort in case of siege or attack. The keep was either a single tower or a larger fortified enclosure. **

D: *Are there going to be a lot of people there?*

K: Oh, probably.

D: *Is it a special occasion or something?*

K: It's a gatherin'. Everybody, they have 'em every now and again. There's been a recent harvest, and everyone is through with their work, and it be time to have a little fun.

D: *Will there be other entertainment besides you?*

K: Ah—there are—acrobats (had trouble finding that word) and jugglers and—a couple on the flute. A few things like that, yes.

D: *Then there'll be lots of entertainment. Sounds like it will be a grand time.*

K: It will not be bad.

D: *Do you think they will pay you good at this one?*

K: Aye. I'll get probably a bag of silver for it.

D: *Oh, that'd be good, wouldn't it? Are you going to dress special for the occasion? Or do you carry any clothes with you?*

K: I'm just dressed in my best blue (blue and next word unclear) and it's a tunic with hose and boots.

D: *Do you wear anything on your head?*

K: I have a hat, ehhh.

D: *This is your best clothes?*

K: It's what I have.

D: *(Laugh) You can't carry much with you, can you, if you have to walk?* (No) *What do you do about food?*

K: I usually play for my supper or sometimes catch a rabbit or something if I'm out in the middle of nowhere.

D: *Oh, do you have weapons?*

K: Um, have a rope and a snare.

D: *That's enough to catch something with? Okay. Well, where do you get your songs that you sing?*

K: Sometimes I make them up, and there are those that other harpers have made up. And harpers get together and trade songs and secrets and little bits of news from wherever they've been.

D: *Oh. Then these are some of the songs that tell of things that have happened?* (Aye) *And you have made up several yourself?*

K: A few.

D: *What are you going to perform tonight? Have you already picked it out?*

K: Not really. It depends on how the crowd will go. I'm not the first to go, to be listened to. Usually the harper stays at the last. And I'll see what the crowd seems to want.

D: *Do you sing love songs sometimes?*

K: On occasion. Again, it depends on the crowd. Most of the men wish to hear about brave deeds that have been done. Of course, the ladies want to hear about lovers, but ah, just whatever hits 'em just right.

D: *Then you won't know until tonight then. Okay. Let's move ahead till the night of your performance, and you're giving your performance. What are you doing now?*

K: I'm just singin' a song.

D: *Okay. Sing it for me.*

I thought this would be an unusual chance to see if we could do this. I always rely on my intuition because these opportunities arise unexpectedly. I never know if something is possible until I try. I wondered whether or not we would be able to get any kind of music. It might be a first.

D: *What kind of a song is it?*

K: I don't know. It's just a song.

D: *About brave deeds, or what? Go ahead and sing it so I can hear it too.*

K: Ah, you would not want to hear my voice. It's not that good.

D: *Oh, yes. You let them hear it. I'm as good as them, aren't I?*

K: Begins to sing. (Song #1.) The first part is in English: "There was a lad, a bonnie young lad. He went to woo a lady."

The rest (timed at forty seconds) was definitely not English, but some other language. A good melody, and the words seemed to follow a pattern. I do not think it was gibberish.

I have a theory about this. Apparently, the regressed subject uses their brain (or mine?) to translate from other languages. This would explain the searching for words that sometimes occurs. Maybe music is different. It may be harder to translate. She started out to translate and then switched. Many of us sing songs in another language automatically. Maybe this is natural, and since it is harder to translate poetry or music, he just left it in the natural state. This phenomenon will have to be investigated further. (These songs will be available to download from a link at the end of the chapter.)

D: *Oh, that's very good. I like that. That's very good. Did the people like it?*

K: They seemed to be in the right mood for it, aye.

D: *Is that one that you made up yourself?* (Aye) *It's pretty. I like it.*

K: It's not bad.

D: *Do you do more than one song at the performance?*

K: Aye. Usually I do two and twenty, maybe more. They all want to hear something different.

D: *Are you going to sing a different one tonight besides that one?*

K: Aye, I be singin' a lot more.

D: *Can you sing me another?*

K: Aye, let me think here.

D: *Because you must think fast when you're doing a performance, don't you?*

She starts singing unexpectedly, in another language. (Song #2. Timed at twenty-seven seconds.)

This was quite exciting. I had traveled back in time and was actually present as a minstrel entertained. It was exhilarating to actually hear music in an unknown tongue. I knew I had stumbled onto something very original and valuable.

D: *Oh, I like that too. What language is that?*

K: It be Celt.

D: *Oh! What is the song about?*

K: It tells about how a lad a long time ago saw a dragon. And it threatened a lady, and so he had to go and kill it. And it goes on and on.

D: *That's a song of bravery then, of brave deeds?*

K: Aye, I suppose you could consider it that. Maybe a love song, maybe. Um.

D: *I couldn't understand the words. That's a language I don't know. Is that one that you made up?*

K: No, it is one that has been passed down fer a long time.

D: *Then that's one that you sing often.*

K: Times.

Another interesting phenomenon took place while she was singing. She moved her hands as though playing a harp that was sitting upright in her lap. Her fingers plucked invisible strings, and her right thumb would run across all the strings sideways in perfect time with the singing.

D: *Well, do you think they will give you a bag of gold tonight?*

K: No, it be silver, maybe. If I be lucky.

D: *A bag of coins though. (Aye) Oh, that's good. I think you deserve it. I like your voice. And you said the people act like they like it?*

K: They seem to be quite happy, but of course, everyone is getting roaring drunk, so pretty soon they won't be able to understand.

D: *Because you're last. By that time, they're really drunk, aren't they? (I laughed.)*

K: There are those who stay fairly sober because the harpist brings news from everywhere. And it's like having your own messenger, you know, from different parts.

D: *Oh, yes, because you travel everywhere, and you know all the things that are happening. (Aye) Well, how do you give the news? Do you sing that or ...*

K: Most of it, yes. Sometimes you talk it and you just play the harp while you talk it. And you tell 'em about what's goin' on, and who's doin' what, and who's gettin' married and ...

D: *Oh. How do you do that? Can you show me? Like tonight, if you were going to tell what has happened, the latest news.*

K: No. Perhaps, ah, they would ask from different counties what's goin' on, and it would go on about—I don't know. It comes to me.

D: *Well, if you were going to talk it, how would you talk it?*

K: I would perhaps talk it in a very sing-song voice, so that it all seemed to rhyme, and it all came together, and the music just kind of added to it.

D: *Is it hard to think of the rhyme like that?*

K: (Laugh) Sometimes.

D: *(Laugh) You have to do it fast without thinking about it before-hand.* (Aye) *It seems like it would be hard to make it all rhyme.*

K: Well, at least if it doesn't rhyme, you have to make it sound like it fits together anyway.

D: *I think that would be hard to do.* (Aye) *You play the harp too. That's a talent that's hard to do too. Not everyone can do those things.*

K: This is true.

D: *To sing it and to make things rhyme and to play the music. You said there are also flutes? Do they play with you or ...?*

K: Usually a harper plays alone.

D: *You said this was a keep. These people living here, do they have a title? Do you know what a title is?*

K: You mean like bein' lords or ...?

D: *Yeah, something like that.*

K: Let me think here. The O'Connell is just the O'Connell. I mean, he be, ah, like the great-grandson or something. Some brother maybe sometimes removed of the king.

D: *You think he might be like a chief or something?*

K: Ah. That's about as close as you can come, because the O'Connell was his great-great-great-grandfather or whatever was king of Ireland. And, you know, that's how he gets his position, as it were.

D: *Well, in your country now, do they have a king?*

K: Eh, the last time I heard, ah, aye.

D: *I was wondering if they had some kind of ruler over the whole ...?*

K: (Interrupted) It be the O'Brien right now.

D: *Over the whole land?*

K: Well, see, they're fightin' as to who has the right to the title.

They got all the houses, those who've *been* royal and those who *are* royal and then—ah, they keep going on about it.

D: *You mean they're having like a war?*

K: Everyone's always at war with someone else.

D: *You never can get away from war, can you?* (No) *These are part of the news that you carry?*

K: Aye. As far as perhaps who's won, and who has died and 'tsuch as that.

D: *That's the only way anyone would know what is happening.* (Uh-huh) *(Her hands were moving again.) Are you singing a song now?*

K: No, I just be playin'.

D: *Do they like that?* (Aye) *Where are you going after you leave this place?*

K: Well, I wouldn't been sure yet. Maybe to the north of here. Or perhaps maybe I'll go to the south and go to Kerry. I'm not sure yet. I haven't really decided. I have a few days to think about it.

D: *You're going to stay here for a few days?* (Aye) *That's good. Do you try to stay away from where the wars are happening?*

K: Well, you see, it's like this. A bard doesn't usually have to worry about who's fightin' who and such, because they all want to hear the news of everywhere else. So, he's kind of considered protected territory, as it were.

D: *I see. Then they wouldn't think you were dangerous. They wouldn't try to kill you or get you into the war.*

K: Right.

D: *That's good. You don't have to worry about that then.—Did you ever have a desire to settle down and have a home?*

K: Sounds rather boring to me.

D: *Well, what about having a wife?*

K: More trouble than they're worth.

D: *(Laugh) So you never thought of having a home and a family, or children.*

K: Every time I think of having a home or a family, I come on some fine happy couple. The wife nags the husband and he's got five squallin' brats, and ah, this changes my mind very fast.

D: (Laugh) Then the idea doesn't appeal to you. (No) *I thought everyone wanted to have a home. Did you* ever *have a home? Long ago?*

K: I remember when I was young that—I used to live with my mother. And then one day my father came to the keep where that we were livin' and she told me that was my father. And that night I packed my bags and when he left, so did I.

D: You went with him? (Aye) *How did she feel about that?*

K: Don't know. I haven't seen her since.

D: Did you travel with your father for a while then?

K: Aye. I think she probably told him just to get rid of me, 'cause I was quite a bit of trouble to her. And she wanted to be "unencumbered" by a growing child. (He sounded a little aggravated by the memory.)

D: Were you trouble to your father then?

K: If I were, he beat me about the head, so I straightened up pretty good. And he taught me the business of harping and how to sing.

D: Oh, then you learned from him. (Aye) *He must have taught you well.—The harp you are playing, does it stand up or is it on your lap or ...?*

K: It sits on my lap. It's a lap harp. (This whole time she had been strumming away at the invisible strings, while she talked to me.)

D: Then you sit in a chair, and it's on your lap? And then you, what, strum the strings? (Aye) *Well, some harps I've seen stand up on the floor.*

K: I've seen them that be that big too, but they're probably more trouble than they're worth. I've never played one that was that large. This is one of the larger ones I've played.

D: You couldn't carry the big ones around. (No) *Well, I really thank you for letting me hear your songs. I liked them and I think the other people liked them too.*

K: It can be hoped.

D: They will give you money and give you a place to stay for a few days. That's very good. Enjoy yourself. Let's leave that scene now. It's a happy scene, a happy time, an enjoyable time.

(Subject brought forward.)

This was an unusual session in many ways. I found the music especially interesting. I will try to get some more next week when we meet at Harriet's house. I wish for her to witness this.

You can download these songs and more from the website:

www.ozarkmt.com
https://ozarkmt.com/product/horns-of-the-goddess-songs/.

Chapter 13
The Minstrel, Part 2
(Recorded May 19, 1983)

Session held at Harriet's house. I hope to get some more music from her to hear. Beginning of tape was part of Hiroshima story, then part of Viking life.

D: *Let's leave that scene, and let's go back further into the past.
Let's go back to the 600s. (Counted back by hundred-year
jumps.) I will count to three and it will be the 600s. 1, 2, 3, it
is the 600s, some time in there. What are you doing?*

K: I be walkin'.

D: *Where are you walking? (It sounded as though I had found
the minstrel again.)*

K: I have no great idea. I'm not quite sure where I am. (Laugh)

D: *(Laugh) Where have you* been?

K: Been down to Kerry and around the lake. Um—just wanderin'
around, seein' a bit of the country.

D: *What do you do for a living?*

K: I be a bard.

D: *Have you been giving a performance somewhere?*

K: Not unless you consider harpin' at the inn a performance, eh,
no.

D: *That's what you've been doing?*

K: The past few weeks, aye.

D: *Well, did you get much from that?*

K: I got some ale and a roof over my head and some food in my
belly.

D: *No money? No coins?*

K: It keeps the body together.

D: *Well, it's something to do till you can find a place that will pay, isn't it?*

K: I'm not worried about it.

D: *The people in the inns don't give you money, do they, no coins?*

K: Sometimes they do, but that is rare. Usually they just feed me and give what I can drink and consume and …

D: *Give you a place to sleep, eh?* (Aye) *Do you have your harp with you?*

K: Aye, it's strapped to my pack on my back.

D: *What else do you carry with you?*

K: A change of clothes, a few extra strings, a knife. That be about it.

D: *You don't need very much, do you?* (Nay) *What about shoes?*

K: Aye. The pair I have on my feet.

D: *That's it.*

K: Why carry around more?

D: *Well, I thought you might wear them out.*

K: Then I can always sing for some new ones.

D: *(Laugh) Sing for your supper, sing for some new clothes then. Then you don't know where you're going or where you're going to be performing next?*

K: Not unless I find out where I be pretty soon. Who knows?

D: *Are you lost?*

K: I haven't considered myself lost. I just don't know where I'm goin'.

D: *(Laugh) You know where you've been though. That's about it.* (Aye) *What do you usually do? Just walk till you find something?*

K: Aye. Till I decide where I want to go. Don't always know. Sometimes I change my mind even then, when I do.

D: *You told me that you do lots of singing.* (Aye) *That's really what you do for a living, sing and play the harp?*

K: And I get paid for the news that I bring too.

D: *You said you make up some of your songs, don't you?*

K: That's true.

D: *Well, would you feel like singing a song for me? You've nothing else to do right now.*

I wanted Harriet to hear the singing.

K: No much. But it be a little bit wet to be singin' out here.

D: *Why is it wet?*

K: It's rainin'.

D: *Oh, you get wet then, don't you?*

K: Aye. But I haven't melted yet.

D: *(Laugh) Then you're not worried about getting in somewhere.*

K: It not be that bad. But I wouldn't want to take my harp out of the pack.

D: *You have to have your harp in order to sing?*

K: Oh, it just would be easier.

D: *But you don't want to take it out because it's raining.*

K: You see, if it got wet, it would warp and then its sound would be ruined.

D: *Do you keep it wrapped up?*

K: In oilcloth, yes.

D: *Then you don't have to worry about it getting wet, just you getting wet. (Aye) Well, let's move ahead till you find a place where you're going to perform. You should find somewhere pretty soon to get out of the rain. Where you'll be nice and warm. I will count to three and let's move ahead till you've found a place where you're inside, and you're going to perform for someone. 1, 2, 3, we've moved ahead till you're inside. What are you doing?*

K: Be sittin' by the fire, and warmin' up.

D: *Where are you?*

K: It be an inn.

D: *Do you know where you are now?*

K: Somewhat. It's called the Yellow Rooster.

D: *Is there a town near there?*

K: No, it be just a crossroads.

D: *Are there any people there?*

K: A few travelers, come to spend the night and get out of the rain.

D: *Are you going to sing for them?*

I had been trying to get him into a position where he could sing some more music for me and Harriet.

K: Aye. Soon somebody'll spy the harp and ask for a song or whatever.

D: *And then they'll want to know the news. That's how you get to stay there, isn't it? (Aye) Otherwise you wouldn't get your free room and food, would you?*

K: That's true.

D: *Could you sing me a song now that you're inside and dry? This would get the people interested too.*

K: What be you wantin' to hear?

D: *Oh, anything. It doesn't matter. I like all the songs. Sing a favorite of yours.*

Here Karen went through a series of intricate motions. She appeared to hold the harp upright on her lap and adjusted or tightened invisible screws on the top. This went on for a few seconds. Then she seemed to be testing the sound by plucking the strings. When this was completed, she sang a slow song. (Song #3. Timed at one minute, five seconds.) Again, her hands moved in time with the music, strumming invisible strings and running her right thumb over the strings. It may have been more plucking the strings rather than strumming. It was very interesting to watch.

D: *That's a pretty song. I like that. What does it say?*

K: (Sigh) I have no idea. It be an old one that the meanings be forgotten. I'm not even sure what it means.

D: *What language is it?*

K: Um, let's see. My father said something about it bein'—ah, Pict. I'm not sure. Something like that.

D: *Pict? (Aye) Oh, then that is older than your language? (Aye) What language do you speak?*

K: Celt.

D: *Celt? Have you ever heard of English? (She frowned.) That's a language. You don't know that one?* (No) *What about Latin?*

K: That be one the priests talk.

D: *Oh, you know that one then.*

K: I have no knowin' of it, but I know *of* it.

D: *But then, this language you were just singing in, is very old.*

K: They say it's as old as the hills. I have me doubts about that.

D: *(Laugh) It's very pretty though. I wonder, it sounds like maybe a love song, but it's hard to tell.*

K: Me father said it was something like that, but it was about— um, let me think now. I'll remember in a minute. Ah, something about a girl that had been—ah, promised that her love would return, and then he never did.

D: *Oh, a sad song?*

K: Aye, something like—you know. Something like life.

D: *Yeah, many of your songs are about life, things that happen, aren't they?* (Aye) *I like that. What did the other people think?*

K: Aye, they seemed to like it all right. It's one that's got a nice tune that seems to carry anyway.

D: *Yes. Would you sing another? (She sighed.) Get you more food.*

K: (Slyly) How well you gonna pay me for this?

D: *Well, how much do you want?*

K: Oh, maybe a few drinks, um, who knows?

D: *What do you drink?*

K: Ale.

D: *Okay. I think I have enough money to buy some drinks. Warm you up on the inside too. (Laugh)*

She sang another slow song. (Song #4. Timed at one minute exactly.) Same hand movements. She seemed to be holding the harp upright in front of her pointing straight out, with a hand on either side of it.

D: *That's another one that sounds a little sad.*

K: It's about a man who lost his kingdom and he laments about it.

D: *What language is that?*

K: Aye, that be Celt.

D: *They sound alike to me.*

K: Ah, they have a lot difference. They're nothing the same. They have maybe a few similarities, but no much.

D: *But to me they sound alike, because I don't know either one. (Laugh)*

K: Be strange. If you not know either one, then you not be from here.

D: *No, I'm not. That's why I've enjoyed your music. (Ah) (I had to think fast.) That's why I was asking if you knew ... Have you ever heard of the country England?*

K: (She frowned.) England?

D: *Or Scotland?*

K: I heard of Scotsland. Across the water.

D: *That's my country. I'm from over that way. So that's why ...*

K: (She interrupted emphatically.) Then how come you don't know the Picts?

D: *Are they from there?*

K: Aye. Surely you be pulling my leg.

D: *(How do I get out of this?) No, I'm not. But I don't think they live where I come from.*

K: Aye, the Picts, they come from Scotsland to over here. You have to know them.

D: *Well, maybe I just didn't know what they were called.*

K: Could be.

D: *England is farther south than Scotsland. It's over across the water too. Okay. How old are you now?*

K: Oh ... I'm about twenty-nine, thirty, maybe ... ah.

D: *You're not very old then, are you?*

K: (Sigh) I be gettin' past me prime.

D: *(Laugh) Have you never been married?*

K: Have no desire to.

D: *(Laugh) Well, what are you going to do when you get too old to sing?*

K: Find a cave and crawl in it and pull it in after me.

D: *(Laugh) 'Cause you know when you're married, you have someone to take care of you.*

K: Ha! That be funny. Usually it be the other way around.

D: *You think so?*

K: I think so.

D: *I thought if you had a wife, in your old age she could take care of you.*

K: (Chuckle) More like nag me into my grave.

D: *(Laugh) Have you ever had a girlfriend or anything?*

K: Not that I stayed around long enough to ... not enjoy.

D: *Ah. Just a wanderer.* (Aye) *But you're not worried about the future then, are you?*

K: The future will take care of itself. I have no worries about it.

D: *(Laugh) Well, you said you travel in Erin?* (Aye) *Have you ever been to any large towns?*

K: There be, ah ... Kerry. It's not too bad. And some of the keeps. You cannot consider them a town, but a few of the keeps, and such like that.

D: *What's the biggest town you've ever been to? (Pause, as though thinking.) You know, where there are lots of people?*

K: Lots of people. I guess the biggest thing I've been to, would be, ah ... maybe the Keep O'Brien, but it's not really what you'd consider ... (Coughs) what you'd consider a town.

D: *You're coughing because you got wet, huh?*

K: Maybe I have a little bit of a chill.

D: *Well, I think of a town as where there's lots of houses all together, and they have names. Do you have anything like that?*

K: Just what's grown around the keeps, that's about it. This way if there be wars or something, they can all go into the keep and not have to worry about it.

D: *It would be safer that way, wouldn't it? (Aye) Well, the inns, are they just out by themselves?*

K: Usually they're on crossroads, or sometimes there's some village of people. You know, where that they gather together, but they're just people who don't like to … maybe, associate with others too much, and they come out here and they live.

D: *But most people live around the keeps then.* (Aye) *Some places there are what they call cities. They're even bigger than towns. Lots and lots of people.*

K: That is not … nothing I've ever been to.

D: *Nothing like that in Erin?* (No) *Well, do you know any happy songs? You've been singing sad songs.*

K: (Sigh) Do they make a happy song?

D: *Do they make more sad songs than happy songs?* (Aye) *I wonder why?*

K: I have no way of knowin'. Seems to be, the people in Erin like to be mournful and sorrowful. It gives an excuse.

D: *I wondered if they ever have anything that was a little lively.*

K: Not that I can think of right off-hand. (She yawned.)

D: *You're yawning like you're getting sleepy.*

K: Aye, it be late. I've been on the road all day. (She yawned again.)

D: *Have you ever heard anyone talk about the "little people"?*

K: You mean the shay (phonetic)?

D: *What is that?*

K: The wee ones. The … um, let's see. Some folks call 'em, ah … leprechauns.

D: *Yes, and some call them fairies. Do you know that word?*

K: We call them the shay. They dance around in the meadows in the moonlight, and they leave their circles, and … Everyone's heard of them.

D: *Have you ever seen any?*

K: Not really remember, maybe when I was a wee bairn, but … Everyone knows that they're real. Maybe mischievous folks though. They pull tricks on people. It's said that they steal children and leave something—a changelin'—in their place that never survives long. But I've never had any dealin's with 'em.

D: *Do you think these are just tales or are they true?*

K: No, they be true! They have people that they say are "pixie-magiced," and they go wanderin' off not quite right. And they do strange things. Dancing naked in the woods in the middle of the night, and different things like that.

D: *(Laugh) Do you think the little people make them do these things?*

K: Aye, because they be mischievous, and they laugh at humans.

D: *You think they just do it for the fun of it.*

K: Perhaps.

D: *What is a changeling?*

K: See ... the fairy, as you call them, or the shay, they have very few children. So, they like little babies and stuff. So, with their magic, they make something in the shape of the child that they be takin'. And leave it there and take the child.

D: *How do they know when it's a changeling?*

K: Well, you see. Usually it's taken sick and then it dies. And it's like just a shadow. And there's different ways that the priests say that they can tell, but I don't know.

D: *Will the changeling live and grow up?*

K: No, it dies soon after.

D: *Then they say that the little people have taken the real child?* (Aye) *I thought maybe you meant that they left another one in its place, and it would live and grow up.*

K: It is said that some have, way back in the past, but I've never heard of it in recent years where that one actually lived.

D: *The priest knows how to tell.*

K: They say they do. Who knows?

D: *Do you ever go to church?* (No) *Do they have churches around in Erin?*

K: They have ... ah, wandering friars or monks or something like that. I'm not sure. But they go around trying to convert people to Christianity and lots of fearin'. And it doesn't sound very good.

D: *Oh, you mean they make people afraid?*

K: They have a lot more don'ts than they have dos.

D: *(Laugh) What do you think about it?*

K: I think I be happy just the way I am.

D: *Are there other religions in the country? You said they're trying to convert, trying to change them?*

K: They say that we're all a bunch of heathens, believin' in Belldain* and things like that, and feys** and shay.

D: *What was the first word you said? Believing about what?*

K: Belldain? (Phonetic. Maybe: Belltain?) It's the fires and all at midwinter and such as like. And keeping the bad spirits away and that the fires always have to be burnin'.

* Beltane is a Celtic word which means "fires of Bel" (Bel was a Celtic deity). It is a fire festival that celebrates of the coming of summer and the fertility of the coming year. These rituals would often lead to matches and marriages, either immediately in the coming summer or autumn. Beltane is the Gaelic May Day festival. Most commonly it is held on May 1, or about halfway between the spring equinox and the summer solstice. *
**Fey: the world of the little people, leprechauns, fairies, sprites, brownies, etc. **

D: *And they say this is bad to believe that way?*

K: It says that you're damning your soul and that it's goin' to burn in the same set fires. (We laughed.) And I asked them how did they know, have they ever been died and been buried and find out?

D: *(Laugh) What did they say?*

K: Then they say that I'm goin' to Hell for sure, so …

D: *Because you're asking questions?*

K: Aye. For which they have no answers. So, of course, I'm in the wrong and they're in the right. Ehhh!

D: *Yeah, it's easy to say that when they don't have an answer. Have you ever heard of the Druids?*

K: (Thinking) Ah … Druids, Druids? Um … no.

D: *I've heard that was a kind of religion too. You don't have them in Erin?*

K: If you're talkin' about religions and things, they're the people who brought the Dancers up and such.

D: *They did what?*

K: They raised the Dancers.

D: *(I didn't understand his pronunciation.) The Dowsers?*

K: No, the Dancers. You know, the Stone Dancers. And they said that they raised them, but I don't … They're gone away or at least into hiding.

D: *Have you ever seen that place or just heard of it?*

K: Oh, they're several Stone Dancers. There's one in the south that's quite a large one that's got some things and … There's several smaller ones in the north. Ah … and then there's a couple of places in the great hills that are coiled in different directions, that they said they're not sure who made them. But it has something to do with some of their beliefs or somethin'.

D: *They must be very old then.* (Aye) *You've seen these places because you travel so much.*

K: Aye. Some of 'em I've just heard about. But the one down south, I've seen it with my own eyes. It's quite a large one.

D: *Can you tell me what it looks like?*

K: Well, the stones, they're all about man height and they're blue. And there's a great center altar stone that they're not sure where it come from. It be coal black and very dark. And it is said that they used to make sacrifices on it, but who has any way of knowin'?

D: *They don't do it any more though.*

K: Well, as least not out in the open.

D: *(Laugh) Why do they call it the Stone Dancers?*

K: Because they're all different angles now, and they look like somebody that's drunk and just kind of dancin' around.

D: *The stones are leaning against each other?*

K: Some of 'em are leanin' this way and some of 'em are leanin' that way, and …

D: *You said there were coils?*

K: Aye. There be coils, you know, great mounds that are in the shape of coils.

D: *How are they made?*

K: (Smiled) I do no make 'em. It is out of dirt and clods (sods?).

D: *Stones?*

K: No, it just be dirt.

D: *It seems like the rain would wash it away.*

K: It's been there forever though, and the grass be grown over it.

D: *Do you think some religion some time made these things?*

K: *Somebody* did. It's not somethin' that just 'appened.

D: *They couldn't just happen by them self. Do you think those are holy places?*

K: 'Tis said that if a man trespasses on them, they make somebody anger, that he has a tendency to disappear.

D: *That'd be a way to keep people away, wouldn't it?* (Aye) *What kind of belief do you have?*

K: I believe in what I can see and feel, and that's about it.

D: *Well, that's a good way to be. Then you're not afraid of all these other people telling you these things.*

K: I'm not worried about it. I figure I'll find out when I die. If there's nothing, I'll be happy, and if there is, I might be surprised.

D: *(Laugh) That's a good way to believe. Anything that happens will be good.* (Aye) *But you don't know any happy songs?*

K: (She yawned.) Can't think of any.

D: *I sure would like you to sing me one more anyway. Would you do that before you go to bed?*

K: Seems like that be the eternal question, "Oh, one more. Oh, one more."

D: *(Laugh) The people always say that?*

K: Usually. (She sounded tired.) Let me think.

D: *Just sing one more and then I'll let you go to bed.*

She paused as though thinking. Then she sang. (Song #5. Timed at one minute, twenty-five seconds.) This was the longest song she sang. It too was slow and accompanied by the usual hand movements.

D: *That's pretty. I really thank you. Tell me what it means.*

K: Oh, let's see now. It's about this place that they say is across the sea that the ... oh, what do they call 'em? Ah, these brothers, that they sailed to and they said that there is an isle of glass. And that they came back and they told of it and no one believed them. So, they went back, and never were seen again.

D: *Was that also in Celt?* (Aye) *Ah, I wonder what the island of glass was?*

K: I have no way of knowin'.

D: *That's a pretty song though. Thanks for doing it. And you said you were getting tired.*

K: I be ready to be stretched out on a mat somewhere. (She yawned.)

D: *But first you're going to get your drinks, aren't you? (She yawned again.) Well, thanks for doing it for me. I think the other people probably liked it too.*

K: At least they're not hollerin' and throwin' things, so they must not have thought too much.

D: *(Laugh) Do you get that sometimes?*

K: Well, upon occasion, it's been known to happen. Aye, they get too drunk and they don't want to hear perhaps what I be singin' or ...

D: *(Laugh) Okay, if they aren't throwing things, then they liked it. 'Cause I liked it.*

(Subject brought forward.)

Chapter 14
The Minstrel, Part 3
(Recorded June 20, 1985)

D: Let's go back to O'Keefe, the harper. The man who played the harp and sang the songs, and traveled to many, many places. He traveled and sang the songs and gave the news. And I believe his name was O'Keefe. Let's go back to the time when he lived. I will count to three and we will be there. 1, 2, 3, we're at the time when the harper lived and played and enjoyed himself in his trade. What are you doing?

K: Sitting by the fire. Just a wee one that I managed to scrape together.

D: Where are you?

K: On the road.

D: Outside? I thought maybe you meant you were in an inn or something.

K: Not tonight, no.

D: Have you been somewhere?

K: I've been a travelin'.

D: Where are you going?

K: Down the road. Nowhere in particular.

D: Have you been to any large keeps lately?

K: Not in the last month or more.

D: You like your work, don't you?

K: It keeps bread in my mouth.

D: Have you done any singing lately?

K: When ere I get the chance.

D: What is your favorite place that you go to?

K: Oh, I don't know. Maybe Taramoor (Phonetic) and Shawnray (Phonetic).

D: *Are those places that treat you right, and you like to go back?*

K: They be nice, yes.

D: *I've been wondering about the country that you have to walk through. Is it nice level land that's easy?*

I had not been to Ireland, and I knew Karen had not. I wanted to see if her description would be accurate.

K: Well, if it were level land, it wouldn't be Ireland. It has lots of hills and valleys and such as that. You just kind of go up the hill and down the next.

D: *Do people live in areas like that, or do they live in the flatlands?*

K: They live all over. Wherever they can scratch out a livin'.

D: *Well, is there anything important that's been going on lately in the country? That you're making your reports on whenever you give the news?*

I was looking for something historical that I could verify.

K: (Pause) Just the different people fightin' back and forth as usual. That's about all. There's always feudin' goin' on. The O'Connor saying that the Bradys are on their land, and fightin' over that, and things like such. Just normal situation being that.

Her accent was so strong it was often difficult to transcribe the names.

D: *Do you ever have any trouble with anyone from outside the country coming in and trying to take anything? Wars or anything?*

K: There's always people who land on the shores that are trying to come in, but mainly … it's kind of like an Irishman will always fight against his brother until somebody starts beating on his brother. And then they band together. So, there's not a lot of trouble in that yet, no.

D: *I thought you would know these things, because you carry the news. Has there been any wars like that that you could know of in the past?*

K: Oh, there's always people coming from the land across the waters. And sometimes they settle down peaceably, and sometimes they fight, but ... not in recent history, no.

D: *That's what I was wondering, if they had any wars that had been going on lately that you would have to report about.*

K: Not from the outside. Just your average Irishman having a good donnybrook. *(I laughed.)* There's not very much excitin' goin' on right now.

D: *You said before that when you go to the keeps you must tell them all the latest news.*

K: That be true, aye.

D: *And that's about all it is right now, just the different ones feuding?*

K: Oh, they've got the two factions that are wantin' to put their man on as king. And that's about the size of it.

D: *What do you mean?*

K: Oh, the O'Connors are wantin' to have their man as king again. And the O'Learys, they're wantin' him back. And they're fightin' over it, as usual.

D: *Then you have one king that's over everything?*

K: Usually it's the man with the biggest stick or the biggest army.

D: *Who is the one right now? Is it one of them?*

K: No, it be the O'Bradys. They take turns for every hundred years, after they've smashed everybody else's in the clans heads in. Ireland has been a series of deeds like that for as long as Ireland's existed. Or had a king over the one as a whole.

D: *And this is how they decide it? They fight with each other.*

K: As a rule, yes.

D: *Do you have any idea which one will get it next?*

K: Whoever's got the most money in the larders.

D: *Do you get to go to these places where the feuding is going on?*

K: Sometimes I do, but I'd like to stay away from 'em. I mean, sometimes a stray harper gets shot in it too.

D: *Oh, yes. That could be. I was wondering, what language it is that you speak? Does your language have a name that you speak in?*

K: You mean, the Gaelic?

D: *Is that the tongue that you speak?*

K: That's what it's called.

D: *I wondered, because one time you sang some songs for me, and you told me they were in one language. And I was just wondering if you sing a different language than you speak.*

This had been suggested by a linguist as an explanation for the language in the songs.

K: Not as a rule, no. Every now and again I get a request for a song that's, say, in Pict or something like that. But as a rule, it's always just what everyone understands.

D: *That's what I wondered. Someone told me that maybe you sing in a language that's different than other people could understand.*

K: No. I mean, why would I sing in something that they wouldn't understand? I mean, then I wouldn't get my silver or gold for singin', because they wouldn't know what I was sayin' to them.

D: *Yes, that's true. And you think it is something that's called Gaelic?*

K: That is what I've heard the others called it, the people that are strangers from here.

D: *Does everyone in Ireland speak the same language?*

K: All the ones I've ever known. I mean, you're got people that are from, say, the north, that speak a little different. But they all have the same language.

D: *One time you were singing about dragons. Do you really think they exist?*

K: That sounds like something that perhaps might have been

invented for mothers to scare little children with. Don't you
think?

D: *You've done so much traveling, have you ever seen anything*
like that?

K: No, nor anybody that's ever set eyes on one, for real. That
was right in the head anyhow.

D: *(Laugh) What about unicorns? Do you know what they are?*

K: Oh, I've heard of 'em. Who hadn't? Course there's always
them peddlers that are selling potions that are said to be made
of different parts of unicorns and stuff. But I no believe them.
I think they're out to just make the money. Each man does
what he can to survive.

D: *You've never seen unicorns or dragons then.* (No) *You think*
they just might be stories then.

K: Who knows what might have existed before we came. There
has to be some truth even in the oldest legends. Otherwise
they wouldn't have started, as a rule.

D: *Tell me about your harp that you play. The one that you carry*
on your back.

K: What would you know about it?

D: *How many strings does it have?*

K: The one that I carry on my back has twelve.

D: *I've heard that some of them just have a few strings, and some*
have many.

K: The larger it gets, the more strings that it has.

D: *Did you make it yourself?*

K: How else would I get it if I didn't make it myself?

D: *I thought sometimes other people make things, and then they*
sell them.

K: Why would a man sell a good harp? Unless he could not play
it anymore. And then he'd probably pass it down to his son
or maybe grandson.

D: *Sometimes people make things just to sell, for other people.*

K: And would you buy a harp that had been made by somebody
that had no music in his fingers? The off key, or sound sour
when it was meant to sound like a bow (The accent was strong
here. I think the word was: bow.) It would not be good.

D: *That makes sense, doesn't it? I was wondering if you could tell me a few words in your language. Just a few simple words or something, to see how they sound.*

I had already been researching the music and language with a linguist. She had made this suggestion. Karen paused and her facial expressions displayed distress. She was confused.

K: I'm not sure I'm understanding what you're wantin'. I mean, I'm speaking to you like this, and you seem to understand me okay. So why are you wantin'… I don't understand.

D: *That's all right. I thought you might have a different word for things that I wouldn't know. That's all right. We're communicating quite well this way, aren't we?*

K: Oh, aye.

D: *Well, I do enjoy talking to you. All right. Let's leave that scene. I'm going to count to three, and let's go to when you are at one of the keeps. I will count to three and we will be there. 1, 2, 3, we're at a keep now, that you enjoy going to. What are you doing?*

K: I be playin' my harp.

D: *Where are you?*

K: I be at Strafmoor. (I had her repeat it. Phonetic: Straf moor.)

D: *Are you in the hall, or where are you?*

K: I'm in the great hall, yeah.

D: *What does the great hall look like? I've never seen it. Can you look around and describe it to me?*

K: It be havin' walls that are raised up out of stones. With very high windows in it. And then the beams across, made of wood, and covered with thatch.

D: *High ceiling?*

K: Oh, aye.

D: *Are the windows very big?*

K: No, they're fairly small.

D: *And they're up high.* (Aye) *You wouldn't be able to look out of them then, could you?*

K: No, nor would someone be able to sneak into them.

D: *Is that why they're so high?*

K: That, and the fact that it allows the smoke to go out, I believe.

D: *Oh. Then they're not covered windows?*

K: They've got oil skin sheets covering them.

D: *Why do they have smoke? Are there fires built in the room?*

K: Oh, aye. There's a great central fireplace in the middle of the room. Otherwise, how would people stay warm in it?

D: *What does that look like?*

K: It's a big raised … in the center of everything. And it's round, and open. It's just kind of a pit fire.

D: *It's raised higher than the floor?*

K: Aye. If it weren't raised up higher than the floor, then the rushes would catch on fire. And that would not make any sense.

D: *(I didn't understand the word.) The dresses?*

K: The rushes.

D: *The rushes? Where are the rushes?*

K: Strewn on the floor.

D: *Why are they on the floor?*

K: To keep things clean and neat. (She was slightly aggravated with me, because I didn't understand.) I ne'er asked why they were there. It is just done.

D: *I mean … I'm thinking of rushes … is it like dried grass?*

K: Oh, aye, yes.

D: *And it's spread on the floor?* (Aye) *I thought it would just be a swept clean floor.*

K: (Chuckle) With the people that are around here, you'd never keep it swept clean.

D: *So they put this, like grass, all over the floor?* (Aye) *And throw it around.*

K: And they just toss their stuff in the rushes. After supper, that's where the bones go, and the dogs fight over 'em and such.

This is not exactly the romantic picture of a castle banquet that the movies give us.

D: *Oh! And they throw the things on the floor then?* (Aye) *And what, there are tables set up around the ...*

K: Tables and trenches, yes.

D: *Trenches?** Are set up around the fire?* (Yes) *In a circle?*

** *Webster's New World Dictionary*: 1. Formerly, a wooden platter for carving and serving meat. 2. Any platter. **

K: No, they're put in lines.

D: *Long tables?*

K: Fairly long. They're longer than a man is.

D: *And what do they do? Bring in the food and set it on the tables?* (Aye) *Who does that? Servants or what?*

K: Aye. The drudges.**

** Drudge: a person made to do hard menial or dull work. **

D: *The drudges bring in the food? And then the people eat, and throw the bones and everything on the floor?* (Aye) *And are there many dogs in there?*

K: There's enough that it gets some kind of a ruckus going on, and they have a squabble over things.

D: *(Laugh) They fight over the food.* (Aye) *What kind of food do you see on the tables?*

K: Things like venison and ... (pause as she looked) oh ... smoked birds. And different type partridge and pheasants and stuff like that. And different types of fish and such. And touvers and such.

D: *And what?*

K: Touvers (Phonetic).

D: *What is that?*

K: (In this sentence I finally figured out what she was saying.) A tuber is a tuber, and I know no other name to call it.

D: *Oh. Is it like a vegetable? Or do you know that word? (Pause) It grows in the ground?*

K: Oh, aye, aye.

D: *All right. That's a different name. I know what you mean now. Do you have very many of those things to eat there, that grow in the ground?*

K: There is sufficient quantity to feed all the mouths there are.

D: *What about bread? Does anyone make bread?*

K: There are flat cakes, if that's what you mean.

D: *Is that a sweet cake, or a ...?*

K: Oh, no, no. It be a ground cake. They be flat cakes. I know no other way to say it.

D: *They're not very thick?*

K: Maybe about as thick as a thumb and a half wide.

D: *I mean, how high are they?*

K: That's how high they are.

D: *How big around are they?*

K: Oh, about like such. (Hand motions) If you span your two hands you could meet around it.

D: *And this is not sweet?* (No) *What color is it?*

K: Maybe brown.

D: *Do they eat that with the meat?*

K: Usually it's used to wipe up the trencher afterwards. And you eat it like that. (Chuckle) It's the only way you can eat it, is with a good little juice on it.

D: *Do you know what plates are? (Pause) Some people eat off of plates.*

K: I have no knowin' of this word, no.

D: *It is a ... do you know what pottery is? Do you have pottery? Or ...*

K: We have goblets, if that's what you're talkin' of.

D: *Goblets. Okay. Sometimes they have things they put food in, and you ...*

K: Oh, they put it in the trenches.

D: *In the trenches. And you have goblets that they pour the drinks in?*

K: Some of the folk have goblets. Others just have ... what you be callin' 'em? Mugs, I guess is a good word.

D: *A goblet is grander?*

K: That be for the high folk, aye.

D: *What kind of drinks do they have?*

K: Oh, there's stout and ale, and mead and such like that.

D: *Does anyone ever drink milk? Do you know what that is?*

K: That be what they give the bairns.

D *(I didn't understand the word.) The barons? Then the common folk don't drink it? (Pause. She showed confusion.)*

K: You're not understanding me. No, that be what they give the babes.

D: *Oh, okay. I thought you meant baron, like a high person.*

K: I have no knowin' of what a baron is. It be a word that's strange to me. Would you explain it?

D: *Well, it's something like a chief. Some people somewhere else might call a chief or a king that.*

K: That's an interesting word, it is, aye.

D: *It's a grand person. Then they give the babies, the babes, the milk?* (Aye) *The people as old as you don't drink the milk?*

K: Not as a rule, no.

D: *Is there anything sweet that they serve at these dinners?*

K: Only if you have lots of money, they have sweets. It 'tis rare, very rare. Made from honeys and such. And it's very expensive.

D: *I thought if they had a big party like this, they would have something sweet. Just special occasions?*

K: As a rule, like weddings and such like that.

D: *Is there any order that they sit in? Would somebody be more important than others?*

K: Aye, there are those at the high tables, and you've got a kind of a descendin' order. And then you've got above and below the sellers and such.

D: *What do you mean, above and below the sellers?*

K: Where that they be keeping the salt. They would have it either above the sellers and below the sellers.

D: *The high tables? Do you mean they are raised above the other people?*

K: Oh, there is one that is. It be the owner of the place. He would have the high table. And all the visiting folk, that are say kinfolk or what have you, would be up there with them. And then it would be a descending order from down the room, as it were.

D: *When you said they were above and below the salt, doesn't everyone get to use the salt?*

K: No. You're only allowed salt if you're of a certain importance or so.

D: *Why is that? Is it rare? Is it hard to find?*

K: Aye. Salt's the same as money in a lot of places.

D: *Then the people that are sitting lower down don't get to use the salt on their food.* (Aye) *Ummm. Then when they get through eating, they just throw everything on the floor.*

K: The dogs clean it up.

D: *Do they have anything that they eat with?*

K: They have their knives.

D: *How are the people dressed? Especially the ladies. Do they dress any certain way?*

K: How you mean, how do they dress? I mean, they wear a dress, a curtle.

D: *A curtle?* ** *(kirtle)*

** Kirtle: a woman's gown or outer petticoat. **

K: What else is there, I mean? I don't know ladies' fashions as such.

D: *Are the skirts long?*

K: Aye, they touch the floor.

D: *Do they wear anything on their heads?*

K: They would have the wimples.**

** Wimples: a cloth headdress covering the head, neck, and the sides of the face, formerly worn by women and still worn by some nuns. **

D: *And they don't wear their hair just hanging down then, do they?*

K: It's usually up in braids or in a caul** of some sort.

** Caul: a woman's close-fitting indoor headdress or hairnet. **

D: *What about the top of the dress? Does it come up high on the neck or ...*

K: Aye. It comes up high.

D: *It's not cut low?*

K: No. You'd freeze to death if it were.

D: *(Chuckle) Oh, it's cold in there, huh?*

K: Oh, winters get a bit brisk.

D: *Are the sleeves long or short?*

K: They be long.

D: *Do they wear jewelry?*

K: The ones that have enough money for it. And if they don't, they don't. Usually it's maybe a ring or a cross. That be about it.

D: *Nothing more fancy than that. What about the owner? Does he wear any special jewelry?*

K: He would have his signet ring, and maybe some sort of a ... (thinking of the word). A type of a ... medal. It sits in the middle of his chest.

D: *A round metal thing on a chain or something?*

K: Aye. That be showing his office. They have different designs and embroidered with his arms and such.

D: *And that tells who they are. (Aye) What kind of clothes do the men wear?*

K: A jerkin** and hose. I mean, I don't know any other way to explain it.

** Jerkin: a man's close-fitting jacket, typically made of leather. **

D   *Does the jerkin come down very far on their legs?*

K: About mid-thigh.

D: *Do they have long sleeves?*

K: Aye. Sometimes they have a shirt inside it. And then the jerkin itself will have the short sleeves, and the shirt will have the long. And that be a lot warmer. It depends on the time of year, I guess.

D: *Do they ever wear anything on their heads?*

K: Various people have different types of hats. Just depends on your mood, I guess, or who you are and what you can afford. Some of 'em are rather strange. I seen one that looked like a bird that was about to take off and wing.

D: *(Laugh)* On a man? (Aye) *That sounds like something a woman would wear.*

K: No, this was evidently a man full of his own importance, I guess.

D: *(Chuckle) He wanted to be different and make everybody notice him.*

K: He was noticed all right, but many of them thought him a fool.

D: *What type of clothes do you wear?*

K: Just hose and jerkin, as a rule. Maybe a cape if it be cold. But that be about it.

D: *Do you wear anything on your head?*

K: Sometimes a cap in the winter or during the rain. But as a rule, I'm bare headed.

D: *Are the clothes any certain color?*

K: Mine are brown, and I've got a pair that's red. But that's for special occasions.

D: *Do the people wear bright colors?*

K: How could they afford the dyes for them? Unless they are occurin' in the things that are around them, they cannot get the dyes.

D: *Then most people would just wear brown clothes?*

K: Or things that are the color of whatever they're made out of. Like if it's wool, it's the color of the sheep that it was shorn from.

D: *They don't dye that then.* (No) *And very few people wear bright colors?*

K: Not very many, not unless they can afford it.

D: *Where did you get your red clothes?*

K: By havin' to pay a dear penny for it. I got it from a tailor. When you go into keeps you got to have a least one pair of clothes that looks like you belong there.

D: *Well, when you're singing, and up there playing your harp, where do you sit in the room?*

K: Usually on a chair that's up by the high table. So, where it can be heard by them, and they can tell me what they want to hear and such.

D: *And you said sometimes there are jugglers.* (Aye) *What about acrobats? Do you know what they are?*

K: I've no knowin' of the word.

D: *It means people who do ... oh, they jump around and do all kinds of tricks with their body. Turn upside down and things like that.*

K: I've seen people doin' that, yes. And then there's mummers** and stuff that may go on. And they play act things out.

** A mummer was a medieval entertainer who was an amateur actor. He performed at different plays in the villages that were held at the harvest time or on some religious occasion such as Christmas. **

D: *Mummers? Oh, you mean they play act without talking?*

I was thinking of mimes.

K: No, they talk. But they use ... say, different voices and such. To make it more funny to people. Do you understand what I'm saying there?

D: *I think I do. You mean they're playing many parts?*

K: Oh, aye, yes.

D: *One person is doing it?*

K: Oh, there's usually a group of them, but they're all playin' several parts, so that you get the whole act, as it were. Between two and three, maybe four people.

D: *Do they put on different clothes when they do this, or just change their voices?*

K: Usually they just change their voices. And some of them I've seen, they've had costumes that they would turn around. Like on one side of this one man, he'd turn it, and it was hose and doublet. And on the other side he had a long curtle? *(I laughed.)* And it was very strange.

D: *He was pretending to be a woman and a man then, wasn't he?* (Aye) *Did the people think it was funny?*

K: They laughed very hard, aye.

D: *And they tell stories this way?* (Yes) *That's the same way you do, only you sing yours.*

K: In a way, aye.

D: *Do they ever have anyone else that plays music, besides you?*

K: Well, there's different harpers and such.

D: *You mean you all play at the same keep? Whenever you are playing, is there ever anyone else who is playing something else? Not when you are, but maybe before you come on?*

K: Sometimes, but not often. Usually if a keep's got a harper, a harper won't stay there.

D: *Oh, that makes sense. But are there other people that play other kinds of things?*

K: Oh, the women sometimes play lutes. But that's not done out in halls and such.

D: *Is there anything that someone would blow to make music?*

K: Oh, there be whistles and such, but they're mostly just things with strings.

D: *Well, right now are you just playing music?* (Aye) *Will you sing for them soon?*

K: There's too much noise goin' on to really sing. Everybody's in a grand mood and getting rather hot under the collar and such. I doubt if they be wantin' to hear music, other than just … music itself. They wouldn't want to hear meself sing.

D: *Is this a large keep? (Pause) I mean, many rooms?*

K: It's got quite a few rooms, aye.

D: *When you come into the keep, how do you come in? Is there a big door or what?*

K: There be a big gate.

D: *A big gate. Does it have a wall around the outside of the keep? Or do you just come right into the keep?*

K: You come into the keep itself.

D: *Some places, I've heard they have high walls that are outside the keep, to keep people from coming in, like in a war or something.*

K: Not this one, no.

D: *Have you ever seen anything like that?*

K: Not around here, no. It just has the gates that would keep them out of the center of it. And from the higher parts you could shoot down at them if they were surroundin' you.

D: *Are there any towers or anything? (Pause) Do you know what that word is? (Pause) It's a part that sticks up higher than all the rest of the building.*

K: But the building is all basically of one piece.

D: *All the same height?*

K: Aye. I mean, it's not short. But it's not great and tall, like you're talkin'.

D: *I've heard of some places that have just one part that sticks up higher than all the rest.*

K: I've not seen it, no.

D: *Do all the rooms have high ceilings, like the grand hall?*

K: No. The kitchen would, to let the soot out and such. But the other rooms, they would have a room above 'em. When the grand hall is just a large room in itself.

D: *You said, to let the soot out in the kitchen? (Aye) What do you mean by that?*

K: The cinders and such from the fires and the ovens and such. If it didn't have a tall roof and places to let it out, you wouldn't be able to breathe in there.

D: *This is how they cook? They have the big ovens?*

K: (Chuckle) As far as I know. I have no way of knowin'. I cannot cook that good.

D: *Neither can I. That's why I was wondering. Well, as you look around the great hall there, is there anything on the walls for decoration?*

K: There be hangin's and stuff that they dearly made, but nothin' really fancy.

D: *What do you mean? Like big pictures or embroideries? Or how did they make them?*

K: They be woven and such. I believe the word's looms. I'm not familiar. I just know they're made. The biggest one it be the crest of the house, as it were.

D: *Like the same thing, as you said, the man had on his neck?*

K: Aye, aye. And it sets behind the head table.

D: *What design does it have on it? Can you see it from where you are?*

K: It's got a red heart in the center with a sword through it. And a crane (?) in the top corner.

D: *A crane?*

K: A crown. In the top corner. And inside it a cross. And on the bottom corner it has ... it looks to be some type of a harp. Although I'm not quite familiar with the type of harp it be.

D: *It has four sides then in the designs?*

K: All crests do, that I've ever seen. And then the other two, he's got one ... blue on the top and the bottom one is gold.

D: *The colors you mean?*

K: In the opposite corners ... I'm not describing it very well.

D: *You're doing just fine. Then you mean in one corner would be a color, and in the other corner it would have a design?*

K: Aye. And in the very center there is the heart with the sword through it.

D: *That seems strange. I wonder why it has the sword through the heart.*

K: Showin' it come down in a hunt or somethin'. I have no idea. And the white heart ...

D: *(I finally understood what she was saying.) Oh, a hart! I see, you mean an animal.* (Aye) *I thought you meant a heart like is in the body.* (No, no) *(Chuckle) The words sound alike.*

K: Aye, they do. But like, if it was a white hart, it would be for purity and such. But the red hart, it's showing strength and such, I think is the meaning behind it. I'm not sure.

D: *Oh, yes, I see what you mean now. That's all part of the design.* (Aye) *And a crown and ...*

K: The crown has a cross inside it.

D: *I'm trying to remember what you said was on the other side. There was a crown, and then there was a ... A harp!*

K: Aye, there is a harp on the bottom, on the one side. And then there is the crown with the cross in it. And then the other side, the top was blue, and the bottom was red. I mean, it's not red. It's gold. Excuse me. I was thinking of the red hart.

D: *The blue and the gold. All right. I think I can get a picture of what it looks like now. And this is the crest of the man who owns the house.*

K: Aye. Strafmoor. (Phonetic. Maybe: Stravmoor. Sounds more like an F.)

D: *That is the name of the people, or the name of the keep then.*

K: Aye. And his name also. It be himself also.

D: *What do the other hangings look like, that are smaller.*

K: Some of 'em are just flowers and such. Nothing important or large or anything. They're just kind of there. They're supposed to put warmth in there. Some of them are so covered with smoke and such, that you can't tell what they are. They haven't cleaned 'em in a while.

D: *They make the room warmer by hanging on the walls?*

K: They're supposed to. I don't know if it helps much.

D: *It gets cold in there with that high ceiling, doesn't it?* (Aye) *You said they had rafters that had thatch on them?*

K: The roof has thatch. There's rafters that are made of wood, and then the roof is thatch.

D: *I thought the roof would be stone like the building is.*

K: How would you put stone up there? I mean, what would hold it? The stone is stronger than wood. What would hold it up?

D: *The walls are stone, aren't they?*

K: Aye. But they're just stacked on top of each other. They just go straight up. What would hold it at an angle like that?

D: *I don't know. It would be hard to do, wouldn't it? But isn't the thatch something that would blow away or ...*

At the time I was not familiar with thatched roofs, but now since I have traveled to England every year, I see many houses that still have this type of roofs. It is a vanishing art in England, because people don't know how to make the repairs. It is tedious and the art is not being passed on to the young people. The roof is very tight and secure and serves the purpose quite well, but it does need repair from time to time (as does any other roof). At the time of this session in 1985, however, I had the mental picture of loose thatch or grass laid on top of a roof, which in hindsight is not very practical.

K: It's bound down very well. Of course, they have to replace it. Usually in the spring, summers. But it holds real well.

D: *I thought maybe the rain would come through, or the wind would blow it off.*

K: It's put on real thick. And tied real good down.

D: *And the roof of the whole keep is made out of this?*

K: The part I've seen.

D: *And stone walls. Are the floors made of stone too?*

K: (Confusion) I don't know.

D: *Oh, it's covered with the rushes. It's hard to see.*

K: I think it's probably just dirt. I don't know.

D: *But the fireplace in the middle where the fire is ...*

K: 'Tis stone, aye.

D: *And it's raised up.* (Aye) *And the smoke goes out towards the windows then. Do they open those oilcloths?*

K: Usually they're just at the top. (Confused as to how to explain.) They're fastened somehow at the top, but they're left to flap, as it were.

D: *Oh, they're loose then. That way the smoke can go out.* (Aye) *But also rain could come in, couldn't it?*

K: It protects it some. But there's not enough of 'em that it would come in bad, unless it was a very windy day outside.

D: *I can see what it looks like now. Do you like playing at the keeps?*

K: It pays better than singin' at inns.

D: *I would like it if you would sing another song for me. You've done it before.*

K: Aye, you might like it, but I think I might get thrown out of here tonight. No, I don't be thinkin' I'll be singin' tonight.

D: *You don't think they'll want to hear the news or anything?*

K: Not tonight. They're rather rowdy right now.

I wanted to get some more songs. I would have to move her.

D: *All right. Then let's leave that scene. Let's go away from that scene. And I will count to three, and we will go to a time that you are giving a performance. When you are allowed to sing. A time when you can sing for me. And you're singing for all the people too. And they enjoy it very much. I will count to three and we will be there. 1, 2, 3, you're in a place now where you're giving a performance, and you are singing for the people. What are you doing?*

K: Playin' my harp.

D: *Where are you now?*

K: Be at the Keep Claire.

D: *Do you like that keep?*

K: Be a fair keep.

D: *Are you going to sing tonight?* (Aye) *Would you sing so I can hear it? Then I'll know what it sounds like too. (She seemed to hesitate.) I'd really appreciate it if you would. (Pause) Can you do that for me?*

K: (Softly) I think so.

D: *Okay. Because I would like it. And you've done it before, and I really liked your voice.*

She sang another slow song. (Song #6. Timed at forty-five seconds.)

D: *I liked that. Did the people like it?*

K: I didn't get nothin' thrown at me, so I suppose they did.

D: *It's got a nice tune to it. Would you sing me another? (Pause) You'll be singing many, won't you?*

K: I sing quite a few. (She seemed disturbed.)

D: *Why does it bother you if I ask you?*

K: Just sometimes it seems hard. I'm not sure why.

D: *Do you have any idea? (Pause) Because I don't want to bother you. Do you know why? I'm trying to understand.*

K: I'm not sure. It seems sometimes it just sort of closes up. And nothin' wants to come out. (A nervous chuckle)

D: *But it doesn't do that when you sing for the people, does it?*

K: (Chuckle) Sometimes it does. It depends on the situation. Like if I've not been to the place before.

D: *Yeah, I know what you mean. I've had that feeling too. You don't know whether they'll like it or not. (I was trying to gain her confidence.) It's a little hard to stand up in front of all those people. (Aye) But I really would like it if you'd sing one more song, and then I will let you go. I would appreciate it. I like the music. It has such a pretty sound to it.*

K: I think I'll try.

She sang another slow one. (Song #7. Timed at about one minute.)

D: *That's pretty. I liked that. You said the word "shelan" (Phonetic) a lot in there. What does that mean?*

K: It be a person's name. It's sort of a lament, as it were.

D: *A lament?*

K: Aye. A crying out for that person.

D: *The person is gone? And they want them to come back? (Aye) Is that a man or a woman that they're calling for?*

K: It's the woman.

D: *They would be unhappy. (Aye) Yes, it sounded sad.*

K: Or full of longin' anyhow.

D: *Many of your songs are that way though, aren't they? (Aye) Do the people in your land dance?*

The only type of Irish music I am familiar with is the modern Irish jig. That music is lively, not slow and sad. Did that type of music exist in that day?

K: They dance a jig every now and again. Or whenever a couple of people get together. We're generally a happy people. But the happy songs you never sing, unless somebody's dancin'. No one would hear you anyway over the clappin'.

D: *Do they have any music that goes with it when they're dancing?*

K: Aye. Sometimes with the harp, sometimes just hands clapping, or using whistles and such. I've never played the whistle, so I don't know how to do it. Sometimes they use the voice to make the song, but it ... it's not many words to it. (Confused again as to how to explain.) It's just kind of to carry a tune.

D: *Have you ever got out there and danced?*

K: Aye, but I think I got two feet that don't know each other very well.

D: *(Laugh) Some can do it better than other people.*

K: 'Tis the truth.

D: *You told me one time that when you were a little boy you went with your father, and he taught you how to do all these things? (Aye) What part of the land were you living when you were a little boy? (Pause) Before you went with your father, do you remember where you lived?*

K: All I remember was it was in a valley, and it was all green. And it had animals and such. But I don't remember much about it. All I remember, it was close to a river. I've never been back since.

D: *I wondered if you ever went back to see your mother, or the place where you lived. (No) What happened to your father?*

K: He died. He just coughed himself to death. (Sadly) He was sick for a long time.

D: *Did that make it hard to travel with him?*

K: At times. And then it got to where he couldn't even sing.

D: *Were you very old when that happened?*

K: (Hesitated) Twenty-three, I guess.

D: *Then you were no longer a little boy. (No) He taught you many things, didn't he?*

K: Oh, aye.

D: *When you travel, are there roads that you travel on, to go to the different places?*

K: Sometimes there's roads, sometimes you have to make your own. Sometimes there's just kind of trails. If you know where you're eventually headed, you can at least ask directions.

D: *And you go back and forth to the same places too, don't you?*

K: As a rule.

D: *Do you like your life?*

K: It's not bad. At least I got food in my mouth, and usually a warm place to stay.

D: *What more could you want then? Well, I do thank you for talking with me. And I thank you for singing the songs for me. I do like them. May I come again sometime and speak with you?*

K: If you be willin' to listen to my blather, I suppose so.

D: *(Chuckle) Oh, I enjoy it. It's interesting to me. All right. Thank you again for speaking with me.*

The only thing that Karen could associate with this life was her ability to sing and play the guitar. When she was quite young, she found she could play the guitar naturally with no lessons. She also often found herself making up songs and singing them when she was working around the house and having no idea where they came from. A small remnant of O'Keefe that still remained to filter through to her present life.

After Karen left Fayetteville and moved to Little Rock, we had only communication by mail or phone. On this date I had to go to Little Rock for a convention, and we arranged to meet at my hotel and have a session. I was mainly interested in contacting the minstrel again, and hopefully getting some more music. I also felt there were a few gaps in his story that I wanted to ask questions about. Karen's keyword worked beautifully, even though it had been about two years since we last worked. She immediately entered into a deep trance.

As we continued, I asked her to move ahead to an important day. She took a long time to answer. When she did, she seemed depressed. There appeared to be something wrong.

K: They ... didn't like what I was singin' about and ... How was I to know? (A deep sigh.)

D: *Who didn't like what you were singing about?*

K: Ah, the Brock. (Phonetic, but the name was unclear.) He, ah ... me singin' a song that be about ... oh, this somebody,

309

I can't remember the name of 'im. Anyway, it's about this glorious deed that he did and this, that and the other thing. And come to find out that he be the enemy of these owners of this keep. And they didn't like that.

D: *Oh. That was a mistake, wasn't it?*

K: Aye. I should have known better than that. I should have kept my ears open a little bit better, perhaps.

D: *What happened?*

K: (Sigh) Oh, they say they're gonna ... strike me head off in the mornin'.

D: *Just for doing that?*

K: Oh, people have been killed for less.

D: *Where are you?*

K: Somewhere down in the bottom of the keep, from the looks of it. Pretty dark back here. We came down these steps that came down, and ... course they had torches and we could see then.

D: *They didn't give you a chance to apologize or say you were sorry or anything?*

K: They have no wish for people to apologize. They don't think that a man should have to apologize for his deeds, so they're not gonna give me a chance.

D: *How do you feel about it?*

K: (Pause) Well ... disappointed. Can't say that it's something that I want to see happen. Never wanted to lose my head this much over somethin'.

D: *How old are you now?*

K: Oh, thirty-five, gettin' on up there. I guess it's not too bad.

D: *You could still walk and do all the things you wanted to, couldn't you?*

K: Aye. But there's no use moanin' about it now. There's not much I can do about it.

D: *Is there anyone else down there with you?*

K: Heard some noises from that direction, but from the sound of it, he's too out of it. He's just a moanin' and goin' on.

D: *And you don't think they're going to just keep you there, a prisoner?*

K: Why should they feed me? If they cut me head off, they don't have to feed the stomach, so ... It's a lot better this way. I'd rather go out at once, than sit down here for months and rot to death.

D: *That makes sense. Well, it wasn't your fault. You really didn't have any way of knowing about that.*

K: Should have been wiser.

D: *That was the wrong people to come and sing for. Have you ever been to that keep before?*

K: No. I have no been here. But what do you expect from these people in the north. They're a bunch of heathens anyway, so ...

D: *Oh, you're in the north of Erin then. (Aye) What's the name of that keep? I want to keep away from there.*

I had her repeat the name three times. It is a difficult name to decipher. Sounded like: Tyrag, Tyrug, Tyrod? phonetic.

D: *I want to stay away from there. I don't think those are people I'd want to go to see. Well, let's leave that scene and move ahead till whatever happens in the morning has already happened.*

I could see no point in making her go through a beheading. I am not a sadist.

D: *And you can look back at it. And it won't bother you to look back at it and talk about it. It's already happened. I will count to three. 1, 2, 3, whatever happened has already happened. Can you tell me about it?*

K: They took this great sword and ... laid my head on the block and ... just cut.

D: *Who did that?*

K: One of the guards. I'm not real sure.

D: *They didn't let you stay down there very long then, did they?*

K: No. 'Tis better that way. 'Tis not a very good place to die. At least they let me see the sunshine one more time.

311

D: *Then they took you out into the courtyard or what?* (Aye) *But it was a happy life, wasn't it?*

K: 'Twas a very carefree life.

D: *Well, how do you feel about it? Are you angry?*

K: 'Twas something that I had to repay. 'Tis only fair.

D: *Do you know what you had to repay?*

K: 'Twas past unfairness and … There is always a life for a life, and this had meaning.

D: *Do you mean what happened to you was repaying something that happened in this life, or from somewhere else?*

K: From before.

D: *And you know that now that you have left the body again?* (Yes) *Do you know what it was supposed to repay? Or do you have that knowledge yet?*

K: Um. I just know that it was for something of equal horror. I do not remember.

D: *It was something you had done in a past life, and now you have to pay back in this way?* (Yes) *I see. Yeah, that's the way it works, doesn't it? At least you don't have any anger. It's very good not to have any anger or feelings of revenge. You understand what happened.*

She no longer spoke in the charming Irish accent. Karen's normal voice had returned.

K: Anger is a useless way of reacting to something. Anger causes much karma to be built. If anger is all overpowering, it brings itself over from the past into the present and causes nothing but problems.

D: *That's good that this time you haven't done that. You've learned something then.*

We left that scene, and I jumped her back another hundred years and she came to the life I later called the "falcon lady." She was a woman who lived in a fortress in Italy and was hunting with a falcon. This life contained much information about those times, and also the art of falconry. The switch from the minstrel to the lady was immediate and complete, as had occurred to all regressions with Karen.

I think that the music on this tape is very important, also the fact that she sang in a different language. I would like an expert to examine this, if one could be found that knows anything about this.

Chapter 15
The Doctor, Part 1
(Recorded May 25, 1983)

Karen has just left the life I called "the falcon lady."

That's good, that's very good. Let's leave that scene and let's go back further into time. This was in the 500s when this life took place. Let's go back before that to the 400s and see if we can find out what you were doing at that time. I will count to three and we will be in the 400s. Sometime in there and see what we can find out. 1,2,3, we're in the 400s, what are you doing?

K: I am making an elixir.

D: *An elixir?* (Yes) *What is that?*

K: There are many herbs in this and it will bring about soothing. It is a—(sigh) something that will relieve pain.

D: *Oh. Who are you?*

K: My name is Alexandro.

D: *Are you a man?* (Yes) *Okay. Where are you living now? Does the place have a name? The country?*

K: It is—somewhere in—ah, it is Alexandria. (Pronounced: Alexandra)

D: *Alexandria?* (Yes) *That's what the people call it?* (Yes) *I see. Okay. What do you do? What is your occupation? Do you know that word?*

K: I am a physician.

D: *You are a physician at that time. How old are you? Are you an old man or a young man?*

K: (Deep sigh) I am very old, I am in my sixties, I'm very tired.

(The accent is noticeably different from the Lady with the Falcon.)

D: *Oh. Have you been doing this a long time?* (Yes) *Where did you get your training for this kind of a job?*

K: There were studyings here, though the school is not what it used to be. Fourteen trained under my master in Thrace. But you just learn by doing, mostly.

D: *Well, do you mostly just use herbs, or do you do other things? To heal people?*

K: Sometimes if there is need you use surgery.

D: *Surgery? Do you know how to do those different things?*

K: Yes. There are different ways of making a person so that they do not feel pain. Some use juice from berries in which that their patient is rendered unconscious. Others use hypnotico and they would put them into a state where there is no pain.

D: *I see. Then they can do surgery that way.* (Yes) *Okay. There's someone here who would like to ask you some questions. Is it all right?* (Yes) *Okay. (This personality, although sounding tired and older, sounds much more confident.)*

Harriet (H): Alexandro, do you have a badge as to, perhaps, the dress you wear or color, hat, something that denotes how much training you've had in this field?

K: I have my medallion that I wear. It is gold on a chain and was given to me by this school. There is a papyrus paper that has my master's signature saying that he has trained me and given me all of the knowledge that he has. And this is who trained him and in what, different things like that.

D: *But you have no certain hat or clothes that you wear that is like a uniform of some kind?*

K: I have my white robes, but other than that, no.

H: Alexandro, are women allowed to be physicians as you are? (Yes)

D: *Then either sex can be a physician?*

K: Yes, there are those who say that women should only teach women, but I do not feel this way. I think that they are just as good, if not better, than some of the men that I have known that call themselves physicians. (A bit sarcastic.)

D: *Oh. You think they do just as good a job. I've heard ... you said you're in the city of Alexandria?*

K: Alexandria, yes.

D: *Is there a library there?*

K: (Sigh) The library burnt down about—maybe a hundred, two hundred years ago.

D: *Oh, it's no longer there anymore, then.* (No) *Do you know something of what the library was like?*

K: There are some of the ruins that are still here and some of the teachings have not been lost. They have been retained. Because of the paranoia that caused the burning of the library, they are kept mostly secret.

D: *Oh. I have heard that all the knowledge was lost with the burning.*

K: This is not true. There were hints that such an act would perhaps take place. And many of the teachers and scholars fled, taking some of this knowledge with them. There is a lot of it that has survived. But a great deal was lost due to wanton destruction.

D: *What caused the fire?*

K: It was deliberately set. The Emperor, I cannot remember his name, he was very ... upset with the way that they were teaching here. He said that there were too much ... liberties and speaking freedoms that he did not want to grant. And it was his decision.

D: *Seems like an awful thing to do, to destroy so much knowledge.*

K: The ignorant do not know of destruction of knowledge. They have fear of others having knowledge, and so they would take away the method of gaining this.

D: *Do you know what the library looked like before it was burned?*

K: It had—tall columns. It was built in the way of the Greek. It had the light, open doorways. Different openings in the roof, in which the light would come in. Each section of the library or school, it was actually a school rather than a library—

D: *Both together?*

K: A lot of both. It was a storehouse of knowledge, in which there was teaching done and also the storage. Each section had the teachings of perhaps, like, astronomy in one, medicine in the other. It is said that one studied all out of these aspects in order to graduate from this school.

(Had to turn tape over.)

D: *Okay. I was wondering what the inside of it looked like. What did the books look like? Have you ever seen some of the books that have survived?*

K: Mostly they were on scrolls, the ones I have seen. They were on papyrus and on wooden notes and scrolls, they were stored that way.

D: *Were they ever put in anything?*

K: It is said that there are some who were bound in leather and sewn with ... pages. (Unsure of that word.)

D: *Well, do you know, was there a main room? (I am asking all these questions because of another regression I had where someone else had described the Library of Alexandria as it appeared before the fire.) Of the library?*

K: There was a room that was used for debates and discussions, if there were large groups of people who were being either lectured to or taught. Sometimes, it is said that they went to here. Most of what I know about this is from the people who said that ah ... their grandfathers or whatever studied. I've been through the ruins, but that is exactly what they are, they are ruins. It is a very sad state of affairs.

D: *I just wondered what it looked like, because I talked to someone else who told me what it looked like, and I just wondered if it were true, or not.*

K: (Interrupts) It is said that it was a very glorious place. A place with ... where that remnants of knowledge was everywhere. And even though many of the teachers and students got into very heated debates, there was always the respect for each other's brilliance of mind, and desire to learn.

D: *Well, do you know, was there a main room in the storehouse where the books were kept?*

K: Yes, it was very tall, and there were several sections. It is said that you would go up one level of stairs and there would be another section there in which more storage was found.

D: *Was the room a particular shape?*

K: I do not know.

D: *Okay. Someone told me it was a round room, where they had the books stored all the way around. Shaped like a wheel, like the spokes of a wheel.*

K: And that things came off of it, sections came off of it or something?

D: *Yes, like the spokes of a wheel. Does that sound right?*

K: (Sigh) I have heard that this is ... one of the ways that it is said, only like I said, I do not know.

D: *I just wondered, because someone had told me this who was there before it was burned. They said it was as though a wheel and the spokes going out, like a round room. And they had all the storage of the books.*

K: I do not know.

D: *Okay. I just wondered, I thought maybe you could help me. Who took care of the library?*

K: There were several librarians, I think which that a lot of the students were in charge of making sure that there was no mildew and damage to the books. If that a scroll or a book was being damaged in some way, they were then copied so that the knowledge would not be lost.

D: *Well, do you know who was in charge of acquiring the books? I mean, would it be some kind of a religious group or a—*

K: I do not know.

D: *You do not know. Okay. I just wondered about it. Okay. She wants to ask you some questions.*

H: *Alexandro, can you tell me, if one of the aspects in your training, do you use the hypnosis technique? Do you use the hypnotic? (She nods.) Can you explain to us what you do?*

K: Usually by talking to the patient, you—the patient is usually in a lot of pain. And so, if you reach (breach?) them to a state where that they are focusing upon your voice, and you give them the suggestion that they are drowsy and that they will have very beautiful dreams. And that they will feel no pain, and that all the pain and worry that they have been experiencing up to now, is floating away from them, upon a sea or whatever.

D: *You make them, what, see this?*

K: Yes, you use imagery, in which their own mind brings up the pictures. And it is like they are elsewhere then and you can do whatever has to be done to the body and the soul will not be harmed.

D: *Isn't this hard to do though, if they are in pain? To get them to focus on your voice?*

K: Sometimes it is easier when that they are in great pain, because they have a great desire to focus on anything to get rid of the pain, if that you promise them that it will go. And they are reaching like a lifeline.

D: *Oh. You mean, like you tell them the pain will go away if they listen to what you say?* (Yes) *And do what you say?* (Yes) *Ah.*

H: *How do you maintain them at that level then, until you finish what you need to do?*

K: Throughout the operation you are continuing to talk to them. Giving them suggestions as far as what they're seeing. Giving them ah, … healing suggestions, saying that once it is through that they will still feel no pain. That the healing will be speeded up. Just different things like that.

D: *Do they stay at—does it work? I mean, they don't ever come back up and feel the pain?* (No)

H: *Do you use colors in helping with the healing in any way?*

K: (Pause) How so?

H: *For instance, would you use certain colors to help the healing speed up? Or … their mental state, for instance, if they were depressed, would you use brighter colors? Does this have any bearing on what they're doing? And also, have you heard of the place, or do you use the sleeping technique where the patient is put to sleep and given suggestions to help improve him?*

K: I have heard that there are those who use colors in … different forms. Whether to tell the person that they are to focus upon this color. I have heard this. I, myself, do not use it. I have not had a teacher in this method. The sleeping method is somewhat like what is used during operations. But, are you saying that it is used when that a person is not being operated on or—

D: *Uh-huh.*

K: You utilize their own inner focus to ... speed up the process of healing.

D: *She means without surgery. You use it without surgery? The sleeping method?*

H: *I have heard in places they have sleep temples where people that are troubled can go and be taken by the sleep healer.*

K: It is said that many, many years ago, that this is true. I have heard of them. But this method has been lost.

H: *Thank you.*

D: *You don't use it any more then? Okay. Then you do surgery this way and it always works, and no one feels pain.*

K: It has always worked up to this point.

D: *You hope, anyway. (Laugh) Then you use drugs too?*

K: If the situation is extreme, and for some reason the sleep is not deep enough, yes.

D: *What kind of drugs would you use for that?*

K: Sometimes the poppy is used. Different herbs that have been blended together and drank. And grapes, distilled (pronounced: distill ed) grapes are sometimes used.

D: *You mix it with the grapes, you mean, or the herbs by themself?*

K: Sometimes just the grapes by themselves, that have been ... fermented. *(Sounds like they get the patient drunk.)*

D: *Fermented, yes. And this works that way too, then. (Yes) I see. Are you teaching any students now? (No) Have you done this?*

K: (Sigh) My calling is not to teach, though I have started a few upon the path of learning. I would rather use my abilities to heal.

H: *How long does it take to train for what you're doing? How many years do you have to train before you are considered complete in your training?*

K: I trained for twelve years under my master.

D: *Oh. Did you start very young?*

K: I was sixteen.

D: *You started at sixteen and it took twelve years?* (Yes) *Is he the only one that you were taught under?*

K: No, I went to several schools afterward but that didn't always … when that I left his training, I was considered a physician.

D: *I see. Did you have any schooling before you went under his training?*

K: No. Just—

D: *I mean, like regular school, just learning other things besides being a doctor.* (No) *Then you went to him when you were sixteen and trained for twelve years?*

K: My master thought that I showed an ability to help with healing, and it was decided that they needed a physician, so they would train me.

D: *I see. Then you said you had some training after that though?* (Yes) *From other people?* (Yes) *Was that in certain things or what?*

K: (Sigh) Perhaps just newer methods. Different techniques, yes.

H: *Alexandro, have you ever heard, or do you use any kind of touch in your healing? And have you heard of magnetic healing?*

K: I have heard that those who use stones … that have these abilities to, when placed upon the part that is ill, that the sickness is drawn into the stone. There are those who use the hands in healing. In that mostly I do not know.

D: *You don't do that though?* (No) *But you have heard of it. Where do you perform your surgery?*

K: I have a room that is off the back of my … home, that is utilized as a … an … (has trouble finding the word) office.

D: *Like an office?* (Yes) *Then the people who are sick come to you?*

K: Ah. It is those who are ill and in need, yes.

D: *They come to your house then?* (Yes) *And you do these things there. When you're doing surgery, do you take any kind of precautions? You know, how do you prepare the patient, the person for the surgery?*

K: Usually I take vinegar and wash off wherever that I am going to perform the surgery. I wash my hands very good and then I rinse them in vinegar.

D: *You mean you put vinegar on the patient's body?*

K: Yes, yes. And then the knives are also laid in vinegar.—This is about it.

D: *I wondered if you had anything like that. Where do you operate? Is it a table or something?*

K: Usually it is on the table, yes.

D: *And it's like a room just for that, you have everything there then. (Yes) Okay. And what do you do after you perform the surgery? How do you close the person back up again?*

K: You use either silk or … sometimes it is, we use the guts of a cat, the sinews.

D: *You mean to sew them back up so they would heal? (Yes) Do you use a needle or what?*

K: Yes, you use a needle that is usually made out of bone.

D: *Bone. And then you sew them back together so they will heal. (Yes) I just wondered, there are so many different techniques that are used by many different physicians. Do you like your work?*

K: Yes, I like the feeling of having made someone better who was perhaps dying or in great pain.

D: *Do you have a family? (No) Have you ever married? (No) Did you ever have any desire to?*

K: (Sigh) I have my work. This was important to me.

D: *Okay. You were happy with that. That's all you cared about, then. (Yes) Okay. I thank you for sharing your information with us. We'd like to come back again and talk with you. Maybe you can help us quite a bit with knowledge.*

K: It can be hoped.

D: *Okay. Thank you. We will leave that scene now. Let's go forward into time. Let's go up to the 700s. I will count to three and it will be the 700s. 1. 2, 3. we are in the 700s, what are you doing?*

We cut the doctor short because Karen had asked at the beginning of the session to be returned to the time of the Druidess. She liked the feeling she had last week of being able to tap into that tremendous energy field. She hoped to do it again and maybe learn something about directing the energy. We agreed to try it. We will return to the doctor next week for more information.

Dolores had spoken many times in her lectures when asked about her own past lives about the life in Alexandria at the Library when it was burned.

To the best of my recollection, she was one of the people who cared for the scrolls that were kept in the library. She was not one who would write on them or study them but was one who would retrieve the scrolls when requested by a scholar or professor. It was her job to protect them.

When the Romans caused the fire that burned the Library, Dolores, as the person from that time, tried to save as many scrolls as possible. In doing so, she was killed and was not able to complete her mission.

Dolores has stated that because of this, she feels she is now trying to get back the knowledge that was lost. Many people ask, "Do you have to rewrite the whole Library?"

While in Russia, Dolores had a session with a young man who also was in Alexandria at the time of the burning. He was one of the scholars who studied the scrolls and was there when the burning started. He also tried to save as many scrolls as he could but was killed by a falling beam that struck him across the shoulders.

I don't know if Dolores ever found anyone else that was there during this time but to find just one was astonishing.

~ Nancy

Chapter 16
The Doctor, Part 2
(Recorded June 1, 1983)

We held this session at Harriet's house, but Harriet had an appointment and did not come back until we were almost finished.

D: *Okay, we're going to go back and back in time. Let's go back to the year, sometime in the 400s. I will count to three and it will be some time in the 400s. That's way back there in time. When the physician lived in Alexandria. At that time. Sometime in the 400s. I will count to three and you will be there. 1, 2, 3, you're in the 400s, what are you doing?*

K: Walking.

D: *Oh, where are you walking at?*

K: Down by the shore.

D: *Where are you?*

K: In Alexandria.

D: *Well, can you tell me what you see as you walk?*

K: I am watching the (sounded like "docks") as they sail.

D: *The what as they sail?*

K: (It again sounds like docks.)

D: *What is that?*

K: It is the boats. They are sailing in the harbor.

D: *Do they come in and out of there?* (Yes) *Are there lots of them?*

K: Quite a few.

D: *What do they look like?*

K: They have a sharp bow that rises up and a sail that comes at a slant, that comes out and then down. The sail is full when it catches the wind.

D: *Oh, uh-huh. Are they big boats?*

K: No. They are small enough that they can be manned by two people. They can hold more, but this is all it takes to run one.

D: *Is there anything else around where you are?*

K: No, I'm away from the city a little ways. It is quiet here.

D: *Oh, these aren't the docks where the boats come in?* (No) *You're outside the city.* (Yes) *What is the weather like where you live?*

K: It is very hot. It is cool with the winds coming off of the water, but there has been much heat lately. (Sigh)

D: *Does it stay hot all year round?*

K: It cools off some during some months, but for the most part it is very hot, yes.

D: *I just wondered what kind of climate it was. Does it ever rain or anything like that there?*

K: Yes, there is … sometimes there is rain. Most of the water that is used here comes from up the river. When that the floods come.

D: *You mean there is a river near there?*

K: It is on the Nile.

D: *Oh. What is the water you're looking at? Is that the Nile?*

K: No, it 'tis the sea.

D: *Oh. and then the Nile River comes into the sea?* (Yes) *And this is where you get your drinking water from?*

K: From the Nile, yes.

D: *You said you had floods sometimes?*

K: Every year the Nile, she rises.

D: *Then what do they do? Store the water?*

K: It is used in the irrigation of the fields. And they have the planting season planned around the spring floods.

D: *Then the rest of the year they can't use the water?*

K: Uh, what do you mean?

D: *Well, you said they use the water in the planting in the spring.*

K: No, it is just that the fields are covered. During spring floods, the fields are covered with water. And then this water is used for that. This is not the only time, but it is the time when there is the most water.

D: *Oh, I see. Well, how do they store the water for drinking? Or do they do that?*

K: Usually there are wells for the drinking water. They actually have wells that are away from the Nile. It is (sigh) water that has come from the Nile, but it has been cleaned. The Nile is very dirty.

D: *Oh, that's interesting. I think it would when it floods, that it would be dirty water. How would they clean the water? Do you know?*

K: It ... when that the well is away from the river, it cleans through the sand, so that it flows into the well clear.

D: *I see. Then if they were to ... they couldn't drink the dirty water, could they?*

K: People do, but you can get sick from this.

D: *Yes, it's better to have clean water, isn't it?* (Yes) *What is your name?*

K: Alexandro.

D: *What kind of a job do you have?*

K: I am a physician.

D: *Have you been a physician very long?*

K: Since I was but a young man, yes.

D: *How old are you now? (deep sigh) Do you have any idea?*

K: I have probably forty-five years.

D: *Have you always lived in Alexandria?*

K: No. I lived in Thrace when I was a child. But this is where my master moved, and he sent me to school here.

D: *Then you came there so you could study under him? Your master?*

K: For him.

D: *For him. Okay, I thought maybe, the master meant that he was your teacher.*

K: No, no, no. My master, he was my ... (hunts for word) my owner.

D: *Oh, I see. That's something I didn't understand. I thought that once you became a physician, finished your schooling, your studies, that you would go off on your own.*

K: It was his money that sent me to school. And then I spent the years until his death in his—as his and took care of the family and the other slaves. And when he died, I had my freedom.

D: *I see. Then you were like a slave, but you still—*

K: I was a slave.

D: *You were a slave, but you were still allowed to go to school to learn to be a physician.*

K: He knew that I had an aptitude toward this and they needed a physician. The ... his physician was becoming old.

D: *Oh, I thought that usually slaves did nothing but labor.*

K: No. There are house slaves, there are many who are teachers and physicians and such, yes.

D: *Oh. That's a different idea than what I've always thought. Well, how did you first become a slave? You said you lived in Thrace?*

K: I do not remember anything before being sold.

D: *Oh, then this man bought you in Thrace or what? When you were a child?*

K: He bought me from a slave trader, yes.

D: *You were a child at that time?*

K: I was about five, yes.

D: *Oh. that's why you don't remember anything before that then. Well, was this man good to you? (Yes) He was a good master then, wasn't he?*

K: He was fair. It is not many masters who leave their slaves a freedman when they die.

D: *This is what happened then? He gave you your freedom? (Yes) And you could be a physician without ... on your own, so to speak?*

K: Yes, then it was my choice.

D: *I wondered. It is different customs than I'm used to, that's why I'm asking questions. Where I live, they don't have slaves and I was wondering.*

K: There are slaves everywhere.

D: *Different customs. But, anyway now, you have your own— what, you have your own home?*

K: Yes. It is through my fees as a physician that I have earned enough to have this. Yes.

The entire session she kept playing (fooling) with her left earlobe. She kept rubbing it between her thumb and forefinger and fiddling with it. She was wearing loop earrings and I was a little worried she might get her finger entangled in the loop and pull on it. As she had pierced ears, I was afraid she would hurt herself. She seemed to be doing it absentmindedly as a habit or something.

D: *(I decided to ask about it.) Is your ear bothering you?*
K: (She jerked her hand quickly away and folded her arms across her chest.) No! (Abruptly)
D: *I just wondered.*
K: It is a habit.
D: *Oh, just a habit? Okay.*
K: The ear, there is a telltale sign that everyone knows you have been a slave.
D: *Oh. How can they tell by looking at your ear?*
K: The ear has been ... cut. (She fingers it again.) The lobe has a V.
D: *In the bottom part there?* (Yes) *Oh, that's what that is on there? (I pretended I could see it.)* (Yes) *That's why you mean, and it bothers you because people see it or what?*
K: It is a sign that someone else owns you. Even after you become a freedman, it is still there.
D: *Then it's kind of a habit, you mean, you still fool with it. You don't have to worry. It doesn't bother me, because you've told me the story now.—That's what they do to all the slaves? They cut the ear?*
K: Yes, it is a mark.
D: *Oh. This was done when you were real young then.* (Yes) *Where do you do ... you told me before that you did surgery. Where do you do your surgery?*
K: I have a room at the back of my house that is used as my ... where I see patients and have those who ... have nowhere

else to go. They stay there and I do my surgery in one of those rooms.

D: *Do you ever go to people's houses?*

K: Upon occasion if they are a wealthy client, yes.

D: *Then you would go there instead of them coming to you then.* (Yes) *What kind of operations do you do?*

K: There are many kinds. Ah, those for disorders of the stomach, when that there are tumors in the abdomen. If a man has a limb that has become gangrene it is then amputated. There are many types of surgery.

D: *Are those the most common types that you do?*

K: I would say yes.

D: *What is a tumor?*

K: There are two different types. There are those that once they have grown to reach a certain size, grow no more. And there are those that keep growing. They are ... (hunts for the word) Cancerous. And they keep growing. They consume what is around them and they must be removed.

D: *Okay. That is the word that you use for it, cancerous? Is that what you would call it when it got like that? (I wanted to know if she was using a word from her language or from Karen's mind.)*

K: Malefic.

D: *Malefic? Is it a little hard to find the word?* (Yes) *But you would probably use a different word then, is that right?* (Yes) *Okay. But you have that a lot with people with tumors in the stomach area?*

K: In the stomach and abdomen there are different types, yes. (Sigh) There are those such as the women would have. A growth upon their ... female organs. (Has difficulty finding the right words.) There are ... stones in the bladder that would be used to ... you would perform an operation to be rid of them.

D: *Well, if you had a, like you said, there was a tumor in the abdomen, how would you remove that?*

K: You would first either ... using some form of either drug to put them to sleep or you would induce them into a hypnotic trance, to where that they no longer felt any pain. You would then take the knife and you would make an incision into the fatty tissues. And cutting with the muscles instead of against it, you would open the abdomen, so that you could reach in and cut the tumor away from whatever it had attached itself to.

D: *Is that hard to do, to take it out?*

K: Sometimes it is impossible, and one must just ... sew them back up. Because it is impossible to get it. (Sigh)

D: *It is difficult sometimes?*

K: At times, yes. We then would remove the growth and take and stitch together the muscles that you had to separate and then stitch the fat together. This is the hardest, because it always wishes to dislodge itself. It is not easy to stitch. And then you would stitch the skin.

D: *Yeah, it would be slick, wouldn't it, the fat would be. It would be hard to sew. (Yes) Do you ever operate on any of the organs inside the body? Or can you do that? I don't know, I'm just asking questions.*

K: (Sigh) Explain this to me. I—

D: *You said you remove a growth. Have you ever cut on an organ?*

K: To remove the stones in the gall bladder, yes, you would open up the bladder. And removing the stones, making sure that none of the ... fluids from the bladder emptied into the cavity. Because it would cause a great risk of ... infection. You would then remove the stones and stitch the bladder up. And again, the same procedure as before, stitching everything up.

D: *How can you keep the fluids from emptying into the cavity?*

K: Usually there is an assistant there who would help you in this. You have the area packed with ... (again has difficulty finding the right words) cotton. They would take this cotton that has been soaked with this, so that it didn't touch anything else. And they would throw it out and empty it.

D: *Oh, because I thought there would be no way to keep it from coming out. (Yes) And then you remove the stones and sew it back up. (Yes) Does it heal all right like that?*

K: I prefer using hypnosis in these cases because you can then induce a state in that person, so it will speed up the healing process. And they have greater chances of survival.

D: *But it seems like there would be pain afterwards. You know, cutting into them.*

K: Then you would leave the suggestion that there would be no pain or discomfort. And the healing would be at an advanced rate, and you would not have as many problems or as many deaths.

D: *Well, I was wondering about other organs in the body, if you ever operated on them. Besides the bladder. If you've ever cut into any of them.*

K: I have heard of those who do other surgery such as this. But to me it sounds like the risk is greater than the good that would come out of it.

D: *Like cutting into the stomach. Or the—*

K: You would cut into the stomach if there was a growth on it and sew it, yes. But I have heard of those who would wish to experiment on the heart. And there is no way to keep the blood flowing and keep the patient alive if you're doing such things as this.

D: *There are people that think they can?*

K: Yes. But then there are those who care not whether they lose the patient or not, because they are just dealing with slaves.

D: *Oh. they experiment to see if they could do it?* (Yes) *Oh, that seems like it would be very dangerous. On the heart.* (Yes) *Well, what about the intestines? Do you know the intestines?*

K: Yes, the entrails, yes.

D: *Can they be operated on?*

K: They can be shortened if one is very careful in this procedure. For again, they have … ah, if any of what is in them is lost into the body cavity, the person would sicken and die. So it is something that is better left alone. But you may operate, yes.

D: *Well, the kidneys? Do you know those organs?* (Yes) *Can they be operated on?*

K: I have never known anyone to perform a successful surgery on them, no.

D: *I just wondered which organs you could touch. You know, and which were dangerous to fool with. Then there are some organs that are better left alone, is that right?* (Yes) *What about the lung? That part of the body? Have you ever done any operating on patients there?*

K: The only reason I have ever operated on the lung was ... one time I had a patient who had had it pierced. And it had to be stitched up and then re-inflated, for it had collapsed. And to do this, we sewed the lung up and then a reed was inserted. And air was blown into the reed and into the lung and re-inflating it.

D: *Where was the reed inserted?*

K: It was inserted ... ah, at about the same place that it would be the fourth rib.

D: *Oh, where you had cut, you mean?* (Yes) *You put the reed in there and ... what? It is blown by the mouth then?* (Yes) *And this works? It inflates the lung?* (Yes) *Oh, uh-huh. This is what you would do, say, if ... oh, what about cases of battle? Or something, if someone was hurt there?* (Frowns) *I'm thinking of battle—where someone was fighting a war. You know. (Still frowning) Do you have any cases ... you don't have anything like that then?*

K: I'm not understanding what you— (Apparently war was rare at that area or time period.)

D: *Well, sometimes in wars when soldiers fight, they have—*

K: You're saying that they would have wounds in the lungs. This is what you—

D: *Or somewhere, yes.*

K: Yes. Ah, basically, probably. This particular injury was due to a ... disagreement.

D: *(Laughed at her expression.) Then you're not having any wars right now?*

K: Not here.

D: *Okay. I thought sometimes battles are going on and doctors are needed in cases like that. Well, are you ever called in when women are having children?*

K: If they are unable to have them, we will perform ... surgery in order to bring the child out. The ... In many cases the mother is not saved, but this is a last resort.

D: *They only do this if there is nothing else that can be done, is that right?* (Yes) *Does the child live this way?*

K: In ... if the woman has been with child long enough and it is almost its time, yes. But if it is too early, its chances are not as great of survival.

D: *Uh-huh. And sometimes the mother will die?*

K: If there has been too much of a loss of blood prior to my being called or if there are many other problems, like the swelling. A lot of women who are unable to have children naturally, toward the end of their pregnancy, they get, um, the fluids in the body do not escape. They do not leave, they are trapped in around the wrists and hands, and feet and ankles, and different extremities of the body will swell with this fluid. And it is dangerous to both mother and child, and in a lot of these cases the woman will need surgery. But ... because of the stress on the body due to this, they will not always survive the operation.

D: *I see. Well, is it dangerous to cut into the body then to remove the child?*

K: Any time that you perform any type of surgery, it is dangerous to the body. It is a shock. It has to be prepared for this shock and ... beating it is taking. Therefore, it is dangerous, yes.

D: *Well, can you tell me how you perform the operation whenever you remove the child?*

K: You take and you would—a lot of times I will cut this way across the stomach. (She motions with her hand, a crosswise cut across the lowest part of the abdomen, in the area now described as a bikini cut.) Lower, so that you are cutting the middle of the utero. And you would then open the stomach up, in which will ah, expose the ... fiber of the utero (pronounced: utro, ut-tro), in which you can see the child through this. And you will very carefully cut so that you do not damage the child in any manner. And then you would lift him out along with the placenta and lay them to one side or give them to your assistant, so they can make sure the child is okay and clean them up. In which time you are then sewing the mother back. And—

D: *Just a moment. (I had to get up and close the window. A lawnmower was having a field-day going back and forth right beneath the window. It was difficult to understand her, and I am glad the tape recorder picked up her words so well, even if I couldn't.) I'm sorry, I was distracted by a lot of noise. Yes, you would have to be careful cutting in, wouldn't you, so you wouldn't damage the child in any way. (Yes) Okay. You said you also cut off limbs sometimes?*

K: Yes, if that they ... a wound has become so bad that the wound is endangering the body. If perhaps the bones had crushed so that there is no use left in this limb. Then you would take it.

D: *Okay. Ah, do you know the word "infection"? (Frowns) (How do I explain?) I was wondering how you would keep—Oh? How you would keep the wound clean afterwards so that it wouldn't get—go bad again.*

K: There are those who, ah, use cauterization, where that they would and, take a ... utensil of some sort and that has been heated to red-hot and seal the end of it in this manner. There are those who use ... different tars to seal off.

D: *Different what?*

K: Tars, resins to seal the wound. A resin, to be less of a shock to the system, you will ... if you cut off someone's leg and then you again shock the system by cauterization, you are doing double damage, because you have already shocked those nerve endings. Whereas if you would use different resins and balms upon this that would stop the bleeding, it is not as much of a stress on the body.

D: *That's what I meant. That sometimes whenever you operate—I don't know if you know the word "germs" or not, that's what I meant by infection—it will go bad. I don't know how else to explain it. (Laugh)*

K: You mean to ... when that there are gangrene pus ... ah ... (She also has trouble finding the right word.)

D: *Like if it came back again, you know, after you operated. I wondered how you would keep it from happening. (Yes)*

Sometimes it does happen.

K: Yes, you must try to keep everything as clean as possible, so that no—ah, re-infestations occur.

D: *Okay. I didn't know how to put it into words that you knew. Well, do you use the balms and the resins?*

K: As a rule, yes. If there are none around … for instance, that if it is an emergency situation where this occurs. Then by needs, you must use the cauterization. But it is not the best method to use.

D: *Well, which balms do you like to use, or tars? Are there certain kinds?*

K: (Sigh) The kind of the balms that is used to … when that the wound is healing. It would get rid of some of the itching, would be the oil of camphor. It soothes the skin, the new skin that is growing.

D: *Which one do you use to stop the bleeding?*

K: Usually tar of cedar.

D: *This is real good for that?*

K: I have used this many times, yes. It is resinous enough that it seals the area.

D: *(I thought she had said oil of cedar.) It's thicker then. I think of an oil as being thin.*

K: You are saying oil. This is not an oil. This is a resin or … sap.

D: *Oh, I see. It is thicker than oil. (Yes) I thought that oil would be thin like water. But it's called oil of cedar, though?*

K: Resin of cedar.

D: *Resin of cedar. You take that and it's spread like a … salve? That's a word I would use. I don't know if … (Frowns) you don't know that word then.*

K: Balm?

D: *A balm. That would be the same meaning. And it's put on the stump, or whatever you call it, where you cut. (Yes) And this stops the bleeding? (Yes) And helps heal? And then you use the oil of camphor to relieve the itching then. That sounds like it will work.—What do you do whenever you, like you say, cut into someone's abdomen and do surgery there? Do you put anything on that? To help with the healing? After you sew it up?*

K: Usually just … oil of camphor or something similar soaked on a cloth. And it is placed over the wound.

D: *This helps to make it heal faster?*

K: Yes, and protects it from, ah, pestilence and … (Finally she found a word that is very near to the word "germs" I was looking for.)

D: *Pestilence? Is that the word you use?* (Yes) *Yes, you are saying the same thing. You just use different words, describing the same thing. That's interesting. I'm always trying to learn new things. When I find someone who can tell me new things, I like to ask questions.—What about the head? Do you ever operate on the head?*

K: I have heard of those who have done, ah, surgery to remove tumors and things. Usually if someone is in this state, I will send them to someone who has experience in this. I—I have no wish to deal in this field. (So, apparently, they had specialists in those days, too.)

D: *You don't like to operate on that part then. But there are people who do operate on the head?*

K: I have heard there are those who have even … had patients to survive.

D: *Then it is dangerous then. There is a tumor on the brain, then it is usually …*

K: Yes. Is fatal.

D: *Yes, it would be dangerous to mess with that organ, wouldn't it?* (Yes) *Then you don't do that type then.* (No) *What type of instruments do you use? Do you have very many that you operate with?*

K: Mostly there are the scalpel, your knife. Um … (has trouble finding the word), the grippers, ah— (Pause, as she thinks)

D: *What do you call it? Just use words that are familiar to you, if it's hard to find the right words.*

K: They would be used to grasp something that you are trying to, perhaps keep away from something else. Or to pull out. *(Okay)* There are the, um, clamps that are used to hold the blood vessels to keep them from bleeding over the opened area.—The needles and, ah, basically that is about it.

D: *You don't have a lot of instruments then that you would use in operations?* (No) *Well, is there any—*

K: (She interrupts as she thought of another one.) A saw.

D: *What do you do if the patient is bleeding too much? Is there any way you can ... anything you can do about that? (Of course, I am thinking about transfusions.)*

K: If it is a serious surgery, you will utilize hypnosis, so that you have better control over the functions of the body. And you will give them the instructions that they will close the flow of blood off to this particular area. And then the bleeding will either cease totally or at least subside a great deal.

D: *Then they can do this with their mind if they are instructed to do so?* (Yes) *But, what if the patient loses too much blood, is there anything you can do then?* (No) *Well, after the operation, do you send them home? Or what do you do with them?*

K: They stay or ... those who are poor, a lot of times they will stay here. If they are those who have a home to go to, then they would be carried home. The very wealthy have the surgery performed at where they are going to stay anyway.

D: *Oh. In their own home then.* (Yes) *Well, when they carry them home, what, on horses or how would they do that?*

K: No, upon a, um, stretcher.

D: *And they just carry them laying down flat that way?* (Yes) *Then do you go and check on them afterwards?*

K: Yes, and make sure that there is no fever or ... problems arising from surgery or the illness itself.

D: *You have to keep watching them until they are all over it then.* (Yes) *What do you do in case of a fever?*

K: It depends upon the type of illness. If it is something to do that ... it is part of its natural, um, progression of illness, then you would just give them a lot of fluids, to help wash out, ah, whatever is causing the fever to be in them. If it gets too high, you would take them and immerse them in cool water to help bring it down. These are in cases where it is extremely ... hot. And there are different types of herbs that you can give them, in which will also help sometimes bring this down. Or again, hypnosis. You can tell them that there is no reason for this high of a ... temperature and reduce it in this manner.

D: *What, do you mix something from the herbs? To give them, or how would you use that?*

K: Usually the herbs are given with, ah, wine, so that they are not tasted.

D: *Oh, in the wine?*

K: Yes. Sometimes, it just consists of something to even just knock them out, so that they would have the rest that they need to help fight, and then the illness will run its course.

D: *I see. What herbs do you use for fevers? Do you know the names of the herbs?*

K: Well, there is different ones, ah, that can be used. (Sigh) Some of the drugs that we would use, would be, ah, just to give them sleep, would be poppy. Ah, sometimes to bring a fever down, you would use the flowers of the garlic that have been ... soaked in vinegar.

D: *Oh? That will bring the fever down? Just the flowers?*

K: Um, it is something that has been handed down. I have seen it work. But a lot of medicine, whether most people will admit to this or not, has to do with the patient believing that it will work.

D: *I think that could be true. Some people can make themselves well or make themselves sick that way. I believe that.—But, you take the flowers that have been soaked in vinegar, and then ... how do you make it so they can drink it? Grind it up or what?*

K: Then the flowers, after they have been soaked, they are then ground and then ... so that it has all of the ... a paste-like consistency. And then they are added to wine, so that the vinegar taste is not overpowering and drunk.

D: *And then they drink that.* (Yes) *That's the main one you use for fevers? The garlic, then.*

K: It is one of them, yes.

D: *Are there others that are good for bringing fever down? (Sigh) Besides knocking them out, like you said.*

K: There are many different types, depending upon what is

available at that time, yes.

D: *I'm curious, because I'm interested in herbs and what they can do. I don't know which—*

K: (Interrupts) Are you a physician?

D: *(Taken aback) Well, I would like to be. If I could learn. I would especially like to learn the herbs and what they can be used for.*

K: Herbs and their concoctions can be very dangerous for those who are uninformed and uninitiated.

D: *Oh. You mean I shouldn't try without having training?*

K: Yes, because they can—in the right quantities—they can be very helpful. But in the wrong, they can be deadly.

D: *Yes, that makes sense. But I at least wanted to know the names, anyway, then I would know what herbs were important. (Pause) I wouldn't try to do it by myself.*

K: This is good.

D: *That's what you're afraid of? That I might do something like that? No, I would be too afraid of hurting someone. I wouldn't want to do it myself. I was just curious what—*

K: (Interrupts) It has been known for those to show curiosity about them and find out enough to use them on others.

D: *Oh, in a wrong way? (Yes) I see what you mean. I was just curious which ones did what, because there are so many. (No answer) Well, you said one time you were making elixirs. Those are medicines?*

K: Yes, they are different things that have been distilled from certain herbs and sometimes, even spices added, yes.

D: *Oh. This makes medicine for people that have different things wrong with them.*

K: Some of it is for people who think they have different things wrong with them. (Smiling)

D: *(Laugh) It works either way, doesn't it?—Do you make your own medicines? Your own elixirs?*

K: Yes. It is so that you know what you are giving the people you are treating.

D: *Oh, then you know it's done right then. (Yes) I've heard sometimes people buy things.*

K: Where would you buy these things? You may buy the different herbs or sometimes go out and find them, but where would you—

D: *Well, I've heard there are some places where people, that's all they do is make elixirs and sell them to people. In other countries, in other lands.*

K: (Sigh) This sounds very unusual. How would I know that I could trust this person who was making them for me?

D: *That would be true. How would you know if they would do it right?*

K: I do not think I would like this.

D: *You wouldn't like that then.* (No) *Some places that's what they do. The physicians treat the sick and then they have someone else to make the elixirs for them. Tell them instructions.*

K: This sounds very unusual.

(Had to turn tape over.)

D: *You know how it is in other lands, there are many different customs. Different ways of doing things.*

K: This sounds to be distinctly odd compared to what I am accustomed to.

D: *Uh-huh. Then you make your own and then you know it's done right.* (Yes) *What kind of—what's the word I want?— sickness, disease? that you would prescribe, that you would make elixirs for, the most often? That people would ask you for the most.*

K: One that is, one that I keep on hand with quite frequency would be, ah, the essence of foxglove. (Foxglove?) It is for people who have the symptoms of ... the heart is being constricted. And it ... assists in the function of the heart in that it ... opens the surrounding area in the, ah, aorti (pronounced: a-ort-i) of the heart, so that it may do its function. (Had difficulty finding the words to explain.)

D: *Okay. That's one that you use the most, the most common?*

K: It is quite frequent due to the fact that there are ... when people get older, there are quite a few who have problems of the heart. You can tell someone who has a problem of the heart, their ... around their mouth will become bluish. They will have a tendency to retain the fluids of the body, due to the dysfunction of several other things that are not getting the right amount of blood to them, because the heart is not functioning.

D: *This is one of the ways you can tell then.* (Yes) *Do they have pain sometime?*

K: They will have tightness in the chest area, and sometimes the pain will get so fierce that it will cause them to ... to (hunts for right word) ... ah, pass out, yes.

D: *Are there any other medicines that you use a lot, like that?*

K: Let me think. The different types of teas. The leaves of the raspberry are used for women who have had problems carrying children to full term. You would give these to them, and they would brew a tea out of this.—The root of the ginseng is sometimes distilled for different types of kidney dysfunctions and different types of things like this. There are those who say that it also slows the aging process, though I do not believe this. I think this is ... (Smiling, waves hand as though dismissing it).

D: *(Chuckle) Do you ever give it to anybody for that?*

K: No. The herbs in medicines are too valuable, and many of them too rare to pass out to someone upon a whim.

D: *Oh. Then they couldn't fool you to get certain medicines like that then?*

K: No. There are ... among some of the more common illnesses that are treated are ... like the "sweet sickness" and—

D: *The "what" sickness?*

K: The sweet sickness. The ... this is mostly in people who have too much fruits and sugars in their diets. It is called this because the ... it is said that the first physicians noticed the sweet odor to the urine. And it is said that the person consumes so much sugar that it is coming out through them in every way that it can.

D: *What do you give for that?*

K: Mostly you control this with diet. And you would ... these people would eat many sweetmeats of calves and oxen. It is said that this helps in that.

D: Do they have to have a regular diet of eating the sweetmeats every day?

K: At least several times a week, yes.

D: Then they have to watch and not eat so much sweets then.

K: Yes, they would have to eat lots of greens, green vegetables, but not many breads or root plants. That would be bad for you.

D: I bet it's hard to make people stop eating sweets since they like it so much. (Laugh)

K: It is themselves that they are causing to pay.

D: What happens if they have the sweet sickness and they won't do what you say? (Thinking, of course, of diabetic coma.)

K: They die.

D: It's that dangerous?

K: Yes. They would go into a, ah, a state where that there is no function of the mind. They are ... they just lie there and slowly waste away.

D: They're asleep, you mean?

K: Ah, it is deeper than that. It is the state where they cannot be reached. A ... coma.

D: Would that be the right word?

K: Coma, yes. (Pronounced with accent on last syllable.)

D: That's a word I would call it or a word you would call it? (No answer) Okay. And then when they go into that state, is there anything you can do? (No) It's too late then, isn't it? Then they die after that, if you can't—

K: (Interrupts) Then they die.

D: Oh, I see. It is a dangerous disease then.—These are all things that you have that you treat then. (Yes) Well, is Alexandria a big city?

K: It is quite large. It is a very busy city, yes.

D: There are a lot of people there?

K: It seems like the people change from day to day, but they always stay the same. There is always the poor and the ... squalid. And the rich, they come and go, and you see different faces. But they ... it is always changing.

D: *Well, what kind of—is Alexandria a—oh, say, have a lot of business there or something?*

K: It is a port city; it is a trade city. It is through Alexandria that many of anything goes up the Nile to the different cities. Many of the anything goes from things from the outside world that are brought in, come through here, and they all get their part of that.

D: *Therefore, it is busy that way, a lot of trade and business.* (Yes) *And you mean boats come in?* (Yes) *They come from all over the world or what?*

K: Yes, there are those from every nationality who come here.

D: *Then, are there many other countries around there that you know of? Where things come from?*

K: Greece and Italy and, um, sometimes they come overland and there are things from Turkey that come by ship or sometimes over land. Even those from way up in the north. The fair-skinned traders who come, Germats (phonetic).

D: *Germats? Is that what you said.*

K: Visgots and, yes.

D: *They come down too then.—Did you say German or Germack? How did you pronounce that?*

K: Germat.

D: *Okay. And those are the fair-skinned people. Well, where you live—are you fair or are you dark?*

K: (Smiling) I am—not quite either. I am, I have brown hair and a light brown skin, but I am not extremely dark. I am not like (accent first syllable) the Bedouins (accent, phonetic) that come from the desert or the—people that come from—ah, the different countries to the South.

D: *They are much darker?* (Yes) *What's the name of the ones that come from the desert?*

K: (Pronounced more like Bud-wins, but she probably means Bedouins.)

D: *They are dark also?* (Yes) *Then, most people where you live, they are the same color you are?*

K: (Sigh) The ones who are here, most of them are probably

darker than I. The people in Alexandria and Egypt, and this area, they are a little of everything. They are not quite exactly Egyptian, but they are not anything else either.

D: *They are a mixture. Okay. Well, I think it's interesting. I just wondered. Let's leave that scene. I will count to three and let's go to an important day in your life. A day that you consider to be important when you're older. 1, 2, 3, it is an important day in your life when you are a little older. What are you doing? (No answer) What do you see?*

K: I see the ... my body that is laying on the bed.

D: *Oh, has something happened?*

K: Um. I have decided to leave it.

D: *Did you have a reason?*

K: Just being—tired.

D: *How old were you? Do you know about how many?*

K: Sixty-nine.

D: *Then you weren't sick or anything?*

K: There was a problem with the heart and so it just ceased to function.

D: *You being a physician and you couldn't—the medicine wouldn't help you?*

K: It would have helped for a while, but I was just tired. (Sigh)

D: *What do you think of that life?*

K: (Sadly) I see ... much sacrifice for others, but a ... almost holding oneself above the others because of a need to feel ... greater or higher than them.

D: *Do you think that's what you really felt?*

K: I see that the serving others was ... trying to get rid of the guilt that was felt on a lower level of being. Um. It was not a bad life, in the fact that there was no harm done to any others.

D: *Well, why should you have felt guilty?*

K: For the want to be better than the others, was why that there was a striving. A lot of this was overcome.

D: *I was thinking, you know, it's not bad to want to be somebody, to make something of your life.*

K: It is not bad to make something of one's life. But to look down upon others who have not, this is ... therein lies the trouble.

D: *Oh, do you think that maybe you did that and didn't realize it?*

K: For a period of that life, yes. It was done to a great extent.

D: *Well, the guilty feeling then was ... you said overcome the guilty feeling, you said.*

K: Yes. This when that—ah, this self-realized that this was a problem. They then offered their self to—the helping of those who are less fortunate, and this was good.

D: *Okay. But then you think you felt guilty, ah, due to something underlying it, you mean, in the early years or—? (Yes) And then you wanted to do this to overcome it. Well, it was not a bad life. It seemed like you did a lot of good for people.*

K: There was a striving toward this, yes.

D: *This is good. Well, you never married, did you?*

K: No. It was felt that—to find a soul mate would distract from the need to accomplish, or greater than the need to help others. If someone was there that would take—energy.

D: *Then your whole life was deliberately spent that way then, to help other people. This is why you had no family. (Yes) I see. I think you did a good job. You did accomplish what you set out to do.*

K: It can be hoped.

D: *Where are you going to go now? Do you know?*

K: I think I will rest.

D: *That would be a good idea, wouldn't it? Rest for a while, to get all of that out of your system. Okay. Well, let's leave that scene now. Let's go back further into time. We have been watching, it has been around the 400s. Let's go back to the 300s, which is back further than that time period. I will count to three and we will be back in the 300s and you will tell me what you see and what you are doing? 1, 2, 3, we are back in the 300s, what are you doing? (No answer) What do you see? (No answer but she is frowning.) Is it something that bothers you?*

K: I see—the students. The students are surrounding the body.

D: *The students are surrounding the body? (Yes) What do you mean?*

K: They are—praying my soul toward enlightenment.

D: You said you were watching the body. Has something happened?

K: I have left—this existence.

D: Where were you at?

K: I was in Tibet.

D: Oh, in the monastery? (I have found the last of the early lives she had gone through and am now able to put it in the proper time slot.) (Yes) You were an old man, weren't you, in that life? (Yes) What do the students do? You said they are preparing the body?

(I had not understood her, she often starts out very softly.)

K: No, they surround it and they are praying for my soul to continue on its wheel of existence toward enlightenment.

D: Oh. What do they do with the body after that? Do they have any certain rituals or things that they do?

Karen was moved back another hundred years and appears to have come in on the last day of this new life. (Hopefully this will be one of the lives we find when transcribing Dolores's tapes/files.)

Dolores had worked with Karen on some additional lives, and we have two more included in this last section.

Chapter 17
The Doctor, Part 3
(Recorded August 25, 1983)

The first part of this tape is Jesus Tape No. 12. We were winding up the sessions on the life of Saudi and wanted to get a little more information about the doctor in Alexandria before we quit meeting.

D: *Let's leave that scene. Let's go forward. We will leave that time and not worry anything about that time anymore at all. Let's move forward into the future. Going up. Let's come up a few hundred years, after you have progressed through a few more lives. Let's come up to the year 400. Sometime in the year 400. I will count to three and we will be there. 1, 2, 3, we are sometime in the year 400, what are you doing?*

K: I am mixing medicine.

D: *Okay. Where are you?*

K: (Big sigh) I am in Alexandria. (The pronunciation is run together.)

D: *Alexandria? Okay. Am I right, is your name Alexandro?*

K: Alexandro, yes. (Pronounced with more of a roll.)

D: *I am not saying it right? (She repeats again with a roll.) Okay. How old are you now at this time?*

K: (Big sigh) Sixty—one, two, ah. I'm an old man, it does not matter.

D: *Oh. you don't keep track of the years?*

K: (Sigh) Who counts anymore?

D: *Okay. What kind of medicine are you preparing?*

K: It is to rid a woman of swellings (sigh) in her wrists and ankles and joints.

D: *Oh. Do you know what is causing the swellings?*

K: (Sigh) She is not eating properly and being pregnant, this—. The toxins of the body are staying in and they are settling in these places. (Accent very strong and different from Saudi.)

Harriet (H): What can she eat to prevent this?

K: Less of the bread, meats, the blood. More of the leaves (pronounced: leafs) and herbs and things, raw fruits.

H: Can you tell us what this does to the system?

K: It helps and ... the whole play behind the continuing of the gathering of the toxins, is the kidneys refuse to function because they are lacking in certain ... elements. And when that they stop to function, there is a gathering of the poisons. And with the introduction of these fruits and herbs into the body, it will help them flush out, so that there is less a problem. This is a problem of malnutrition (pronounced strangely) to have this problem in pregnancy. (The words introduction, malnutrition and pregnancy pronounced rapidly with a strange accent. If I had not known the words, it would have been difficult to recognize them.)

H: Why is it that the fluids particularly gather at the wrists and the ankles? Why not another part? I know it will eventually, but why at those two places do you notice it first?

K: They are the ones that is noticed first because with the fate in the rest of the body, um, these bony areas you notice the swelling faster than any other place. I'm not particularly sure why it chooses in these places, except for that reason, you would notice it first.

D: *What kind of medicine are you preparing? Does it have a name?*

K: It is an elixir; it has several herbs and things that I will use.

D: *What, a drink or to rub on—*

K: It is to drink.

H: Is a medication or something of this nature, is it more helpful to have it rubbed on the body or to take it internally?

K: It depends upon what you wish it to do. There are certain things that are best to be taken through the skin. Some are better if they are put into the stomach and work their way out. It all depends upon the illness and problem.

D: *What would happen to her if she didn't get relief from—*

K: (Interrupts) She would die! And so would the child.

D: *It can be that bad?*

K: Yes, it is poisons. (poisonous?)

D: *Oh, I thought maybe just fluids.*

K: (Interrupts) So if you took—ah—hemlock, would you not die? It is poisonous. The body keeps the poisons and if that they are not flushed out of their system, there is death.

D: *I see.*

H: *Are the joints of the body—do they have any particularly closer input into the internal system? In other words, if you had an ointment to rub on, would this be absorbed more quickly at the joint area than over the tissue area?*

K: Yes. In most cases this is true.

H: *What about particular areas in the body! For instance, under the arms and in the groin. Would this be more accessible, or would it make any difference what joint area?*

K: Well, there are some things that would be rubbed at the neck and that would be—and the chest area, depending upon what they are. Others are better on the gland areas, there, in which they would go into the glands and be carried throughout the body. Some, you would take the feet and would be soaked in this … ah, concoction, elixir, whatever, and you would use this area in which to bring it in the body.

H: *Can you tell us a little bit—I'm very interested in the feet, because the feet take so much of the body's weight. I'm very interested. Is there anything that you can tell us that we could soak our feet in to bring just relief to the general body?*

K: (Sigh) Water in which sea salts have been added is very good, just for a general comfort of the body. It has many minerals and such. Or if you can just take sea water and soak the feet in, this is also very good.

D: *For how long of a time?*

K: Not very long, maybe—quarter of hour.

H: *I see. For a short time then. What about the tissue on the face? So often the face is exposed, the skin on the face is exposed so much more than the rest of the body. Is there anything that we can place on the skin to protect the skin and keep it from deteriorating or wrinkling or hardening or toughening?*

K: There are certain plants that are good to use of this. You take the oil—of the coconuts, yes, or ground coconut made into a paste and spread over that. Or—let me think here—the ... different types of oils from the fat of animals that has been rendered, would also be good if it was an extreme case of dryness.

D: *These are some things that you would use?*

K: Upon occasion, yes.

H: *Would the coconut be the better of the—*

K: (Interrupts) If it is not a severe case and you would start early enough, yes.

D: *Do you have mostly men patients or women patients?*

K: Both.

D: *Both? What about children? Do you treat children also?*

K: Upon occasion. Most children are very healthy.

D: *Why? Is Alexandria a healthy place to live?*

K: (Disgustedly) No!

D: *Why not?*

K: Too many people. Too much dirt, filth. 'Tis not a clean city. This is why I live away from the ... inner (pronounced: inter) city, because it is dirty. (Sounds displeased.)

D: *Oh. Where you live is not in the main part then? (No) Okay.*

H: *Do you know of the buildings known as the pyramids and the Sphinx? (Yes) Have you ever been there and seen them?*

K: Once.

D: *What did you think of them?*

K: There is an immenseness of power there. It is unbelievable.

H: *Is it helpful in any way, in a healing capacity, for people to be in this area? Around them?*

K: There is a drawing of goodness toward them, yes. It would be very helpful.

H: *Any particular one building more than any of the others? Or the whole area?*

K: The northern, in the queen's chamber.

D: *Is this one of the larger pyramids? (No answer) You were only there one time, you said? (Yes) Could you—you know, I've always been curious about Alexandria. Can you give me a description of the city? I wondered what it looked like. (I had read recently about a large lighthouse that stood in the port.) Before, you told me that you would sit on the ... by the ocean and looked out at the sea and the ships. What does the main part of the city look like?*

K: The main part of the city is built around the docks. There is the dock area and then the marketplace opens up into that. So, it's hundreds and hundreds of booths and people hollering and—the rats scurrying everywhere. And the yellow clay of the buildings. Everything is short and there is nothing tall and fine about this. This is a— (deep sigh) again, a very dirty city. It is very crowded, everything is on top of each other.

D: *The buildings are all small?*

K: Yes and crowded next to each other.

D: *Aren't there—are there any large buildings in the city?*

K: Yes, the houses of government and the library and the school. Those buildings are large, but they are not downtown in Alexandria, they are more to the edges.

D: *I wondered if there were any large buildings in the city. What about around the waterfront? Is there anything there that is large? (I am thinking of the lighthouse.)*

K: Ships.

D: *And nothing—*

K: The docks sometimes are very long. They go on for a ways, but they are not—I do not go down there very often, it is not a good place.

D: *There is nothing, no outstanding feature about the dock area? (She seems to be thinking.) You see, I wondered, I heard there was a lighthouse there.*

K: It is out to—there is an island, it's in the middle of the bay, that there is a house.

D: *Can you see that from the city? (Yes) What does that look like?*

K: It is very tall and slender. It looks to be made of some white stone, I do not—I have never been out there, I do not know.

D: *How large is it?*

K: To be seen from here, it is very large. (Yawns)

D: *How would they keep the light burning up there? That's what I was curious about.*

K: How should I know?

D: *(Laugh) You've never heard?*

K: I've never been curious.

D: *I'm just curious about different things, I suppose.—But you live out from the city then.*

K: Somewhat.

H: *I know that you treat with herbs and other—perhaps using a knife occasionally. Do you ever use color or stones to treat any of your illnesses with?*

K: There are many uses of stones in healing.

H: *Would you share some of them with us? I'm very interested in this.*

K: Certain types of cancers can be cured with stones.

H: *What particular type of stones?*

K: It is what some men call a lodestone. It has—magnetic properties with which to draw toward it.

D: *Would you have to wear the stone or—* (Yes)

K: (Interrupts) It would be placed over the area in which the cancer was growing.

H: *Can you tell us how this acts on it?*

K: It is said that it draws it out of the body. I'm not exactly sure.

D: *Well, how long of a time would you have to put it over the stone?*

K: Until the swelling was reduced.

D: *You look tired.*

K: (Intake of breath.) It has been a very long day.

D: *Is it nighttime?*

K: No. It is toward the dusk.

D: *How would you treat a cancer?*

K: If it had gone so far that it would not—make any change by giving herbs and such, then I would attempt an operation to remove it.

D: *Is this advisable? And could a person live afterwards?*

K: (Deep sigh) In some cases, yes, and in some cases, not. But since he would die anyway, this would at least give him a chance to life.

H: *I'd like to question you further. Do you ever use color in treating your patients? And if so, how?*

K: I, myself, do not use it to a great deal. I know of those who do.

H: *Have you ever seen it done? (Yes) Could you share this?*

K: (Abruptly) No!

D: *Is that something that's not normally spoke of?*

K: (Sigh) I'm not at liberty.

D: *(Change the subject.) Are there any other kinds of stones besides the lodestone that would be valuable in healing?*

K: Many different stones known as gems are used, in different ways, manners. (Yawns)

D: *What about crystals? Have you seen them? (Yes) Are they valuable in healing? (Yes) (She will not volunteer any more information on those areas.) Is your patient coming for the medicine tonight?*

K: She is here.

D: *Oh, she's there now? (Yes) That's why you're working late?*

K: (Yawn) I always work late. I'm getting too old for this, though.

D: *You think so. Well, is the patient going to stay at your house, or will she go back to—*

K: (Interrupts) She will stay for a day or so, until the herbs begin to work.

H: *Do you have a special place for your people that stay after they've taken medications? (Yes) Can you describe what it's like where they stay?*

K: It is on the back of my home. 'Tis a fairly open room. There is much light. There are—(Yawn) several cots that may be lined out as—with screens between them, so that they would have somewhat privacy.

H: *Is the position of the cot oriented in any particular direction, or does this have any bearing on it?*

K: North-south.

D: *Do you have very many patients at a time that stay there?*

K: Not usually.

H: *Is it significant at which end—is the head placed at the north or to the south?*

K: The north.

D: *The head's to the north? Do you have a specific reason for doing this?*

K: Alignment with the poles.

D: *Oh, this makes it easier then. Well, when they stay there, do they stay by themselves, or do other—*

K: My helper would stay with them if there is someone who must remain overnight. This way if there was any change, I would be called. (Yawn)

D: *Tell me about your helper. Is he a—is it a man, woman, young?*

K: It is an assistant, it is a young man. He's being trained.

D: *Learning medicine. (Her voice sounds increasingly tired.) (Yes) Does he stay there with you all the time? (Yes) And do you have any other patients in this—*

K: (Interrupts) Not at present.

D: *Not at present. Do people come to you or do you go to them?*

K: It depends. If they are rich enough, I will go to them.

H: *If they are rich enough? Does this mean that they pay you in coin for your services? How are you—what do they do for you when you heal them or give them help?*

K: If they cannot afford it, then there is no charge. If they are poor but have income, then I have a small fee. Sometimes in barter, food, whatever. But if they are very wealthy, then they are charged. They can afford my services.

D: *What do they normally pay you with?*

K: I have no set fee. I decide—sometimes it is in (word difficult to understand. Sounds like: dring?) ... sometimes, other valuables.

D: *Okay. But I was wondering what kind of coins.*

K: Gold, sometimes silver, depending upon what I ask for.

D: *Do you have a name for your coins in that country?*

K: Drachma. *(I had her repeat.)*

D: *Is that what you call the coins?*
K: They are the ones I prefer. They are of Greek origin. (The word sounded like either origin or order.)
D: *Okay. There are other coins then besides those?*
K: Yes, there are shekels and everything. There is Roman money.
D: *Are there many Romans in your area?*
K: Their power is fallen.
D: *Oh, they're not as powerful as they used to be?* (No) *Why?*
K: Their roofs are crashing about their heads.
D: *(Laugh) How do you feel about that?*
K: (Sigh) To each civilization comes its own time. It happened to the Greeks when that the Romans stepped in. Now it happens to the Romans.

(Turned off tape while I read a note passed to me by an observer.)

Other D: Do you know any of the names of the gems we were talking about a while ago that are used for healing?
K: Jade is.
H: Are any particular color of jade more powerful than the others?
K: There is of great rarity among the purple jade or royal jade, as it is known of. And there is a lot of good in the green color. The yellow is not as settling. The white is also permissible.
H: What about the red stones?
K: No. The energy in them is very unsettling and too wild.
D: *It's not a good color then, to use.* (No) *Okay. You know, in Alexandria, is there a ruler there, or a leader or something over the area?*
K: There are elders and—ah—well, I guess you would call it a ruler. There are—a prince, whatever, they would rule what happens in the city, and the—. It is not a prince—magistrate.
D: *Magistrate?* (Yes) *Well, does Rome have anything to say about what's done in Alexandria? (I was thinking magistrates are usually representatives of Rome.)*
K: Not any longer. (Smiling)

D: *What do you mean? Did something happen?*

K: Rome has no power any longer. They are falling about their heads. They cannot come and say, "Well, you must do this, because we decide that this must be done." Therefore, they do what they please now.

D: *Oh. There's no danger then of them coming in and saying, ah, starting trouble because you won't do what they say?*

K: They have enough troubles of their own, why mess with ours?

D: *(Laugh) Did something in particular happen?*

K: I have heard that there was an invasion to Rome. I do not know. This is what I heard. I do not pay attention to politics very often.

(She suddenly grimaced as if in pain and catches her breath.)

D: *Is something bothering you?*

K: I shall—be all right.

I know that the doctor died of heart trouble. I suspected that was what was the matter. I gave calming suggestions that nothing would really bother her. Harriet also picked up on what was wrong and was signaling me to move her forward. I knew if I did, the doctor would no longer be alive. But I couldn't let Harriet know without writing a note. Harriet had not been present during the death of the doctor, so didn't know how he died. I decided to go ahead and move her anyway because I wished to get her out of the discomfort.

D: *Let's leave this scene and let's go forward—a few years. I will count to three. 1, 2, 3, we are a few years older in that life, what are you doing?*

K: There is nothing now. There is no continuance.

D: *Okay. (This is what I thought would happen because the doctor had been in his sixties when he died of heart trouble.) What happened to you?*

K: (Sigh) The heart ceased to function.

D: *Okay. But it was an easy death, wasn't it? You'd lived a long time.*

K: The release was a well-looked-for one.

D: *You had had a good life there, hadn't you? You lived a long time and helped a lot of people. That's all right, it was a good life. Let's leave that scene. (I decided to take her back into the life because we still had questions to ask. But I wanted to take him to a younger age when he hopefully wouldn't be so tired and worn out.) I will count to three and we will be back at the age of forty. Alexandro in Alexandria, the physician at the age of forty. Let's go back to that age. I will count to three and we will go backwards to the age of forty in the life of Alexandro. 1, 2, 3. Alexandro is about forty years old, what are you doing?*

K: I am walking.

D: *Where are you at?*

K: Looking out over the coast.

D: *What, out at the water?* (Yes) *Do you like it there?*

K: It is very peaceful here.

D: *What do you see out there?*

K: (The word for those boats again that I have trouble transcribing.) The ... (sounds like docks and another one that sounds like scoops or skips?) mostly just the water.

D: *Oh, not very many boats out there today?* (No) *Can you see the city from where you are?*

K: Yes, but who wants to!

D: *You don't like that city very much, do you?* (No) *If you had your choice, would you go somewhere else?*

K: (Sigh) Yes. (Her voice now sounds younger and more vibrant.)

D: *Where would you go if you had anything to say about it?*

K: (She says a name I had difficulty understanding.)

Harriet said it was Gaza, but she pronounced it with the accent on the last syllable. (Had her repeat.)

D: *Oh, is that near?*

K: Not too far.

D: *Why would you want to go there?*

K: (Pause) To learn more.

D: *Oh, I thought Alexandria was the center of learning.*

K: It 'tis the center of outward learning.

H: *Gaza is where the Sphinx and the pyramids are. Am I correct?* (Yes) *And this is the center of the inner learning?* (Yes) *Thank you.*

D: *Are there people there who could teach you? (The encyclopedia says the Sphinx and pyramids are at Al Jizah. Could this be what she was saying? The pronunciation was strange.)*

K: My teachers are there. (She had a rather wistful sound in her voice.)

D: *Oh. Do they live near the pyramids?*

K: I will not speak of this.

D: *Okay. (This has happened many times in other lives when you approach too close to forbidden knowledge.) I just wondered. That would be where you would like to go if you could go.* (Yes) *Yes, it's just like you said, Alexandria is just a dirty city?*

K: Yes, so much pestilence and dishonesty and thieves. 'Tis very corrupt.

D: *Do you have trouble with thieves?*

K: No. I just said that I would put the curse of leprosy upon them and they do not bother me.

D: *(Laugh) They leave you alone then. But if the city is full of pestilence, they need doctors, they need physicians.*

K: Yes. (Sigh) But some of them I do not wonder at, whether it would be better for the world if they were not around.

H: *Why do they come in in the first place?*

K: (She says a questioning word here that I cannot transcribe.)

H: *Why? These people who do not observe the laws of health and care about their city, why do they come in? Why are they, why do they incarnate? What is their purpose, do you know?*

(I thought maybe Harriet had forgotten we were talking to her during a life. This was the sort of question we normally asked her in the between-lives state. But Harriet said later she just wanted to see what the doctor would have to say, if he knew anything about these things.)

K: A lot of the people that are of the lower ... forms, whatever, what term you wish to place upon it are slaves. And some of the slaves or freedmen don't really care about themselves. And many people who are tired of striving and looking for a living that is easy.

D: *Oh, just anything that's easy ways of getting things, is that true?* (Yes) *Well, I was thinking, you couldn't look down on slaves, you were a slave yourself, weren't you?*

K: Yes, but there are many types and differences between slaves. There are those who aspire toward something higher, and those who are just in the mire and wish to stay there.

D: *In your case, you wanted to go higher, didn't you?*

K: There was a striving toward that, yes.

H: *Will there be a rapid exit for those who do not care to strive? Will their time here be shorter?*

K: Sometimes. Sometimes it will seem to go on forever. And perhaps they shall learn from this that if you are in a bad situation, if you do not make better of it, it could go on for a long time.

H: *I see.*

D: *What religion are you? In Alexandria. Do you have a religion? (Pause) Do you know what I mean?*

K: We are the followers of the One.

H: *What does that mean?*

K: It is—the path I follow.

D: *I mean, do you worship Egyptian gods?*

K: No. I worship the one God.

D: *Oh. Then you don't worship the Roman gods then.*

K: No. And neither do I follow the priests of—the people who call themselves Christians (pronounced: Christ-ians, the word is separated deliberately), who say one thing and then do something else. This is wrong.

D: *There are Christians in Alexandria?*

K: There are communities of them, yes.

D: *What do you mean, they say one thing and do another thing?*

K: They are—hypocrites. They tell you to believe in one thing and go on saying—that you should do this, and then they turn around and are greedy and grasping just like the others.

H: How did they get the name of Christians? Do you know that?

K: They took that from the Cristos.

D: (Asked her to repeat.) What does that mean?

K: It was a name given to the one the Jews know as the Messiah.

H: Who was this? Can you tell us about it?

K: His name was Yeshua.

H: Did he live here in the world or in Alexandria, or— (She is obviously trying to see what her answer will be.)

K: Yes. He lived in Israel.

D: Well, ah, do you think this is a bad religion?

K: The pathway that they follow is, yes.

D: What about the Christian communities? Are they accepted in Alexandria?

K: Yes, to a great extent. They have much power.

D: Well, you said that you follow the way of the one God. Does that religion have a name? (No) What about the Jewish? Do they believe different than you believe?

K: There are many different beliefs that they have that we do not.

H: Have you ever heard of the people called the Kaloo? (This is from the Jesus material.) (Yes) Are they any place in this area, or— (Yes) They are? Thank you.

D: Could you tell us anything about them? We've heard of them. (No) I've heard they've been around for a long time.

K: They have been here since the beginning.

D: In that area, communities? (Yes) If we went to look for them, would we be able to find them?

K: No. It would not be allowed. They would seek you out. You would not find them.

D: Oh. Okay. Well, in Alexandria, are there churches or synagogues or things like that? (Yes) What would you call— do you go to a building like that for your religion? (No) Okay. You do not go to the synagogue or anything. (No) You said you follow the one God. Is that God Yahweh?

K: He has no name.

D: He has no name. Okay. I wondered about that, because you sound as though you're talking about Judaism. (No) *It's not that. Okay.*

K: It's much older that Judaism.

D: *Oh, it goes back much further than that. What about the Christians, though, were they persecuted for a while?*

K: Yes, so I have heard.

D: *This is not the things that are happening now then.* (No) *Okay.*

(Trying to think of some more questions.)

D: *Do you have very many patients at this time?*

K: I have about four at the house and I have about fifty that I would see on a weekly basis.

D: *Oh, that's a lot, isn't it?* (Yes) *Do you have to see them every day?*

K: Some every day. Different ones. And at once a week, all of them.

D: *At least once a week, you have to see them all?* (Yes) *Are they near, to where it's not hard to get to them?*

K: Most of them come to me.

D: *They come to the house? That makes it not so bad. Do you have anyone right now that you're seeing that is a bad case? Or are they all ordinary things?*

K: Nothing out of the ordinary.

D: *What type of cases do you have right now?*

K: Many different things. Everything from, um, from colds to boils to … upon a man who, every time he gets angry his skin breaks out in rash. This is about the most unusual. He is— every time he gets angry, it's just as if it bursts out all over.

D: *(Laugh) Only when he's angry then.*

K: (Laugh) But he stays angry most of the time.

D: *Have you ever seen cases like that before?*

K: Yes, when I was with my master.

D: *Well, how do you treat something like that? Just keep him from getting mad?*

K: You try to convince him that this is what is causing it. Which is the difficulty. Because he is so opinionated, he does not want to take anyone else's opinion.

D: *He doesn't believe you then.* (No) *He wants you to give him some kind of medicine.*

K: (Sigh) He wants to have an instant cure-all. A pill that he could take and be rid of this forever. (We laugh.) It does not work this way.

D: *He doesn't believe you then. That's the most unusual one that you have?* (Yes) *You mentioned pills, what is that?*

K: Where that certain types of medicines are—compounded together into a small dose that you would be able to swallow.

D: *Do you make these yourself?*

K: Yes, I make all of my medicines.

D: *Would that be harder to make than a drink?*

K: Yes, because it has to be compressed.

D: *Okay. That's one thing that you can do though.—Do you ever have anyone come to you with a broken arm or a broken leg?*

K: Yes, and they must be set or just bound with splints, if they are not out of place.

H: *How do you know when they're broken? How can you tell?*

K: You can tell by feeling. You would be able to tell when that you would run your hand along the arm or the leg. And you would feel the energy, where that it does not continue on, it is a breaking.

D: *Oh, you can tell by feeling the energy?*

H: *And this is also the way that you set the limb? So that when the energy flow is complete, then.*

K: Then it is in place.

D: *Oh, you can tell it. Because I know it's very painful. I didn't know how you could tell a broken leg from one that was just sprained. Had the muscle pulled or something. (Pause) Have you ever had a case where someone had a broken back?* (No) *I wonder if you would be able to do anything in a case like that.*

K: I do not know.

D: *What if someone would come to you like that? Would you know how to treat them?*

K: It is possible they would never make it to the doctor, because they would die.

D: *From the broken back?*

K: It would sever the cord in the back and it would be death.

D: *What about a broken neck, would that be the same thing?*

K: Again, very few live.

D: *I wondered if there was any way you could fix anything like that.*

H: *That spinal column is a source of great energy. Is this one of the reasons?* (Yes)

D: *What would happen if someone lived—could someone live with a broken back?*

K: I've never heard of it, but this does not mean that it is not possible.

H: *When a limb is set, is there any way of increasing the flow of energy around the break area, in order to help it speed its healing?*

K: The first thing you would do, would be to put the patient under hypno, so they would be in a state so they would not feel the pain of setting the limb. And you would have them utilizing their thoughts to bring about a—I prefer using a green light around that break. And they would do this themselves and send energy from their own body into this.

D: *Well, you said you use splints? What do you make those out of?*

K: Just wood.

D: *Just wood? Just to make it so they can't be moved.* (Yes)

H: *When they are under hypnosis and they are utilizing the green light, how long of a period does this go on for? Or do you have them do it periodically?*

K: I would put the suggestion into their mind that every time a certain word was spoken, that it would be done. And have one of their family periodically use it.

D: *Oh, they could say the word and this would make it—* (Yes) *A different person I see. We're just very curious about these different things so we can help each other. I hope you don't mind answering my questions?*

K: No. I'm just very tired.

D: *Has it been a long day?* (Uh-huh) *With fifty patients, I think you would be. (Laugh) But you said you don't see them all every day, do you?* (No) *Sometimes, are you able to keep your patience with those people?*

K: Pardon?

D: *You know, keep from being angry. Are you able to stay calm?*

K: For the most part.

D: *(Laugh) That's the hard part, isn't it?*

K: Sometimes. (Sounds tired.)

D: *Okay. Well, I think you do very good at it. A very good person. Thank you for talking with us. I'd like to come again and speak with you again sometime. Would that be all right?* (Yes) *Thank you. We will leave that scene now.*

(Subject brought forward.)

Chapter 18
The Girl Who Saw Fairies

I had just finished taking Karen to 1350 and as I finished counting, I saw she was frowning deeply. I asked what was the matter?

K: (Her voice was soft.) Fire! (She sounded frightened.) My house! (Heavy breathing) It—is—burning! I do not want to watch!

Most of the time when a subject tunes in on a life they will come in on a normal, everyday scene. But occasionally they will come in while something traumatic is going on. This seemed to be one of those cases. I quickly gave her calming suggestions so she would be able to talk about it.

D: *What happened, how did the fire start?*
K: They started it. The people in the village. They were afraid of me. (Her voice was very soft and meek.)
D: *Why were they afraid of you?*
K: Because I was different, and because that I was not like them. I used to—listen to people that they said weren't there. (She had a distinct accent, either Scottish or Irish.) And see things before they'd happen.
D: *Where did this happen?*
K: 'Twas in Scotland. We're just outside of the village Glenmara.
D: *Were you a man or a woman?*
K: I was a woman. (She sounded so sad.)
D: *What was your occupation?*

K: I made lace.

D: *I can't see any harm in that.*

K: No. But I was different. I had second sight.

D: *Did any one incident happen that made them this angry?*

K: (Sigh) They—when I tried to tell them that there would be a problem this year with the crops, and things. And when it came to pass, they said that it was I that cast an evil eye on the crops. And made the sheep all lamb too early and they all died. (Sigh) And they said it was my fault. (Sadly) I would never harm God's creatures. I thought that it would be good for them to know.

D: *They sound like ignorant people, they didn't understand.*

K: No, they had no wish to.

D: *Did you live there by yourself or did you have a family?*

K: I was alone. My mother died several years ago. And there was just I.

D: *Were you very old when this happened?*

K: Maybe twenty-two, maybe less. (The accent is very pronounced.)

D: *You were still young then. Had you ever married?*

K: (Coughing) No.

D: *What happened to you when they burned the house?*

K: (Matter-of-fact) I died.

D: *I wonder how the people will feel now?*

K: They will probably feel grand. They will think they've done a glorious thing in the name of the Lord.

D: *Had you told them things before that they didn't understand?*

K: Oh, a few just day-to-day things about people and maybe what—if that they would watch out that things wouldn't happen to them. And of course, if I saw anything that was maybe bad, they would say that I had done it. Just to prove that I could see the future, and they would blame it on me.

She began coughing more, probably from the smoke of the fire. So to relieve her from any discomfort I decided to remove her from the scene. Besides, I wanted to find out more about the earlier life of this young girl and how she came to this sad state of affairs. I seldom have a subject come in at the end of their life, but it sometimes happens. I took her backwards and asked what she was doing?

K: Making lace.

D: *Is it hard to do?*

K: 'Tis not very hard, if you take the time to do it. It can be a very simple thing to do. I had a very good teacher, my mother taught me when I was a little girl.

D: *How do you make it? Do you use a needle or what?*

K: It is a—a bobbin, and you knot it around it and—how can one explain it, it is—I don't know. It is very interesting.

D: *What do you do with the lace when you are finished?*

K: We sell it to very nice ladies. They come and they buy it.

D: *Do you charge very much?*

K: A few pence.

D: *Is that much money?*

K: Not really. It gives us money for food though. And we can eat very—not too bad. And we raise a little food so that we won't starve to death.

D: *It seems like with so much work involved in making it, you would want to charge more money.*

K: Why would they pay us to do it for more money? They wouldn't do it.

D: *But it takes a lot of work to make something beautiful.*

K: Aye, but grand ladies are very stingy with their money. And there are lots of lace makers.

D: *What is your name?*

K: It is Sarah MacDonald.

D: *Who are you living with?*

K: My mother.

D: *Does she also make the lace?*

K: She used to. She can't do it anymore. Her hands are too bad. If you can't bend your fingers, you can't make the lace. She's doing very poorly. It may not be long before she's not with us any longer.

Her voice was so soft, she seemed very shy and quiet. She had an odd way of using her mouth when she talked and especially when she smiled. She would pull her lips back exposing a lot of her teeth, and the upper lip would protrude out from the bottom one. I had the impression she had buck teeth. I also felt she was very self-conscious. I would have to be very gentle with this personality. She seemed very fragile.

D: *That must be very time-consuming. I think you must be very smart to be able to do that.*

K: (Seemed embarrassed. She smiled and blushed.) I don't know.—No one ever called me smart before.

D: *Is Glenmara a small place?*

K: It's not too big.

D: *Are you happy there?*

K: Who knows? Who's to say what happiness is?

D: *Do you think you will ever marry?*

K: I—I don't know. I haven't got much money and there's not many—eligible bachelors around. (She sounded sad.) It is for the good Lord to say.

D: *Are you still having trouble with the people in the town?*

K: Aye. They think that we're strange livin' out here, and doin' strange things. But—I'm not very different than they are. Sometimes I wish I was just like one of them and didn't have to worry about what people thought of you.

D: *Why do they think that you're different?*

K: Well, you see, in my family, the women are all born with the sight. And my mother said that you're supposed to help people with it and when we try to do that, they all think that we're witches and doin' things that are wrong out here. But we're not! (Her voice was so soft, I thought she must be a very beautiful person.)

D: *They just don't understand. Some people can be very ignorant.*

K: And ignorance can hurt other people, but—it's just not very fair.

D: *I think they would really like you if they got to know you.*

K: I'd like to think that.

D: *(I was speaking to her this way to gain her trust, but I also liked the poor girl.) I think you're a good girl. I wish I could do half the things that you do.*

K: (Blushing) Thank you. You could if you tried.

D: *It's not wrong to be able to talk to things that aren't there, to be able to tell people things—*

K: (Interrupted) It's not that they're not there, it's just that no one else sees them. They're very real, it's just some people aren't open to the things that exist around them. And because we see them, they think that we're strange or different.

D: *Who are these people that others can't see?*

K: I have friends among the fairies, they come, and they sing for me.

In order to maintain her trust I had to accept anything she told me as truth and not question it, even though it seemed strange. Whether fairies are real or not, is not the question. They apparently were very real to this poor girl.

D: *Have you seen the fairies all your life?*

K: Oh, aye. They used to come and play with me when I was a wee bairn.** I used to tell the children when we went to kirk that, you know, that they would come and see me. And they thought that I was crazy.

** Bairn (Scottish, northern English): a child. **

D: *That means you must have had a lonely life because they didn't understand. What are the fairies like? I'm interested, I want to know.*

K: Well, they're really very small and they're very shy. And they have, the women have wings that are just like glitter, and— they're just very happy people.

D: *How big are they?*

K: Oh, maybe six to nine inches tall.

D: *I've heard of such things, but I always thought they were just stories.*

K: People think they're just stories because mostly they don't come out anymore. But some people still see them. But they are accused of being so mischievous that, you know, anyone that talks to them is considered—bad. And maybe pixie-touched, as it's said, maybe a little crazy, and do strange things.

D: *Well, are they human, flesh and blood?*

K: No, they're—they have existence but they're not human. They're much, much older than human and they've been here forever.

D: *Like a spirit?*

K: No, they have existence, but—

D: *I wondered if they have a body like a human has.*

K: Sort of, but it's not the same. It's—you can't look at them through human eyes and say that this is like me, because it's not. It's something that's totally different, but that doesn't mean that they don't exist.

D: *Are there male fairies, too?*

K: Yes, but they're not as gay and colorful as the womenfolk.

D: *Do they have wings also?*

K: No, just the females.

D: *I've heard of the leprechaun, is that the same kind?*

K: I have no way of knowing; I've never met a leprechaun.

D: *And I've heard of elves.*

K: They are closer to being to the fairies. The elves are bigger, but I've never met an elf, either.

D: *Or a gnome? I've never seen these either, but I've heard of them.*

K: See, the gnomes are the people of the hills. And it is said that if a gnome is ever touched by daylight that he turns to stone. But I don't know, that's just a legend.

D: *But you have seen the fairies, I think that would be an honor. They wouldn't show themselves to everyone.*

K: They're very shy.

D: *And they come and talk to you?*

K: Yes, and they tell me things.

D: *What are their voices like?*

K: Like the whispering of the wind across the harp strings. They're very soft and very beautiful. It's like music. When they sing, it is like the birds singing in the trees.

D: *Maybe that's what people think it is when they hear it.*

K: Sometimes, yes.

D: *Did they ever try to teach you anything?*

K: You mean bits of magic?

D: *Well, anything.*

K: Well, they used to teach us how to find things. You know, if they were lost, and things like that. If that's what you mean.

D: *Is that hard to do?*

K: Not if you can think yourself to be the things that's lost.

D: *And you think where you would be if you were that thing? Does that work?*

K: Oh, aye.—And they'd tell me stories—about Queen Mab and her court and just different things like that. Long, long stories.

D: *Where do they live?*

K: Some of them live in trees and protect them as spirits. And some of them live—what are known as water sprites, live in water and wells and springs and things like that. And different things.

D: *Do they live a long time?*

K: Hundreds and hundreds of years, yes.

D: *Do they look old?*

K: No, they look like little children.

D: *Well, I guess they're probably wise to hide.*

K: They know that man is cruel. They have a very long memory. They remember a time that—they lived here and that there were no men. And they used to roam the forests and go about making life happy. And they tell me stories of then.

D: *If the fairies were here before people, what do they think about people?*

K: They don't like them very much. Because they say that, once that men used to be very fine and have all sorts of high motives and that they've just—been drug down by different circumstances and things. That they're no longer all fine and that there's a lot of meanness and cruelty. And they don't—

that's why they hide, that's why that very few people see them anymore.

D: *I can see why; they'd be afraid of what the people would do.*

K: Aye. Besides there's so many myths and legends about them, like—um, fairy gold. And they try to catch them and find their treasures and things like that. And it can cause nothing but harm.

D: *I suppose the fairies were friendlier in the early days when people first came.*

K: Aye, the fairies used to help them and taught them different things. But, you know, back then the people were open to different things than they are now. But they started being drug down and then they were no longer nice. And they tried to take things from the fairies, like misusing their trees and different things like that. And that was when that the distrust started.

Harriet (H): *Did they ever teach you about growing plants or things like that?*

K: They tell you if that you talk to the sprite that has the plant, that you can talk him into growing or—you know, ask him to help you. And it will make the tree a lot greener or whatever it is. But you have to acknowledge that they're there. And let them know that you care about their individual plant or tree or whatever it happens to be. And then they will do all sorts of things.

D: *What do you mean by a sprite? Is that a spirit just for that plant or what?*

K: It's the protective spirit for that plant, aye.

D: *That's interesting, I didn't know that. What kind of a spirit is that? Does it always exist or—*

K: I don't know. (She laughed.) I never asked.

D: *(We laughed.) What would happen to the sprite if the plant died?*

K: He perhaps might find another plant to go to.

D: *One that's just beginning to grow?*

K: Perhaps, I don't know.

D: *But you have to acknowledge that the plant has a spirit?*

K: It's like talking to plants, when that you let them know that you care, they do better.

D: *I bet you apply that when you grow things. I think you're smarter than those people in town.—If someone wanted to be able to communicate with the fairies, is there anything that they would have to do?*

K: I don't know, because, you see, it's always up to the fairy whether or not they want to come around. And that if you try to be high-minded, I suppose, if that—maybe it might attract one. But I don't know.

D: *Are the fairies everywhere in the world or just where you live?*

K: I don't know, I've never been everywhere in the world. How would I know if they're there?

D: *(We laughed.) That's true.—You said something about Queen Mab. Is she still the queen or—?*

K: Well, you see, as far as I know, all the queens have been called Queen Mab. It goes from daughter to daughter and maybe granddaughter.

D: *Oh, then they do die.*

K: Yes, but they have to be very old.

And so this sweet, shy and gentle young girl whose only crime was to believe in fairies and second sight was cruelly killed by the ignorant, superstitious townspeople. Karen had many lives where she was misunderstood, especially when she showed evidence of psychic abilities. On one last occasion, we landed on the day she was dying in the fire. It seemed strange how she kept being drawn to that day even though it was traumatic and upsetting to her. She did not want to watch. I convinced her it would be good for her if she could talk about it without watching it. She sighed and agreed, "This body's time is over. I—I wish to speak of it about this time."

D: *How do you feel toward the people who burned your house?*

K: (Big sigh) Disillusioned.

D: *Are you angry at them or blame them?*

K: No. They were just ignorant, and ignorance breeds fear. They have to live it. Knowing that they killed someone, and they know that I was innocent. They just needed someone to take it out on, as it were. And I was handy.

D: *Yes. But you don't bear them any anger or any— (I am always trying to establish karma that might be carried over to other lives.)*

K: (Her voice was very firm.) Why should I halt my progress just to feel anger towards someone who is so ignorant to do something this bad anyway?

D: *That is good. That shows you are more intelligent or more evolved than they are.*

K: Maybe it's just I care deeper.

D: *That is a very good thing, to care. One day they might learn.*

K: I can but hope.

D: *At this stage they don't, and they've done something they will have to answer for.*

I gave her suggestions that nothing from that life would bother her physically or mentally and brought her forward.

Chapter 19
The Greek Priestess

We join this story at the point when Dolores is asking Karen to either go forward or backward in time. In this case, she is letting Karen make the choice.

D: *I'll let you pick the place; let you pick the time. I will count to 5, and you will go back and back and back. And we will discuss it. 1, 2, 3, going back and back and back, 4, 5. What do you see?*

K: See the temple.

D: *What kind of a temple?*

K: It has white pillars.

D: *Sounds like a pretty place.* (Yes) *Where are you?*

K: Out in the courtyard.

D: *Where are we? Does this place have a name?*

K: (Pause) Thrace. (Repeats) Thrace.

D: *You're standing in the courtyard?* (Yes) *What do you look like?*

K: I'm slim—brown hair—cut short.

D: *What is your name?*

K: Diane.

D: *Okay, then you are a female.* (Yes) *How old are you, Diane?*

K: Sixteen.

D: *What are you doing at the temple?*

K: Learning to be a priestess.

D: *Have you been there very long?*

K: Since I was ten.

D: *Why did you come there?*

K: Because both I and my parents wished it.

D: *Is that normal? Do a lot of young girls like to go to the temple?*

K: Some want to, few succeed. (I didn't understand, and she repeated.) Some want to, but not many succeed.

D: *Then you are proud that you got to go there?*

K: Am happy.

D: *Then you've been there, oh, about six years now.* (Yes) *What are you studying there?*

K: Everything. About the world. About life.

D: *What are you going to do when you're finished?*

K: Hope say become a priestess.

D: *Will you leave the temple then?* (No) *Will you stay in the temple and be a priestess there?* (Yes) *What kind of a temple is this? Is it to a certain god or goddess or something?*

K: Just to the oracle. (This is the oracle.)

D: *The what?*

K: The oracle.

D: *I mean, are there any statues in the temple?* (No) *Any paintings or pictures?*

K: Two line-like paintings—on the wall.

D: *What are they paintings of?*

K: Different scenes with people who have come to the temple.

D: *Are they in color?*

K: Oh, yes. They are very beautiful.

D: *But no statues?* (No) *Is this temple near a city? Or in a city?*

K: No. You must cover very far to come to it.

D: *Oh, isolated.*

K: It is a chosen place.

D: *Where do you eat in that temple?*

K: It is a single room.

D: *Are there other people there?*

K: All of the initiates eat in one dining room.

D: *Are there very many?*

K: About twenty new ones a year.

D: *Who teaches you?*

K: The teachers and the priestess.

D: Tell me what the place looks like where you eat.

K: It has high ceilings. It has a brazier in the middle of the room.

D: A what in the middle?

K: A brazier. It warms the food, and the room.

D: What kind of tables do you eat at?

K: Wooden ones. With stools for each one to sit on.

D: What kind of food do you eat?

K: Grains and vegetables …

D: Do you eat any meat? (No) Why not?

K: It keeps you Earth-bound.

D: And you eat, what, just fruits and vegetables? (Yes) Well, what do you do when it's cold and you can't get fruits and vegetables?

K: It's never cold here.

D: It doesn't get that cold there? (No) There's always something growing?

K: In the wintertime we eat a lot of prepared olives and the grains we have stored.

D: Things you have saved, like that. (Yes) I thought that the trees wouldn't bloom all year round. What kind of fruits do you have there?

K: Lemons and oranges. Some nuts.

D: What?

K: Some nut trees.

D: Where do you get vegetables from?

K: We grow our own.

D: What kind?

K: We have cabbage and lettuce and cauliflower.

D: I always wonder about eating habits. Where do you sleep at in the temple?

K: We have a room where everyone shares a mat. And they lay it down and I sleep there.

D: You mean everyone shares—it's all in one big bed?

K: No, just the room. *(What?)* Just the room, not the mat.

D: You said they lay it down.

K: They lay their mats down.

D: And they sleep on their mats? (Yes) In the one big room.

Ummm, that sounds interesting. (Pause) Diane, do you know how to read or write?

K: Of course.

D: *What language do you write in?*

K: Greek.

D: *I wonder if you would do me a favor. Would you write something for me? Do you think you could do that for me? (I got paper and marker and handed it to her. She took the marker in her right hand and held the paper with her left. When she wrote she did not open her eyes.) Please write something for me. It doesn't have to be anything very much. Just a few words for me. I'm very interested. Can you see it all right? (Her eyes are still closed.) Very good. Did you learn this at the temple? (Yes) What does that say, can you tell me? A name?*

K: It is just the symbols they have over the door, over the doorway.

** When Dolores was able to, she would ask the person to write something if they knew how to write. In this case, we have not been able to go through all of Dolores's files to find this writing/drawing. But if you look in *Five Lives Remembered*, chapter 6, Dolores was able to get two signatures from the person while under trance from two different lifetimes. When a handwriting analyst was asked about the writing, the reply was that it could not have been done by the same person. **

D: *The doorway of the temple? (Yes) Okay, thank you. I'm always interested in things that are different. You do know how to write, don't you? Very good.—Okay, Diane, I'm going to count to three, and we will go ahead in your life to a day that you consider to be an important day. When something important has happened to your life. 1, 2, 3, you're older now, and it's an important day. A day that you consider important in your life. What is happening?*

K: I gave my first reading today.

D: *Oh, how old are you now?*

K: Twenty-three.

D: *Have you learned enough now that you can give readings?* (Yes) *Was it a good one?* (Yes) *Was the teacher proud of you?*

K: I think so. It's hard to tell. They let so little out.

D: *They don't show emotion?* (No) *Did you do the reading for one of the students, or for someone who came?*

K: For someone who came.

D: *How do you do the readings?*

K: We use the smoke.

D: *Smoke?* (Uh-huh) *There are many techniques. How do you do it with the smoke?*

K: You sit there with the tripod in front of you, and you watch the smoke. And you tell what you see.

D: *In the smoke?* (Yes) *Have you ever tried this before?*

K: We were not allowed. This is the first time.

D: *Now you think you're ready?*

K: They say that I am.

D: *Was it an accurate reading?*

K: As far as anyone can tell. We shall see.

D: *We shall see. Do you enjoy this?*

K: It is what I live for.

D: *Very good. Well, I will count to three and we will move ahead till you are much older, to an important day in your life. 1, 2, 3, it is an important day in your life. What is happening, Diane?*

K: The king has come to visit.

D: *The king has come? Why did he come?*

K: Because he wants a reading.

D: *Well, then that must really be an important day. Is everyone excited?*

K: As far as anyone gets excited, yes.

D: *But no one really shows their emotions though.*

K: It's not proper.

D: *What is the king's name? Does he have a name?*

K: Theodus. (Repeats) Theodus. (Phonetic)

D: *And he is the king of the whole land?*

K: No, just our area. There are over a hundred kings.

D: *Oh, there are many kings.* (Uh-huh) *And this is the king over*

Horns of the Goddess

this area.

K: Yes. They are always fighting.

D: *(Laugh) Seems like there is always fighting. Who is going to do the reading for the king?*

K: The high priestess.

D: *Oh, you won't get to, then.* (No) *Are you going to watch?*

K: All of the students watch.

D: *What kind of a method are they going to use?*

K: She uses the leaves in the brazier.

D: *How do they do that?*

K: You take them and crumble them up and you toss them in the fire. Then you watch the way that the flames rise and crackle and tell what you see in the flames.

D: *This is different from watching the smoke, then.* (Yes) *What does the king want to find out?*

K: Whether or not he will be victorious.

D: *What does the high priestess tell him?*

K: She tells him that he will. He is very pleased.

D: *What does he do when he is pleased? Does he give money or anything?*

K: He gives gold.

D: *What would happen if she had given him a bad reading?*

K: He would have just left.

D: *He wouldn't have given her any gold then?*

K: Don't know.

D: *But you said he was pleased that she gave a good reading for him.* (Yes) *What does the king look like? What is he wearing?*

K: He has a purple robe with ? sandals that come up to the knee. He has a band around his head. His hair is cut short. And curled.

D: *What kind of a band around his head?*

K: It looks gold, but his hair covers most of it.

D: *You said his sandals came up to his knee? How do they do that?*

K: The front leather pieces forward and they bind in the back.

D: *That sounds like an odd pair of shoes. And he has a purple robe on?*

K: Tied at the waist.

D: *Does he have anyone with him? Or did he come alone?*

K: His advisors. And his guard.

D: *Do they talk to the high priestess?*

K: No. No one but the king.

D: *He talks to her and she tells him what she sees, then?* (Yes) *Very interesting. How old are you now?*

K: Twenty-three.

D: *Oh, the same age. Okay, you are twenty-three years old now, Diane. I will count to three and you will go up to when you are thirty-three. Take you ahead in your life and see what has happened to you. An important day when you are thirty-three. 1, 2, 3, you're thirty-three years old. What is happening?*

K: I am going out to choose students.

D: *Oh, are you teaching now?* (Yes) *The same temple?* (Yes) *Where do you go to choose your students?*

K: Throughout the country. You find people, young girls, that seem to have promise. And bring them back.

D: *How do you know when you have found the right type?*

K: You just do.

D: *Have you been teaching?* (Yes) *Very good. Where do you go? To any certain town, or just anywhere?*

K: Wherever our footpath leads.

D: *Just in the area?* (Yes) *Do you have to find any certain number before you come back?*

K: No. Just one at least.

D: *How long will you be gone?*

K: As long as it takes.

D: *To at least find one. Then you will come back to the temple?* (Yes) *What if you don't find anyone who wants to go with you?*

K: We will. Otherwise, we would not be sent.

D: *Who is sending you?*

K: The high priestess is the one who chooses.

D: *And she tells you to go out and find some other pupils and bring them back. How are you telling your readings? Are you still using the smoke method or some other method?*

K: Sometimes we just stand and listen to the leaves and hear what they say.

D: In the fire?

K: No, just listen to the trees. Everything has a voice.

D: And that tells you what to tell the people? (Yes) *Earlier, you said the king had wanted a reading and wanted to know if he would be victorious. Was he victorious?* (Yes) *Then they were accurate, weren't they? It was an accurate reading.*

K: Of course! The high priestess has never been wrong.

D: Oh. Are you that accurate? (No) *Do you sometimes make mistakes?*

K: Sometimes.

D: Well, you're still learning, aren't you? Okay, we're going to move forward, Diane. I want to take you up to the last day of your life—as Diane. I will count to three and we will come up to the last day of your life and tell me what happened to you. You will just describe it, you don't have to experience it. You will not feel anything, nothing that will bother you at all. This way you can talk to me about it with no problem. 1, 2, 3, it's the last day of your life as Diane. What happened to you?

K: I decided it was time to relinquish the body. (Sounds old and tired.)

D: How old were you?

K: Seventy-seven.

D: Oh, you were very old, weren't you? You lived a long time in that temple, didn't you? (Yes) *Were you happy there?* (Yes) *Did you have many students?*

K: Many successful ones, yes.

D: That was good. Did you ever regret coming to the temple? (No) *You liked it there, then that's very good. It was a good life, wasn't it?* (Yes) *You never grew tired of it, did you?* (No) *Maybe that was why you lived so long; you had many things to accomplish in that lifetime.*

K: I had much to learn.

Subject given instructions and reinforcement for keyword suggestion and brought forward. During the German lifetime, subject had a childish voice and sometimes a noticeable German accent. During the Greek one, her voice seemed to change and mature as she grew older. There were at times a strange pronunciation, that made words difficult to understand. Especially a way of rolling the r. She also had a different way of using words.

Dolores had left notes to give reference to one of Karen's other lives as a Viking. Hopefully, in the future, we will have all of Dolores's files/tapes transcribed and be able to share with you the many adventures she took over the span of time when she was working with the many different subjects that came into her life.

The session we did on June 20, 1985, was the last time I ever worked with Karen. She eventually stayed in Little Rock and got married. Later she had two little girls by him. He was a hemophiliac and required much care. Karen gave him much loving attention and traveled with him in his work. Years later she moved back to Fayetteville, but we had no interaction. Then I heard that her husband died suddenly because his blood wouldn't clot. She was left in a very good financial situation because of her husband's pension. Thus, she didn't have to work, but could stay home and care for the girls. Our paths did not have a reason to cross again, and it is probably just as well. I heard in later years that she denied any of the sessions and experiences ever happened. I had given her copies of the tapes, and transcripts of them, but she never wanted to listen to them or read them. When she would awaken from the session, she would laugh, and ask, "Where did we go today?" When I told her, she would say that it seemed interesting, but she wouldn't ask any more about it or pursue it further. I usually would take her back to work, and her focus returned to her everyday life. Because of her deep somnambulistic state of trance, she did not consciously remember the many adventures we had had over the two years we had worked off and on. Thus, it was probably easy for her to imagine that they had never occurred. To her they must have seemed like dreams which fade upon awakening. It was probably for the better. She lived a normal and happy life. It was as though her part was to give me the stories, and then for her to return to the normal world. I can truly say with all confidence that the sessions did not interfere with her normal life at all. All of the other lifetimes were like a blur to her. It is strange for me to have been a participant in a shadow world that she did not know existed. And if it had not been for the tape recordings that have survived, and the witnesses to the sessions, I might have doubted their reality also. But I know it happened. For a brief while I was an invisible participant in moments in history as an unwitting time traveler. And as the storyteller and the reporter I must tell what I found.

Parting Message

Dolores opened our eyes to wonderous and mysterious worlds. She dared to go into the forbidden realms of what the mind contained. If it had not been for her insatiable appetite to want to know more and to ask the many, many questions, we might never have known of the lost knowledge she found with her sessions. She found information years before we uncovered it in this lifetime. Example being the ruins of Qumran. When the archaeologists came forward with their findings and they differed from what she was told in the session, at this time she had a very tough decision to make. Does she just throw out what she was given, or does she have the faith that what she received was the truth? If you have read her book *Jesus and the Essenes*, then you know she kept the faith and presented what she had received. Later the archaeologists discovered there was an error in their findings and what Dolores had written was correct. Another example is in *Five Lives Remembered* when Dolores and Johnny were exploring the "in-between life" and were given information about their future. In this book it is said that Johnny was seen sitting in a chair with his grandchildren around him while living in a hilly area. This event was true. We receive numerous letters and emails from people saying how Dolores has changed their lives. This is something we are very proud of and are very thankful to hear the wonderful things that are said.

When she left us, she was working on several books. This is something that was very common for her to do. People would ask "what is the next book?" Her answer was that she never knew and that it would be whichever one found its completion first. This book was one of those that she was working on and it has now found its completion.

We hope you enjoy.

-Nancy

About the Author

Dolores Cannon, a regressive hypnotherapist and psychic researcher who records "Lost" knowledge, was born in 1931 in St. Louis, Missouri. She was educated and lived in St. Louis until her marriage in 1951 to a career Navy man. She spent the next twenty years traveling all over the world as a typical Navy wife, and raising her family. In 1970 her husband was discharged as a disabled veteran, and they retired to the hills of Arkansas. She then started her writing career and began selling her articles to various magazines and newspapers. She has been involved with hypnosis since 1968, and exclusively with past-life therapy and regression work since 1979. She has studied the various hypnosis methods and thus developed her own unique technique which enabled her to gain the most efficient release of information from her clients. Dolores taught her unique technique of hypnosis all over the world.

In 1986 she expanded her investigations into the UFO field. She has done on-site studies of suspected UFO landings, and has investigated the Crop Circles in England. The majority of her work in this field has been the accumulation of evidence from suspected abductees through hypnosis.

Dolores is an international speaker who has lectured on all the continents of the world. Her seventeen books are translated into twenty languages. She has spoken to radio and television audiences worldwide. And articles about/by Dolores have appeared in several U.S. and international magazines and newspapers. Dolores was the first American and the first foreigner to receive the Orpheus Award in Bulgaria, for the highest advancement in the research of psychic phenomenon. She has received Outstanding Contribution and Lifetime Achievement awards from several hypnosis organizations. Dolores's very large family kept her solidly balanced between the "real" world of her family and the "unseen" world of her work.

If you wish to correspond with Ozark Mountain Publishing about Dolores's work, please submit to the following address with a self-addressed stamped envelope for a reply: Ozark Mountain Publishing, PO Box 754, Huntsville, AR 72740, USA, or email the office through our website: www.ozarkmt.com.

Dolores Cannon, who transitioned from this world on October 18, 2014, left behind incredible accomplishments in the fields of alternative healing, hypnosis, metaphysics and past-life regression, but most impressive of all was her innate understanding that the most important thing she could do was to share information. To reveal hidden or undiscovered knowledge vital to the enlightenment of humanity and our lessons here on Earth. Sharing information and knowledge is what mattered most to Dolores. That is why her books, lectures and unique QHHT® method of hypnosis continue to amaze, guide and inform so many people around the world. Dolores explored all these possibilities and more while taking us along for the ride of our lives. She wanted fellow travelers to share her journeys into the unknown.

A Very Special Friend
Big Sandy Press

Five Lives Remembered
Published by: Ozark Mountain Publishing

Between Death and Life
Published by: Ozark Mountain Publishing

Jesus and the Essenes
Published by: Ozark Mountain Publishing

They Walked with Jesus
Published by: Ozark Mountain Publishing

Conversations with Nostradamus Vol. 1-3
Published by: Ozark Mountain Publishing

A Soul Remembers Hiroshima
Published by: Ozark Mountain Publishing

The Custodians
Published by: Ozark Mountain Publishing

Keepers of the Gardens
Published by: Ozark Mountain Publishing

Legacy from the Stars
Published by: Ozark Mountain Publishing

The Legend of Starcrash
Published by: Ozark Mountain Publishing

The Convoluted Universe Book 1-5
Published by: Ozark Mountain Publishing

Three Waves of Volunteers and the New Earth
Published by: Ozark Mountain Publishing

The Search for Hidden Sacred Knowledge
Published by: Ozark Mountain Publishing

OZARK
MOUNTAIN
PUBLISHING

For more information about any of the above titles, soon to be released titles,
or other items in our catalog, write, phone or visit our website:
Ozark Mountain Publishing, Inc.
PO Box 754, Huntsville, AR 72740
479-738-2348/800-935-0045

If you liked this book, you might also like:

Starseeds What's It All About?
by Alexander Quinn
A Golden Compass
by Nikki Pattillo
The Birthmark Scar
By Paul Berg & Amanda Hemmingsen
Dancing with Angels in Heaven
by Garnet Schulhauser
Beyond All Boundaries Book 1-3
Lyn Willmott
Time: The Second Secret
Kathryn Andries
Croton I-II
Artur Tadevosyan

For more information about any of the above titles, soon to be released titles,
or other items in our catalog, write, phone or visit our website:
Ozark Mountain Publishing, LLC
PO Box 754, Huntsville, AR 72740
479-738-2348
www.ozarkmt.com

For more information about any of the titles published by Ozark Mountain Publishing, Inc., soon to be released titles, or other items in our catalog, write, phone or visit our website:

Ozark Mountain Publishing, Inc.

PO Box 754

Huntsville, AR 72740

479-738-2348/800-935-0045

www.ozarkmt.com

Other Books by Ozark Mountain Publishing, Inc.

Dolores Cannon
A Soul Remembers Hiroshima
Between Death and Life
Conversations with Nostradamus,
  Volume I, II, III
The Convoluted Universe -Book One,
  Two, Three, Four, Five
The Custodians
Five Lives Remembered
Jesus and the Essenes
Keepers of the Garden
Legacy from the Stars
The Legend of Starcrash
The Search for Hidden Sacred
  Knowledge
They Walked with Jesus
The Three Waves of Volunteers and
  the New Earth
A Very Special Friend
Horns of the Goddess
Aron Abrahamsen
Holiday in Heaven
James Ream Adams
Little Steps
Justine Alessi & M. E. McMillan
Rebirth of the Oracle
Kathryn Andries
Time: The Second Secret
Cat Baldwin
Divine Gifts of Healing
The Forgiveness Workshop
Penny Barron
The Oracle of UR
P.E. Berg & Amanda Hemmingsen
The Birthmark Scar
Dan Bird
Finding Your Way in the Spiritual Age
Waking Up in the Spiritual Age
Julia Cannon
Soul Speak – The Language of Your
  Body
Ronald Chapman
Seeing True
Jack Churchward
Lifting the Veil on the Lost

Continent of Mu
The Stone Tablets of Mu
Patrick De Haan
The Alien Handbook
Paulinne Delcour-Min
Spiritual Gold
Holly Ice
Divine Fire
Joanne DiMaggio
Edgar Cayce and the Unfulfilled
  Destiny of Thomas Jefferson
  Reborn
Anthony DeNino
The Power of Giving and Gratitude
Paul Fisher
Like A River To The Sea
Carolyn Greer Daly
Opening to Fullness of Spirit
Anita Holmes
Twidders
Aaron Hoopes
Reconnecting to the Earth
Patricia Irvine
In Light and In Shade
Kevin Killen
Ghosts and Me
Susan Urbanek Linville
Blessing from Agnes
Donna Lynn
From Fear to Love
Curt Melliger
Heaven Here on Earth
Where the Weeds Grow
Henry Michaelson
And Jesus Said – A Conversation
Andy Myers
Not Your Average Angel Book
Holly Nadler
The Hobo Diaries
Guy Needler
Avoiding Karma
Beyond the Source – Book 1, Book 2
The History of God
The Origin Speaks

For more information about any of the above titles, soon to be released titles,
or other items in our catalog, write, phone or visit our website:
PO Box 754, Huntsville, AR 72740|479-738-2348/800-935-0045|www.ozarkmt.com